Walking Britain's Skyline

45 Classic Routes

WALKING BRITAIN'S SKYLINE

45 Classic Routes

Tony Greenbank

Foreword by
Chris Bonington

The Crowood Press

First published in 1992 by
The Crowood Press Ltd
Ramsbury, Marlborough
Wiltshire SN8 2HR

British Library Cataloguing in Publication Data

A catalogue record for this book is available from the British Library.

ISBN 1 85223 287 0

Acknowledgements

I would like to thank all the friends who helped and sustained me in so many ways, and also those who suggested alterations to the illustrations and text (any remaining errors are mine), particularly Pete Sellers and Delyth Evans, Andy Ligema, Davie Sanderson, Paul Cornforth, Chris Bonington, Frank Davies, Gunars Libeks, Colin Downer, Paul Ross, John Porter, Adrian Liddell, Iain Williamson, Ed Grindley, Tony Peak, Elliot Blaylock, Ali Kellas, Will Holligan, Trevor Jones, Chris Bacon, Neil Allinson, The Big Fellow (*see* Aonach Eagach), The Brigadier, Adjutant Captain & Corporal; Harry Griffin, Pete Long, Peter Myers, Paul Nunn, Vic McClelland, Richard McHardy, Colin Mortlock, Andy Hyslop, Derek and Carole Thomas, Doug Scott, Luke Steer, Alistair Hopkins, Rick Graham, and John Lockley.

Thanks also to Al Phizacklea – a pillar of strength – who drew the three-dimensional maps just as I requested.

Thanks also to The London Dungeon, and *Climber and Hillwalker* for permission to reproduce letters and an article.

And where in the end I failed to obtain eight of the 150-plus photographs I required, I must also thank Chris Bonington for allowing me to use a slide of Ben Nevis from his collection (but which I took using his camera) AND Jim Perrin who kindly provided me with seven slides to fill up the remaining gaps.

Frontispiece

The North-East Buttress of Ben Nevis, viewed from Carn Mor Dearg Arête.

Dedication

For my youngest daughter Hannah for all the untold help she gave in a year as palindromic as her name (1991). And – fortunately not quite as rare as such a year (though at times it was a close-run thing) – Wilf and his occasional good mug of tea.

Picture Credits

All photographs by Tony Greenbank, except those on pages 193, 215–16, 218 (top left), 219 and 221–2, which are by Jim Perrin. The photograph on page 124 (bottom right), by Tony Greenbank, is reproduced with the kind permission of Chris Bonington.

Typeset by Acūté, Stroud, Glos.
Printed and bound in Great Britain by BPCC Hazells Ltd, Member of BPCC Ltd.

Contents

Part Three   Wales

Note From the Artist

Let's get one thing straight right away: the illustrations in this book are not accurate, and more to the point, they are not *meant* to be accurate. They cannot be used as maps, and if the reader wishes to obtain some figures on the distances and heights involved, there are many good-quality maps available for that purpose. They have been drawn simply to provide the reader with some indication of the layout and nature of the terrain which will be encountered on these walks.

The sketches have not been produced from any special viewpoint or from aerial photographs; they are actually partly figments of my imagination. I studied the Ordnance Survey maps and then visualized the layout and shape of the hills before roughly sketching out what I imagine the hills to look like, so in a way they are my own interpretation of the terrain. These rough sketches were then improved by studying photographs of the areas and adding the details lost due to the small scale of the maps. Many features that exist have been enhanced out of proportion to emphasize that particular area of mountainside, and the exaggeration of the heights has been a deliberate distortion to satisfy Tony's incessant requests to 'make 'em really dramatic, man!'

This has been a most enjoyable pastime for me, as I have ascended less than half of the hills in this book, so it has been a good introduction to those unknown areas of our country. As a draughtsman, and not an artist (there is a world of difference in the drawing ability of the two) I hope that my clumsy attempts at portraying your favourite mountain will be received with a little understanding.

Al Phizacklea

KEY

P CAR PARKING

R OFFICIAL MOUNTAIN RESCUE POST

Y YOUTH HOSTEL

△ CAMP SITE

S HUT OR EMERGENCY BOTHY (SHELTER)

➔**N** ARROW INDICATES APPROXIMATE DIRECTION OF NORTH

Foreword
by Chris Bonington

There is something especially attractive about walking or scrambling a skyline ridge, climbing a path into the sky with the land dropping away on either side, each hummock, pinnacle or bend in the ridge bringing in a new vista. The very symmetry of walking the skyline of a mountain corrie or cwm, of completing the circle without repetition, of reaching the heights and returning to the same point is a metaphor for the paths of our lives; a striving to reach heights of joy, enlightenment, success, self-awareness with a return to day-to-day life.

A guidebook that is just a set of instructions is an empty thing. This is the strength of Tony Greenbank's *Walking Britain's Skyline* for he shares with us his moods and emotions, brings to life companions and friends, as he walks some of the most magnificent ridge-lines of Britain. There are the moments of depression, even of despair, that most of us have known, and there are moments of rich humour, of joy and wonder at the sheer variety and beauty of the British hills.

Tony is one of my oldest and best friends. We first met in 1962, when he was living in a caravan parked in the Yorkshire Dales and just starting his career as a freelance writer specializing in the great outdoors. It has not been an easy path to follow, but he has achieved success through hard work and the quality of his writing. Over the years, we have had many great days on the crags and hills in summer and winter, have been benighted all too many times, have played endless games of darts and drunk many a pint in pubs up and down the land. From the very start, I found his boundless enthusiasm for the hills and climbing infectious, and this enthusiasm comes across strongly in his writing.

This book captures the very essence of walking Britain's skylines, with just sufficient detail to pick out the route without losing the adventure of finding one's own way, but more important it gives the mood and feel of the walk through anecdote and personal experience. It is a book that can be used as a guide, as an inspiration and one to dip into when dreaming of escaping to the hills.

Introduction

29 May 1985

Dear Tony

Jeremy Harrison denied everything attributed to him in your seaside story for *Titbits*. This means the feature is not as I'd hoped in either length or content. This will also be the case with the amount on your cheque.

Yours sincerely

Grant Lockhart
(Features Editor)

Maybe I wasn't cut out for this kind of work I said as I put the letter down. It was a bit late to find that out. I had been doing it full-time for twenty-five years. To get rid of my angst I went for a walk. Not only did I walk up Wansfell, a small hill in the Lake District, but I kept walking (as the man said when I asked him the time in Times Square and he screamed, 'Keep walking, fella, keep walking!'). And on and on I went. Along the summit ridge to the top of Kirkstone Pass, and on past the Kirkstone Pass Hotel *en route*, where I would dearly have loved a pint except that I had only intended walking a short distance initially and track suit bottoms and lightweight tops do not carry pockets for loose change and, much to my dismay, the £5 note I was sure I had slipped inside my socks – a trick, incidentally that I learned through living near Times square – had disappeared.

On then, regardless, up Red Screes and down into the col beyond and up again on to Dove Crag. Along to Fairfield, down to Grisedale Tarn, on up Dollywagon Pike, over Nethermost Pike and on to Helvellyn. Then along to Raise and over the Dodds, large hills each and every one and verging on 3,000ft above sea-level or over. Until at last I staggered down into Threlkeld looking for all the world like a corpse from a Durer engraving, an illusion sustained when I tripped over some roadworks and fell into the coffin-like trench, badly wrenching my knee in the process.

In the bar of the Salutation Inn, a man said the King's Head pub at Thirlspot was closed for the day because the landlord was a miserable bastard. 'Who is he?' I asked in all innocence. 'Me,' he replied.

It was the following morning as I recovered that I thought of it: I would write a book on skylines. Not on individual mountains, you understand, but rather on their combined horizons, like my route of the previous day where I had had no intention of coming down to earth before I had strung together as many tops as possible in lofty succession (and in the process unstrung myself). For that is the thing about skylines. Once you have made the initial effort to climb the first peak, everything else that follows is progressively less strenuous – as a general rule. This would be a book, then, on the linking together of the best peaks, wherever this was possible in the British Isles.

And it is so possible in the British Isles. Here, of all places, the compactness of the landscape is such a strength. Also, conveniently, many of our mountain skylines form horseshoes, incorporating peak after peak and bringing you back full circle to where you began, thus creating outstanding skylines in three particular areas, North Wales, the Lake District and the Scottish Highlands and Islands.

Mountain regions all, these skylines are so superbly delineated, thanks to the geology of Great Britain, that I decided to do them along the same lines I had done that initial one from the summit of lowly Wansfell, and which had given me the inspiration for the book, that is off the cuff, extemporizing along the way and letting the quality of ridges guide my feet as though I was running on rails. I had after all been on mountains all my life, and Wansfell was in my backyard. I did not think the spirit of the game was improved by over-preparation. An element of impulsiveness helps preserve the adventure of it all.

Just do sufficient for the day. That was the idea, and with the minimum of equipment commensurate with safety. I would also take the photographs to prove I had actually been there and not simply at my work-station shoving aside yet another article for *Titbits* or *Secrets* or *Red Letter* to make way for a chapter on a particular skyline, to be written without first-hand experience but solely by copious reference to the works of Wainwright or a Scottish Mountaineering Club guide or whatever.

Not that, incidentally, I did not refer to these guidebooks to keep me on track, because the book I envisaged could never have taken their place. For example that magnificent book of reference, *The High Mountains* by Irvine Butterfield (Diadem) with its detailed data, compelling reading and visual appeal that should be read assiduously every winter, from deep within armchairs, in the planning of yet more skyline excursions.

To do the skylines is only one of the delights; planning and preparing for them can be as fulfilling as the execution. But it is more than this. It is a must. You cannot, in my view, prepare for the big mountain like Ladhar Bheinn from one guidebook alone. You require a guidebook and a map, and, preferably, additional guidebook material to act as a double-check. (There are, incidentally, at least six Ladhar Bheinn guidebooks all of widely varying prices and this goes for other great mountains in Britain and, while you cannot be expected to research every one, it does no harm to know of their existence and peruse as many as you can lay your hands on prior to a visit to your chosen dream.) By this I do not wish to contradict what I said previously about over-readiness but, on a cold winter's night, to turn up the heating and pore through the Wainwright, the Butterfield, the SMC journals or the Ordnance Survey maps is a necessary part of safe travel, just as a sailor will consult the charts.

The sea is the equivalent of traversing mountain skylines. Only it is easier to underestimate the skylines, quite forgetting the currents and vortices of air and cloud and precipitation that swirl around their jagged or domed ridges and which will produce additional problems, like the need for an ice-axe and crampons on the tops, even though it may still be clement weather in the valleys. The only answer is adequate preparation. But not so much please that you forget to smile.

Now for a serious note: the most common cause of accidents on the Hill is erroneous navigation. To this I must plead guilty, the accounts of my erring and straying (quite literally) giving, I hope, an object lesson in not following my example certainly in the case of the skylines of Beinn Eighe and Blaven. Not that I actually made a map-reading error *per se* on the actual skyline in either case so much as the crime was in not evaluating the terrain beforehand and thus having at least an inkling of what to expect.

And what the mountain can throw at you! The automatic weather-station on the summit of Cairn Gorm has recorded a wind speed of 146 mph and on that occasion wind speeds of over 100mph were recorded continuously for more than seven hours; speeds of more than 60 mph (storm force 10) were recorded for more than twenty-four hours and the temperature on the Cairngorm plateau ranged from $-30°C$ to $+4°C$. In such conditions, anyone benighted or lost would find it difficult enough to think, let alone preserve body heat or navigate. No one knows this more than those who service that weather-station.

It cannot be stressed too strongly that the highest level of navigation is totally necessary from all involved, not simply the leading light of a hillwalking or climbing team. This can only be achieved by practising in conditions of poor visibility, preferably on more amenable terrain and within easy distance of the road.

The most common cause of injury or death is slipping on steep snow or ice, and lacking the ability to arrest the fall immediately. That hillwalkers carry ice-axes in winter is true, such is the publicity that has been given to the dangers of travelling without. However, very few take the time out to practise their emergency use. It is something that requires a sufficiently steep slope with a safe run-out at the bottom (free from rocks and boulders and streambeds), and it should be repeated at the beginning of each winter, so you are confident in the art of arresting a fall from every conceivable position, whether upside-down or head over heels. Nor is this sufficient for complete safety. The routine should then be repeated wearing crampons so you learn the safe way to keep them at all costs clear of the snow and avoid a horrendous somersaulting flight downhill caused by these spikes snagging on the snow and ice.

Then there are the common emergencies of avalanches and benightment.

Avalanche conditions cause a number of accidents in Scotland each year, the underlying cause of why climbers are caught up in them being an ignorance of snow structure. The best way to study snow structure is to cut a pit into a section of old snow and inspect the layering process. Also, though, you should pay attention to temperature increases because it is then that avalanches occur. At such times, gullies should be given a wide berth. This is something that is instilled into the hearts and minds of those who attend courses at centres like Glenmore Lodge, the National Training centre at Aviemore.

As for benightment, it usually happens because of a late start. For four months every year the Scottish day in particular is very short and it is vastly preferable to begin the day in darkness with the assistance of the headtorch — now a piece of equipment (thanks to its potent lightweight power-pack) as universally carried by climbers and hillwalkers as the ice axe — than to finish the day struggling through a cruel wind and merciless spindrift when reserves of strength and energy are waning at the very time when concentration is of the essence.

This is not the kind of book that gives you lots of potted information. You will find scant mention of 'attractions' such as the regular appearance of eagles on such and such a peak or the presence of a stone-axe factory or of rare plants. I have tried to let the hills speak for themselves as they surely will if you allow them all respect. Should you happen to see an eagle sailing above or happen on ancient archaeological remains, then great. But you will not be steered towards them by me. To this end also – namely that of treating the hills with reverence and realizing the immense scope they offer to the venturer in tune with them – I have tried to avoid over-stating the use of certain footpaths. While obviously skylines tend to be places limited by definition to more or less one way along their crest, many small variations are possible, and I would like to leave it to the reader to plot their own hill-going destinies for themselves rather than to lead them by the hand (or nose) along one specific route unless it is a matter of safety.

Even the times of the walks I give are very general, and I tend to err on the pessimistic side. This is safer I feel than being too optimistic and offering times that a fell runner might be expected to achieve.

As Al Phizacklea explains in his note of how he drew the diagrams, the three-dimensional maps in this book are drawn nowhere near to scale but serve simply to give an artist's impression of what each skyline looks like when viewed on a clear day from some celestial vantage point.

This book is the wrong size and shape to be carried about on the Hill. However, those of us who may consider they too are similarly unsuitable for the Hill – being the wrong size and shape (and don't we all think this at some time?) – you may be pleasantly surprised to find that, far from it, you are by no means ineligible.

So, in the light of what I have just said, why not try an easy skyline? A Cader Idris or a Helm Crag or a Quiraing could whet your appetite. Of course, there are certain skylines in this book which are clearly for the experienced mountaineer, and it will be obvious from reading the text as to which these are. There are many others though which are not so extreme in their demands but which will prove highly rewarding, just so long as you have taken note of the lessons to be drawn from my own dismal performances on several occasions, and also first ensured you have as kindly a weather report as possible to help you on your way.

It happens frequently with books of this nature that a skyline on which I personally struggled – those mistakes and struggles being recorded from my memory of the event and from my notebook's mad scrawl – may not seem that way to you all. Perhaps you are at your fittest and cruise around a horseshoe or along a linear walk where I experienced a hard time. Bear with me then, and do not be too scathing on this humble author. So unpredictable and gloriously temperamental are the skylines, thanks to the agents of the weather and the personal fitness of those who travel along them, that if you found one particular skyline you had been expecting great things from easy, beware that some other ridge that I found not too troublesome does not swing back at you with its bludgeon or cut-throat razor when you least expect it.

Lastly, although I sound uncompromising on the few ridges which include rock climbing – like the Woolpack Round for instance – do realize that the spines and knife-blades of these great horizons (and they can be the whale-backs of the Cairngorms or Carneddau too) can frequently be terminated at specific points along the way. These escape routes will give you a shorter and more abbreviated route, but will still be serviceable – like snapping off a section of those craft-knife blades where, after you have blunted one such section, you go on to the next knife-edge.

So it is with *Walking Britain's Skyline*. Most of all, I hope it will light a fire within your soul, just as the traverse of that initial skyline from Ambleside to Threlkeld did for me (especially when I found I had not lost the £5 note after all, as it had stuck to the sole of my foot thanks to my trainers letting in water). If so, I will be delighted.

Part One

The Lake District

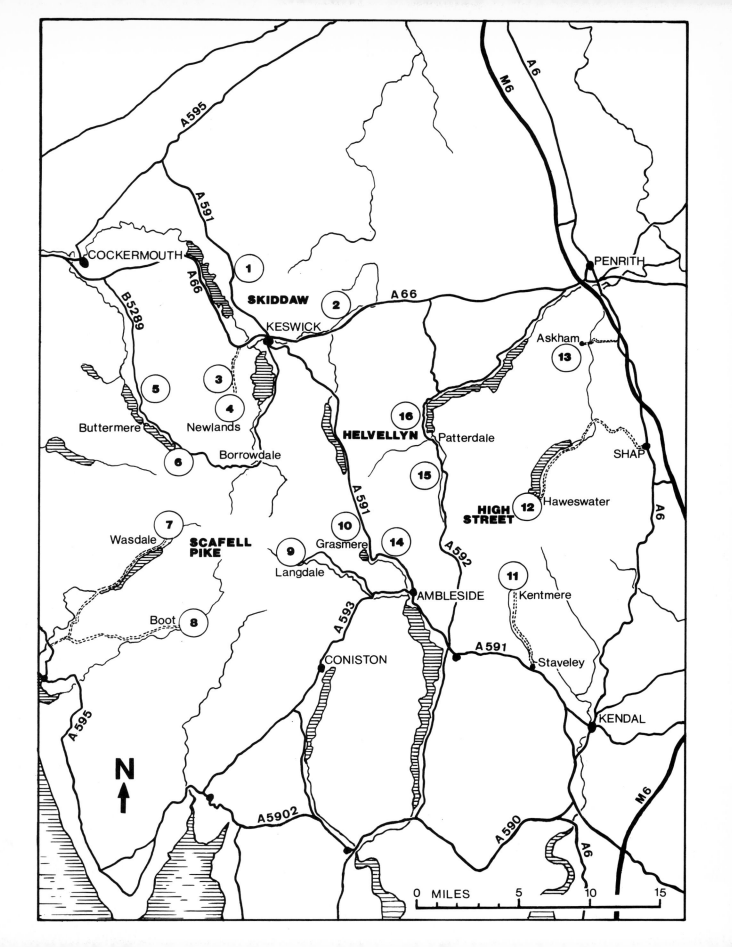

Chapter 1

SKIDDAW BY THE EDGE OF ULLOCK PIKE AND DEAD CRAGS

Skiddaw is a great mountain, whichever of its various routes you ascend by, but it is made all the more so if you traverse it by Ullock Pike, Longside Edge, Carl Side and Dead Crags. The Edge of Ullock Pike and Dead Crags are just two of its highlights: the former, a floating rib that appears irresistible from Bassenthwaite village; the latter, a stack of inhospitable ramparts shadowing Whitewater Dash and alive with a constant stream of the negative ions that are emitted by waterfalls and said to refresh and stimulate jaded appetites. Packaged together with the summit of Skiddaw as the culmination, they provide the cutting edge to a mountain formed 50 million years ago from the sediment in a shallow sea that exists today as essentially a huge mound of smooth, splintery slate.

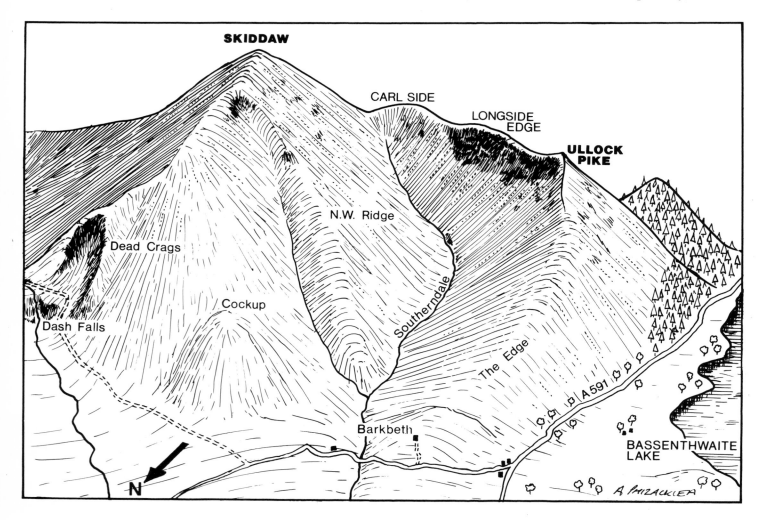

A friend who sells Cumberland pork pies in Greenwich Village regularly writes from Manhattan to the manager of Carlisle United, with this advice: 'Run the team up Skiddaw, a prize to the first one down, and watch out for the First Division'. So far he has yet to receive a reply (although he has been writing since 1972), and Carlisle still languish in the Fourth Division. But Skiddaw is that kind of mountain. It is big, sprawling, and is seemingly built for endurance. However, while the route to the summit from Keswick or Millbeck would conceivably be suitable for a squad of professional soccer players, our intended route here would be inappropriate.

'MONUMENTAL COCKUP!' could well be the subsequent headlines among a certain section of the Press following such a venture. The scene: the complete Carlisle FC squad successfully achieve the rigours of The Edge but then become disorientated in mist so dense that even the coal-black ravens of Dead Crags are stilled into silence. Succumbing to the dreaded effects of hypothermia, the players are finally discovered at their last ebb on Cockup after a rescue call-out where SARDA dogs scent wafts of embrocation drifting on the breeze. Now Cockup is a satellite of Skiddaw in the vicinity of Dead Crags, and that is the danger of this route in bad visibility. While part of it is a knife-edge, it does eventually merge into a large expanse of featureless mountainside some way below the summit, a mountainside moreover that in mist goes on and on seemingly without end.

Whether you view it from the end of Derwentwater in the willow-pattern setting of Borrowdale or from the crowded bazaar centre of busy Keswick, the mountain stretches out as far as the eye can see, furrowed and creased with great rifts that corrugate its sloping flanks. Both these aspects are from the south, but you can also obtain a similar effect of a mountain that commandeers the skyline from many other vantage points. Yet, thanks to Ullock Pike and Dead Crags, all is not lost for the hilltop climber who prefers something more atmospheric and eminently stirring.

Ullock Pike, the hill which incorporates The Edge, and the subsequent peaks of Longside and Carl Side are quite separate from Skiddaw itself. But so perfectly are they grafted on to the northern flanks of the more famous mountain that the join is seamless. Winging higher in the sky with mist lathering its blade like shaving cream clinging to a razor blade, their skyline offers a challenge of close shaves for the hilltop climber. Ullock Pike is, of course, what you're climbing in the first instance, but Skiddaw is the goal.

'Are you sure,' say the cynics, 'that you aren't mistaking Ullock Pike for the Hornli Ridge of the Matterhorn? Or even the Mittelegi Ridge on the Eiger?' All right. I confess. I have exaggerated. But clamber up its edge as the wind tangles your hair, stings tears from your eyes and whistles like a boiling kettle through the aluminium tubes of the child-carrier on your back, while the infant within, cocooned against the weather, gurgles happily away, and the mountainside can fall away on either side below you with devastating suddenness.

Such were the conditions when Paul Ross and I embarked on this lonely mountain traverse, and one, unfortunately, where we came to grief, thanks to a monumental error on my part.

We had begun from the usual place; not, as the map suggests, from Barkbeth farm on the narrow road from Bassenthwaite Lake (the only 'Lake' in the Lake District, incidentally) to Orthwaite, but from a nearby layby. Markers on fence posts and stiles directed us through sloping fields to the Hobbitland of secluded Southerndale, waiting invitingly beyond the furthermost intake wall. Below us to the left, waterfalls spouted down a gorge. Ahead and up to the right, The Edge reared into the sky, tapering to a provocative outline and adorned with the tattered banners of ragged white mist.

We experienced a sense of eager anticipation as we began to climb, first up the fellside to the right, then along the horizon before it began to take off into the cloud. With the appearance of the ridge now limited to fleeting

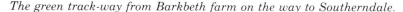
The green track-way from Barkbeth farm on the way to Southerndale.

majestic glimpses above, we might have been on Everest. As it steepened to the point where pressing down on alternate thighs with both hands helped to jack you up the next bit, the cloud enclosed us in its impenetrable grasp. Yet though we couldn't see beyond a couple of yards, the way before us was clear; there was only the narrow crest ahead.

Steep twists and turns in the kinking path made it necessary to use our hands for balance. Although the view to the left was a cauldron of boiling vapour, sudden rents in the cloud gave sombre views towards the Grasmoor complex of fells to the south-west, and also to the right where the dark waters of Bassenthwaite – normally the beneficiary of steady breezes rather than the fierce winds that can funnel through mountain passes to sweep across other lakes – were alive with silver shoals of gusting catspaws.

It was on the summit of Ullock Pike, after several false stops along the way, that we braced ourselves for Longside Edge. This loomed ahead as vaguely as a fog-bound motorway lane from which you know you stray at your peril in case the juggernaut of an articulated lorry comes thundering up behind.

However, as we teetered our way along the rim, it was to be me who would play the part of the oncoming 'artic', all 6ft 2in and yard-of-pump-water physique of me. Just as Paul stopped ahead to peer down an awkward step of slippery steep black slate, I unwittingly chose that moment to step forward, bump into him, send him flying and then, losing my balance, land heavily on top of him.

'Hell, Paul,' I shouted into the wind as we got up like a couple of drunks, disentangled our limbs, checked for mutual injuries and picked up the loose change, wallet and credit cards that had cascaded from his pockets on the rim of what in the mist looked as deadly as a lift shaft. 'I *am* sorry. I was miles away.' He had just found the most serious injury of all and was looking deeply troubled. Thinking he hadn't heard, I was about to repeat the distraught apology when he spoke: 'Perhaps it would have been better if you had been'. Then in a tone of utter resignation, 'All right, then, where's the Elastoplast?' Unfortunately, Band Aids dampened by blobs of rain failed to clamp together the gold wire of his spectacles, which had suffered in the fall. As if this catastrophe was not bad enough, we began to argue.

After our path had descended further narrows, dipping into a depression (complete with tiny tarn beyond), no longer – we suddenly realized – were we on a knife blade. Instead, bulking ahead, was an expanse of mountainside that seemed boundless in its utter blankness.

Paul – now *hors de combat* through no fault of his own – began to sound not entirely unenchanted as I struggled with the map. 'You need glasses, that's your trouble,' he shouted as I strained manfully to pinpoint our position despite the howling wind and the wildly bucking sheet of the Ordnance Survey map.

'I don't,' I said defensively (or words to that effect). Damn it, I'd had false teeth for years and my hair was rapidly going that way too. A pair of spectacles was the last thing I wanted. 'Nothing wrong with my eyes,' I shouted into the wind, the details on the map floating in front of me as meaningfully as the whorls of fingerprints photographed by the police investigating your burgled flat. 'Anyway, how about you getting a hearing aid, I'm sick of having to shout everything.' And then as he roared 'YOU WHAT?' just to show me how wrong I was, I blundered on: 'You're deaf as a post, man.'

Fuelling even more the ludicrous prospect of two fifty-year olds engaged in a heated scene of lost youth and sinful vanity on a bare mountainside, he yelled back, 'If only you could see yourself. The way you're holding that map, you look like you're pushing a pram. Your arms just aren't long enough, are they? And you think you'll look ridiculous wearing spectacles!'

Unable to constrain his growing fury any longer, he snatched the map from my hands, squinted hard, jabbed a finger at the paper and determined that we were on the col close to Carl Side tarn, near the summit of Carl Side, and just off to one side. The

Skiddaw from the south-east and St John's in the Vale.

The Edge of Ullock Pike with a snow-bound Skiddaw in the background, from across Bassenthwaite Lake.

popular path from Millbeck (near Keswick) joined our route nearby and what we had to do, according to his calculations, was to strike slanting upwards to the south summit of Skiddaw from where a level ridge would eventually arrive at the main summit.

We began to scale a vast dune of slates pierced only by a tenuous path which shifted and slid with each laborious upwards step. The angle eased at what we presumed was the south summit (and where it is possible to mistakenly walk straight over to Jenkin Hill and Latrigg above Keswick). Groping our way along a stretch of further chinking Skiddaw slates, we finally reached the very summit trig point which was bearded with hoar frost.

It was then I made my second mistake. Insisting I could see the map, I veered north-west across pathless scree, skirting the tottering mass of Randel Crag (though I did not know it at the time) to guide us at last out of the billowing clouds and down on to a wonderful little ridge covered in grasses as windswept as the coat of a Yorkshire terrier in a gale. The north-west ridge bordering the other side of Southerndale Beck, it brought us back to the entrance of Southerndale just before the topmost intake wall, so naturally and gently that I thoroughly recommend it.

It wasn't, however, our intended route and so I returned a month later, with my new reading glasses and now able to see the map clearly once more. This time the day was clear and cold, following torrential rain. Visibility was perfect. From Skiddaw's summit I dropped down into the north col, continuing down to the waterfalls of Whitewater Dash by the old fence which, from 2,700ft, leads unerringly down past Dead Crags to the Skiddaw House road, once a packhorse track and now part of the Cumbria Way.

Great white feathers plumed down the waterfalls, their thunder reaching my ears before I actually saw them. With the shadowlands of Dead Crags setting off this lonely recess of Skiddaw to perfection and, refreshed and stimulated by those negative ions which, as the mail order catalogue claims about its Ionizer (£22.95 inc. P & P) 'Invigorate the air you breathe for a penny a month', I made my way back to the car beneath the outline of that most marvellous skyline (including the eminence of Cockup) which had kept me so occupied and absorbed from beginning to end.

Chapter 2

BLENCATHRA BY SHARP EDGE, FOULE CRAG AND DODDICK FELL

View the cruel steepness of Sharp Edge and Foule Crag from the M6 motorway on a winter's afternoon as they score a gaunt silhouette against a wild sky and you can feel an involuntary shiver. By the time you reach the lights of the White Horse Inn on the busy A66 from Penrith to Workington, five great ridges loom above but Sharp Edge has already slid by behind the grim bulk of the mountain. Yet fine as Scales Fell, Doddick Fell, Hall's Fell, Gategill Fell and Blease Fell undoubtedly are, it is the *way* Sharp Edge and Foule Crag have just reared up ever closer through the windscreen as you approached the mountain that remains freshest in the memory.

Sharp Edge and Foule Crag not only create the best ridge on Blencathra, but also the finest winter skyline expedition in the English Lake District. Foule Crag, incidentally, may sound like something from the Tales of

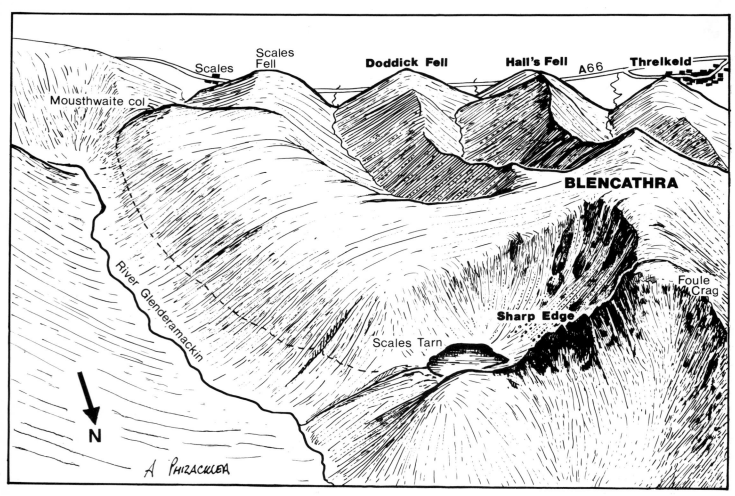

Tiny figures accentuate the bulk of Foule Crag above the slender knife blade of Sharp Edge.

accidents happen here. Besides, there is no avoiding the final rampart bordering Foule Crag, another place where people are occasionally killed or injured. All in all, the crest of Sharp Edge is the safest way to go, all 700ft of it. Perched as it is at an elevation of 2,000ft, it commands extensive views – except of that arterial highway below, which is screened by the mass of Scales Fell falling away beneath – and gives the distinct impression that any cry for help will be readily absorbed by the cavernous depths surrounding you.

Why do accidents happen on Sharp Edge? Part of the reason may be because Blencathra tucks its *bête noire* out of sight from where you park your car below. So you pulled off the A66 by the White Horse Inn at Scales, drove along the minute road signposted to Souther-fell and parked on the tiny common where a stream runs down from Mous-thwaite Combe? Great. But if you too were lulled into a sense of security by the surrounding greenery only to find

Chaucer, and it can indeed trigger the kind of Anglo-Saxon language you find in the *Miller's Tale*, yet its beetling aspect is inextricably linked with Sharp Edge. It is Foule Crag (true, breached at its perimeter but still vertiginous) that adds the final flourish to Sharp Edge, and which makes it look so highly improbable.

Rewarding as Sharp Edge and Foule Crag are, they also create the most formidable of the narrow Lakeland skylines. Broad Stand on Scafell – encountered on the Woolpack Round – is more tricky, but Broad Stand is a rock climb. Striding Edge is certainly a knife blade of solid rock, but Helvellyn's finest challenge is less serious a scramble than Sharp Edge, and though neighbouring Swirral Edge can prove a deathtrap in winter, the difficulties are not as sustained as on Blencathra's *pièce de resistance*.

Blencathra is hewn by the forces of nature from the Skiddaw Slates that

predominate in northern Lakeland, north of a line drawn from the southern end of Ullswater, along the east and south of Derwentwater and across towards Ennerdale. This rock was laid down as sediment in shallow seas, then raised by violent land movements. In the process it became squeezed and crumpled into slates, quite different from the more rugged volcanic rocks to the south (and formed from the lava, dust and ashes thrown out by the volcanoes once active here). The mountains north of the line consequently have a smooth, rounded appearance, and so do the rocks too. Bald, slippery and devoid of the kind of pockets ideal for urgently prying fingers, Skiddaw Slate is not to be trusted.

Difficulties along the crest of Sharp Edge may be avoided for a time along paths that traverse the hillside to the right and at a lower level. However, these have become heavily eroded. The going underfoot is crumbling and

The crucial, exposed and awkward section of Sharp Edge.

that higher up the fellside your first sight of Sharp Edge gripped you to the eyeballs, you are by no means the only one who has experienced such a trauma.

Many are they who have walked through the bowl of Mousthwaite Combe, and climbed by the track that rakes its furthest slopes to a col on its lip, still in blissful ignorance. These were the ones who had had no preview of what Sharp Edge would be like through the windscreen before they arrived because they had travelled from the other side of the mountain (from Keswick), for example, or they *had* driven from Penrith only to have their long-distance views obliterated by cloud. However, at last, as they cut back leftwards from the Mousthwaite Combe col towards the track skirting the flanks of Scales Fell, they too – like you – will have seen Sharp Edge flying up into the sky ahead. Perhaps sheathed in its wintery raiment of glistening ice, as green as a breaking wave.

For those who sensibly feel that already this view is too outlandish – 'I can't believe it! It looks horrific! I just don't have the experience!' – all is not lost. Scales Fell itself gives the fine alternative ascent of Blencathra, and one that is popular and worthwhile. It also proves a fine way down, easy angled and safe. All you need to do is to make a diversion from the path up the treadmill slopes there to the left and you will break out on the backbone of the friendly ridge above. You won't emerge immediately from its incline, I might add, for this is a long, stiff pull, but you will reach the backbone of this ridge, and then the summit of Blencathra, a lot more safely than on a wet or icy Sharp Edge. And a Sharp Edge, too, that in a hard winter becomes a graded winter climb requiring an ice-axe, crampons and expertise.

'This distinctive mountain (Blencathra), sometimes Alpine in appearance, gives the finest ridge climb in the region,' says the guide to *Winter Climbs in the Lake District* by Birkett (Hyslop

& Bennett, 1979). The impact of this on climbers is predictably heady. I saw what effect Sharp Edge had on one hillgoer who arrived at the Horse and Farrier in nearby Threlkeld after attempting it. It was Darts night and when the woman selling the raffle tickets was called away, the visitor was taken up on his offer to continue selling the tickets. He held the pint glass for the coins in one hand and the book of tickets with the other as he went around persuading everyone to buy. 'Was Sharp Edge good then?' I asked. 'Good?' he replied, 'Good?' He raised his glass. 'It was wicked!' Tipping his glass, he threw back his head and the coins poured down his throat.

He later told me his back was not only painful because of the blows it had received (to make him cough up the money rather than to prevent him from choking to death and also doubtless to show him you didn't try those tricks on in Threlkeld), but also because he'd fallen on Sharp Edge that same

afternoon. Slipping on icy rock, he had tobogganed down the flanks of the mountain towards Scales Tarn.

To anybody who knows the mountain, this was a horrific fall. 'Death Row!' was how the man described it, pronouncing 'Row' to rhyme with 'cow'. He had crossed swords with his companion who had insisted on following the crest of Sharp Edge rather than – bearing in mind the wintery conditions – taking the more prudent alternative of retreating before they were committed. Roped together, they each began to tug the rope in opposite directions. His companion had won, pulling him on to the edge and from where he had promptly fallen, dragging the two of them down together like puppets on a string, their cries echoing from the corrie walls. Finally, the visitor had managed to stop himself with his ice-axe and, when the rope twanged tight, his partner as well. Amazingly, nobody was seriously hurt.

If you still feel you are in with a

A distant Sharp Edge and Foule Crag seen from the approach footpath above the River Glenderamackin.

chance, the way to Sharp Edge continues easily ahead, following the course of the tiny River Glenderamackin that runs some distance below, until the moment comes when you begin to distance yourself from the silvery thread. This is the point where waterfalls tumble from Scales Tarn, still some distance above, down a scenic ghyll that crosses your path. It's also the place where, after crossing the cascades, you clamber steeply up their right-hand side and at long last into the crater surrounding the sombre tarn itself.

The outlet of the tarn provides a popular place to recover from the climb so far, and take stock. Sharp Edge and Foule Crag are overhead and up there to the right. A steep and shaly path leads unerringly to a grassy shoulder at the lowest point of the ridge. This shelf has wonderful views across to the Pennines and Eden Valley, but it is the outline of that spine of rock ever rising ahead in the opposite direction that occupies so many of those who take a final rest here. Like the decks of a great surreal submarine just breaking the surface after torpedoing them, and viewed by the survivors from a life raft, Sharp Edge has an air of menace to those sprawled on the grass immediately below. And not just Sharp Edge, for the upthrust of Foule Crag beyond could be the giant conning tower or fin, with a commander appearing on top about to give the order to open fire.

Sharp Edge is airy, narrow and uneven, but it can be safely traversed by anyone who has a head for heights and who takes care. While the agile and cool headed will balance their way like seasoned matelots tightrope-walking the slippiest catwalk in a stormy sea, anybody who is timid and fearful can tackle the scary parts on all fours or shuffle along on their behinds. Which type are you? And does it matter? Frankly, no. All that really concerns you is that you retreat in good time if you find yourself wobbling like a jelly

or freezing into immobility, for it is the final upward flourish of Sharp Edge as it merges into the periphery of Foule Crag that poses the most problems, so near and yet so far beneath the summit. If you suddenly go to pieces on this final headwall you may find it very difficult indeed to preserve the status quo, or to climb back down.

The problem is that there are many different ways ahead. If so far you have had no other option than to follow the vertiginous and exposed crest, now you can go left or right or straight on up. However, all these ways are so much of a muchness: steep, polished, equipped with few definite grips for hands or feet. Is a rope the answer? Unfortunately not; so suspect is the soundness of the Skiddaw slate that solid belays are rare. Consequently, if you fall on Sharp Edge, there is a good chance that any flake of rock to which your companion is attached will snap away under the strain. Thus you pull the two of you down together.

Sharp Edge finishes near the summit of Foule Crag and from here the walk to the summit of Blencathra is gentle. First, you continue easily upwards and across the wide depression that from a distance gives Blencathra its other name of Saddleback. When the summit finally arrives, you may not be able to believe you really have reached the top, this being a small eminence above Hall's Fell Ridge, the fourth along from the east. It can take several glances to double-check.

Although Hall's Fell Ridge is regarded as the complementary ridge to Sharp Edge – and make no mistake, it is an excellent mountain trip – for those who found Sharp Edge near the limit of their ability, then Doddick Fell is a worthy contender. It is an unsung ridge, rarely given its due in the guidebooks, and yet in places it is sharp-edged but with a difference. Only occasionally are you on rock; the way down Doddick Fell is a pathway through the heather, along a delightful path that is flanked

A group of cagoule-clad hillwalkers descend the roof tree of Doddick Fell in sunlight.

on either side by deep ravines and with inspiring backward views of the mountain rising above Doddick Gill to the very summit overhead.

Doddick Fell is reached by retracing your steps down Scales Fell, though this time keeping to the escarpment that overlooks the depths of Doddick Gill. The profile of Hall's Fell shows to great advantage from this viewpoint. Then suddenly the way divides: Scales Fell continuing on down below while Doddick Fell veers off sharply to the right and down a steep section of slabby rocks, to lead you unerringly down its crest towards the road. Near the foot of the ridge the path veers to the left, bringing you down through a tiny gorge, across Scaley Beck (yes, Scaley) and back along the base of the hillside towards the White Horse Inn. You are now within earshot of the traffic on the road below, but still up there above you is the magnificent mountain you have just climbed by a truly memorable way.

Chapter 3
THE COLEDALE ROUND

A great twisted horseshoe bent all out of shape, the Coledale Round might have been furiously beaten by the hammer of a demented blacksmith who finally hurls it into the furthest recess of his forge whilst still glowing red-hot. Here is a deeply bitten and riven ridge of high ground from Grisedale Pike to Causey Pike, including the peaks of Hopegill Head, Crag Hill (the highest 'Hill' in England), Sail and Scar Crags in between. It is magnificent. Offering as it does the greenest turf on which to walk and the steepest rocks up which to climb, it can both entrance and bewilder.

Those who have done this skyline traverse in perfect weather may well say, 'The Coledale Round? What's the problem?' But you, dear reader? You have been warned . . .

Somewhere along its length I had been told (although my attention wandered as the person telling me took a somewhat unscheduled short cut through the garage forecourt at Tyndrum in the Highlands when he had meant to take an acute bend in the road itself), there was a dangerous section. 'Dangerous?' I do remember shouting. 'Yes,' he yelled back, hauling on the wheel like the helmsman of the Flying Dutchman in a tempest, while

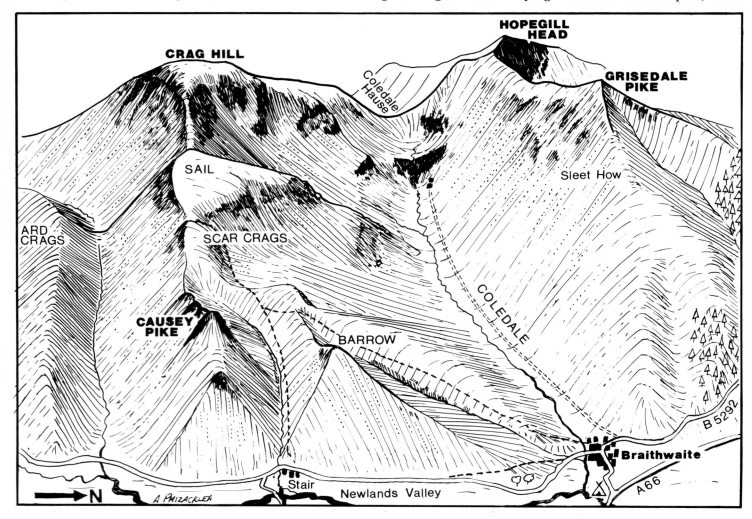

the kilted pump attendant dived for safety. 'Dangerous! People have been killed there.'

Before I came to do the Coledale Round, I found this hard to credit. Dangerous – really? Alfred Wainwright never mentions anything here as being a hands-on occasion (like the ascent of Broad Stand, Sharp Edge or Striding Edge), and surely you associate risk on mountains with scrambling where the hands are as busy as the feet.

Stand on the shingle beach of Derwentwater and you too might wonder. This is a hyperactive skyline where the rise and fall of shapely hills knows no rest. But hazardous? There is not a crag in sight. Didn't John Ruskin (who not only had an Oxford college named after him but also the comprehensive school at Coniston and a dock-lands' back street in Barrow-in-Furness) rate this view from Friar's Crag as one of the finest in Europe? And at a time when any mountain remotely precipitous was a turn-off. Do not top-deck travellers on the big red buses descending steeply into Keswick obtain another stunning prospect of the Coledale mountains? One where the skyline of Causey Pike becomes a giant 'Desert Orchid' in full gallop, 6,000 hands tall and with ears fully pricked?

I had no doubt the person giving me this information would be correct. Completing Zero Gully on Ben Nevis, he and his partner sought shelter from a blizzard in the summit bivouac shelter. In the cramped confines of this metal box, they began to work out a compass bearing to the Red Burn. Two souls already bivvied there shouted, 'Compasses? Hell, no. Tin walls!' The fact that you can use a Silva compass purely for its plastic protractor had never dawned on them. So quickly did it become obvious that my friend and his partner knew only too well what they were about that the other two quickly packed and followed their saviours out into the twilight white-out and down safely to the glen.

However, as to danger on the Coledale Round, I would just have to find out for myself the hard way.

A short drive from Keswick along the freeway of the A66, the village of Braithwaite nestles, just off to the left. Guarding the entrance to a fold in the hills, Braithwaite is the place to park (the best car-park being recessed into the fellside a short way up the narrow B5292 over Whinlatter Pass). It is from here that the terraced steps of a path lead up on to the backbone of the great ridge bordering Coledale (that crease in the hills) and which shows itself to such advantage from the Keswick direction.

So wonderfully gradual is the ascent of Grisedale Pike along this ridge, taking in the eminences of Kinn and Sleet How along the way, that it defies detailed description. However, I have a lasting impression of a strip of luminous green baize that has been inlaid through the bracken like a magic carpet. Sometimes bordering sweet-scented woodland, occasionally jinking here and swerving there, and at several points decidedly steepening in angle, this path defines itself so perfectly that a billiard ball rolling from the summit must surely find its way downwards into Braithwaite until it drops into a pocket of the Royal Oak pool table.

Grisedale Pike finishes with a flourish. A good path swoops up its northeast arête with an abundance of space on both sides, and at a steep enough angle to bend you double with the effort. But risky? Hardly. Perhaps my friend *had* been mistaken I decided, continuing on down from the summit of Grisedale Pike, over a subsidiary peak to the south-west and into a col. Then I heard the shouts.

At first the calls were faint but there was no mistaking their urgency. All around, mountain vied with mountain, their summits powdered by overnight snow, while how green were the valleys below, and how gold the western sea-

Grisedale Pike viewed on the approach up its marvellous ridge from Braithwaite.

board. The scenery was majestic, breathtaking and peaceful. Perhaps people were stuck on Hobcarton Crag? Impossible to climb enjoyably as its rock is rickety, Hobcarton Crag is the haunt of abseiling botanists. Yet surely not in winter? And as for walkers unavoidably cragfast on the Coledale Round, I didn't think so. You do not even have to continue around to Hobcarton Crag (below Hopegill Head) to complete the Coledale Round. Coledale Hause lies down to the left and that is the next stage of the journey. But the sounds were coming from somewhere. Wasn't that the sound of a whistle?

Turning my attention towards the south, the spectacular swell of mountains on the other side of Coledale Hause had not particularly grabbed

The footpath up Grisedale Pike (shortly after leaving the car-park on Whinlatter Pass).

my attention, but now they did. Almost directly across the Hause, an aspect of Crag Hill that had previously been hidden came into view with a vengeance. Here was a veritable Eiger, sunless and sombre and bristling with frowning rock bands and steep scree, and I knew I had arrived at the place my friend had mentioned.

Leading invitingly up scree into the heart of the cliffs was a very obvious track, a direct route to the summit of Crag Hill approximately 1,000ft above. Compared with the usual path, which avoids the cliffs first by cutting across immediately beneath the scree (to the shallow col between Crag Hill and Grasmoor and overlooking Buttermere) and then swinging back left for the summit, there was no contest. The dia-

The path up Grisedale Pike with a view towards the head of Coledale.

The dangerous path slanting up the screes of Crag Hill – especially hazardous in winter.

gonal path up the scree *looked* the part. Presumably it explained why now there was a crisis above.

Someone in a bright red cagoule and carrying a large black rucksack was stuck, unable to go up or down. As more people converged on the screes below from different parts of the fells, those already there were trying to help by shouting, but seemingly to no avail. The scree was unstable and a skidpan of slippery boulders. Besides, the lofty rock bands were inaccessible because of ice on the rock. It transpired that the walker had been descending from the summit and, like a cragfast sheep, had slithered down several yards of crag before coming to rest on a sloping platform above the edge of space.

The shouting continued. Could the victim continue down? Only as he already had – at 32ft per second (I was glad to see that however catastrophic his position he had managed to preserve a sense of humour). Could he then climb up? At first he called 'No!' Then, after it was suggested that he might find it possible if he removed his boots and ascended in stockinged feet, he yelled down he would try. There was a problem: his hands were too cold to untie the laces. Someone asked if perhaps (like Clint Eastwood in *The Eiger Sanction*) he had a penknife. Yes, a Swiss Army model. Next problem: his frozen fingers refused to open it. Then, when they did, he cut a finger while sawing at the laces. But down came his boots, landing with thuds as those assembled on the scree scattered to avoid the missiles and a fusillade of icicles that accompanied them.

A tinkling clatter suggested his penknife had slipped down the crag too (it had and it is still there somewhere among the rocks together with magnifying glass, tweezers and the rest). By now his body was visibly shaking with the effort. Spreadeagled against the face in exactly the position which preludes a fall, he began to claw his way upwards. Suddenly his body lurched. No longer able to watch, I looked away. Glancing up again I was horrified to see a dark shape falling through the sky. This time I closed my eyes. There was a sickening bang. 'Oh, God,' said a voice, 'he's done for – Oh, no!'

When I opened my eyes, it was not clear what had happened. The figure in the red cagoule was still clinging to the rock above. But now someone else was lying prostrate on the scree with blood oozing from his head. And then it became clear. Our 'climber' had thrown down his rucksack to lighten his progress, and it had burst open in the descent depositing packets of sandwiches, a vacuum flask (now sounding like a cocktail shaker full of ice) and various bits and pieces, one of which had evidently struck someone looking for the missing penknife and who had been immediately underneath.

'Looks bad'. The nearest helper on the screes shook his head. 'He's white as a sheet and what a cut! Man, you can see his brains'.

'Thanks a lot,' said the casualty, coming to life with unexpected alacrity, 'You're making me feel better no end'.

'Eeeh! It's not his brains,' said another helper. He carefully wiped the victim's forehead, crouching down to peer.

'Well, what is it then?'

'Ah don't know, man, but it's not brains'. He sniffed at his finger and recognition dawned as he tasted it gingerly with his tongue. 'Coo! It's lemon curd'.

To be struck down by a flying jam jar is a rarer hazard of the fells, but so is climbing frozen rock in stockinged feet. While the recipient of the head wound was receiving a first-aider's attention, the intrepid venturer above, quite unaware of the mayhem he had caused below, was scrambling out of the danger zone to safety and now complaining of being unable to feel his toes. His boots, meanwhile, had been passed on to two fell runners who, making for the top of Crag Hill by the ordinary route, promised they would whisk them up to him within ten minutes – and they had spare laces too.

The strength of this ridge walk is such that, despite the excitement of such an episode, the rest of the skyline was not an anti-climax. Quite the reverse, in fact. Indeed the rest of the way along to Causey Pike was a joy despite the rather interminable slog up those gentle slopes of Crag Hill that bypass its crags. The first gem you meet is the view from Crag Hill. It is one of Lakeland's best.

A string of pearls follow: the utterly delightful ridge walk that leads you unerringly first down the steep, narrow and rocky crest into a col below Crag Hill, then up again on to Sail (at 2,530ft higher than more famous hills like Langdale Pikes). In mist, incidentally, a cairn marks this descent at the south-

The author climbs the final ridge towards the summit of Grisedale Pike.

Looking from Crag Hill along the ridge towards Causey Pike.

east corner of Crag Hill's top. From Sail, another descent continues down into Sail Pass before climbing up on to Scar Crags and along their rooftops to Causey Pike.

The descent is sufficiently steep to allow you, it seems, to peer down the chimney-pots of the cottages far below, but not for long. Your full attention is needed on the steep scrambling (which includes a short rock chimney) and fell-side below as you corkscrew your way down by Sleet Hause and Rawling End to the road. The walk back to Braithwaite begins here, but soon a bridle path strikes left through delightful scenery that is all the more so for being in the shadow of the great hill cirque you have just completed and which allows you to finish your day with a lovely sense of peace and satisfaction.

Chapter 4
THE CATBELLS HORSESHOE

Catbells is one of the best-loved hills in the British Isles. It is also one of those peaks that is just a fraction taller than the red light on top of Manhattan's Empire State Building. However, in terms of stature, it is dwarfed by the sheer size and weight of the mountains that surround it on all sides: to the north, the frowning and malodorous bulk of Skiddaw (at least in Lakeland rain); to the east, the sprawling heap of Castlerigg Fell; to the west the great massed silhouettes of the Derwent Fells (like Crag Hill and Grisedale Pike); and to the south? To the south loom the peaks of Maiden Moor and High Spy, and Dale Head, mountains, in fact, which make up most of the glorious horseshoe to which Catbells gives its name, and of which it is a part.

The remainder of the skyline, now curling back and returning almost to Catbells itself, though on the far side of the Newlands valley, includes the tops of Hindscarth and Scope End, where gold was mined centuries ago. Taken in all, the skyline is superb in every detail, even solid gold you might say. While Scotland's mountain ridges and the brawny arms of Snowdon or

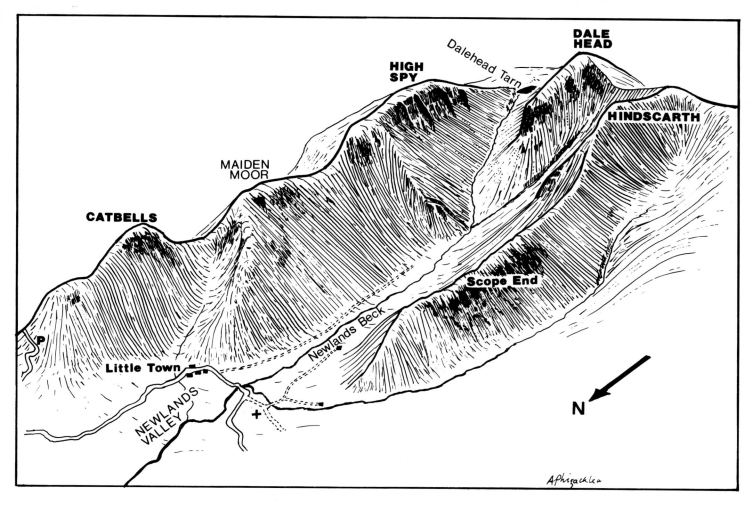

The Catbells skyline rises above Derwentwater . . .

A mountain bicycle and its rider on Catbells. This is an example not to follow as he is off-limits – only bridle paths are acceptable for this form of travel.

the Glyders would lose Catbells among their respective massifs, its skyline as a whole will stand comparison with mountain giants on the strength of its other attributes, not least being its shapeliness and accessibility.

Catbells, like Grasmere's Helm Crag, is all too easily considered a solitary peak. It is the shape that does it. Like the Great Bell of Kiev in Mussorgsky's *Pictures from an Exhibition* it sends out a peal to the heart that is irresistible. Whenever you look from the vicinity (or even the town centre) of Keswick, you can distinguish Catbells from the other mountains by its shape. Even if you have no experience of fell-walking, you may still crave to take up its challenge. Then, having success-

. . . and the start of the ridge from near Hause Point.

fully reached its rocky summit, you see the skyline beyond, which has been hidden from view behind Catbells until then, and you immediately want to venture along it to see more.

This is the danger of Catbells. True, there are other hazards like ancient mine workings and open shafts and pits in the hillside which can unexpectedly open up ahead of you in mist should you stray away from the path, but these are nothing compared to the risk of you suddenly taking off unprepared without windproofs or food, along a skyline that will presently rise to well over twice the height of the Eiffel tower. And all because you only intended to climb Catbells. May I give you an example?

There are four summits to Catbells, each one that little higher than the previous one, and it was just beyond the first summit that I sensed danger. 'Hannah!' I said, 'Hey!' Having no intention of being spoken to like a sheepdog, my youngest daughter Hannah, aged nine, her head full of Beatrix Potter's Mrs Tiggie-Winkle (written when the Lakeland authoress lived in the Vale of Newlands down there to the right and where we had previously watched smoke climbing from the chimneys of the cottages below), disregarded my shouts. Instead, she stepped on to the brink of a dripping mine shaft in the col below the second peak.

We had started from the car-park at the toe of the ridge below, not far from

the Hause Point landing stage on Derwentwater (and reached, if driving, via Portinscale, Braithwaite or Grange-in-Borrowdale). Hannah had led the way from the start, hoisting herself up the steepest bits where the path zigzags, and loping easily along the more amenable gradients. Then, fuelled by curiosity, she found the cutting in the hillside. I would have given anything to have been able to pull her back like a yo-yo on a string.

Like a snooker ball that slowly rolls to the very edge of a pocket before it finally drops in, my daughter disappeared, swallowed into the bowels of the earth. 'Hannah!' I yelled, breaking into a run. The relief of finding her standing just inside the mine on a carpet of moss

'Hannah had led the way . . . hoisting herself up the steepest bits where the path zigzags and loping easily along the more amenable gradients . . .'

could not alleviate my feelings of impatience. 'What the hell . . . !' I think I said. 'But Dad,' she said, 'Dad! Beatrix Potter mentions it . . .' She tailed off miserably, adding that she thought that the hole was the chimney of the little house deep within the hillside that Lucy had stumbled upon when she discovered a door beneath a boulder. Beyond which she had heard someone singing.

'I'll give you Beatrix Potter,' I said, immediately regretting it as she turned her face away, a tear falling on a training shoe. Feeling dreadful, and knowing it wasn't just what I had said but the way I had said it, I tried to make amends. 'Please be careful, Hann, people have been killed down these holes.' I stopped, unzipped the rucksack and rummaged for the sticky bag I knew was somewhere inside. 'Would you like an Acid Lemon?' but she shook her head and again became interested in the magical view of Derwentwater's wooded islands below.

What does a father do? I think I began to whistle. I also tried to help her as the path became more awkward, ascending rocks up the final turret to the summit. Reaching up, I held her foot on a tiny ledge as she hesitated. But she took it sharply away. This caused her to slip and she banged into me, scraping her hand in the process. 'Let's have a look,' I said, reaching for the hand. Hannah kept her face averted and didn't answer. When we eventually reached the summit a stinging rain shower caught us and we pulled on cagoules – only for the deluge to stop just as quickly. But Hannah was shivering. I put my arm round her and this time she didn't try to pull away.

'You might have been right,' I said, 'It could have been the chimney to the house in the hillside, the one with the clothes-prop outside cut from bracken and with the clothes-line made from plaited rushes, but I'm just not sure it

was in the right place.' I waited. 'What d'you think?' She didn't answer but I felt her head nod. 'I'm sorry,' I said. 'I shouldn't have shouted, but I thought you'd fallen down a mine shaft.' Again her head moved. 'I was just worried sick,' I continued, 'That's why I yelled'. 'I know you did, Dad,' she said, 'I know you did.' We sat there for a few moments in a more contented silence. 'Should we?' I finally asked. Hannah saw where I was looking, and followed my gaze first down the other side of Catbells into the saddle of Hause Gate and then up the steady incline, climbing to Maiden Moor beyond. 'Go on then?' She nodded 'Go on, then, Dad.'

Some way below the summit of Maiden Moor, Hannah wanted to go back. No longer scrambling in front, she now trailed behind, and so we retreated. With no thanks to me: 'A party on the hills is only as strong as its weakest member' goes the saying. By keeping her in the dark as to my real intentions, i.e. the eventual traverse of the complete ridge to take photographs for this book rather than just the ascent of Catbells as I'd originally promised, I had put Hannah in the position of the novice who succeeds in climbing Catbells, only then to be drawn on unprepared by the continuation of the ridge.

The next time I climbed Catbells I was on my own. Continuing along the ridge past Hause Gate and striding up Maiden Moor in my trainers, I revelled in my new-found sense of freedom, but I missed my daughter. Down there in Newlands to the right was the community of Little Town. This was where, Hannah had explained, Lucy had climbed the fellside as fast as her short legs would carry her to a point so steeply above the houses below she could have dropped a pebble down any of the chimneys. 'Good old Hannah,' I said aloud. 'I beg your pardon!' said a voice. I glanced up in consternation. A couple on the path immediately ahead were looking at me enquiringly and trying to make themselves heard through a freshening south-west wind. 'Just rehearsing for a play,' I replied, hurrying past to hide my embarrassment. 'I wonder if he's famous?' I heard the woman say. 'Max Wall', said the man.

The sou'wester began to gust so violently that it stopped me in my tracks. I paused in mid-stride to pull the cagoule from my day sack, gripped the sack between my knees to prevent it blowing away and clamped my mitts between my teeth. Facing into the wind, I was about to slip a hand down a sleeve with the garment streaming behind me like a windsock, when the wind tore it from my too casual grasp, blew it far away and continued to knife through my clothing with renewed vigour.

Arms folded across my stomach to cut down the chill, I staggered on, punchy and confused. Where was the next escape route? Of course, Hause Gate. I could retrace my steps with the wind behind me with no problem. Then I heard the voice (this time from safely within me): 'No!' it said, 'You have the photographs to take'. It is under such pressures that accidents happen on mountains, as I was about to discover.

Long before I reached this summit, the wind took its toll, tearing shrilly across the exposed ridge, bitter and far more numbing than a dental anaesthetic. Though I must have known, I didn't actually acknowledge to myself that this was the killing cold that makes newspaper headlines about mountain tragedies. It was only because the footpath over Maiden Moor and High Spy is easy to follow and not unduly steep that I continued to climb, unable to stop because this option – I felt – would chill me even more. By now the photographs were a memory, although gleams of sunlight nourished a forlorn hope.

At one point I became so disorientated that I was convinced I *was* returning towards Catbells until it finally dawned on me that the mountain looming ahead was Dale Head; I was descending from High Spy to Rigg Head. Rather than retracing my steps northwards to take a photograph from Blea Crag – a subsidiary peak midway between Maiden Moor and High Spy, past which I'd blundered without even realizing – I was still continuing southwards and, with my body unprotected from its blast, into the teeth of the gale.

Teeth, I managed a fleeting thought, that seemed to be losing their grip. Then I realized why. As I was turning around the head of Newlands, the wind was now coming from the quarter and actually helping me on. But it did not get any warmer. By the time I reached Dale Head Tarn I was hungry, yet, hearty eater as I am, I could not have stopped. Standing still in the cold was an endurance test in itself. Movement was the only way to keep the circulation going. Furthermore, I knew that my swollen, gloveless hands (for in trying to grab my fleeing cagoule my mitts had also blown away) would have been incapable of unzipping my rucksack, let alone opening a vacuum flask.

Things had become so bad that I preferred to let the wind blow me up the steep track towards the summit of Dale Head rather than take either of the two escape routes from the tarn; one down to Borrowdale, the other into Newlands. Leaning back against the blast, my back protected from it by my day sack, and with a fraction of the effort normally required, I was swept on so violently up the extremely steep flanks of the mountain and towards the summit cairn that there was no stopping me. I did try, by digging my heels frantically into the turf and attempting to fling myself on the turf. Dale Head cairn sits on the brink of space and for several agonizing moments I was in danger of being frog-marched straight past it and on into eternity. However, luckily, the wind veered, plastering me up against the column of stone instead, breathless and exhausted.

I don't know how long I was there. I do know I had to crawl along the ground to gain a position sufficiently far down the slope and into the wind before I could stagger to my feet with any certainty of not being given the bum's rush back towards that cairn again. Mercifully, I somehow found my way down to the top of Honister Pass by the escape route that follows a line of old fence posts, but this gentle downhill stretch took two hours. By the time I reached the road (and obtained a lift back to Keswick) it was completely dark.

And the Catbells Horseshoe? I completed it the third time. But I reflected, as I continued around Newlands from the summit of Dale Head (negotiating a sharp-edged ridge and finally making a dog-leg away to the right and on to the gravelly top of Hindscarth, before descending down three miles of roof-tree perfection to Newlands church), I could not say 'Third time lucky'. I had been lucky the second time. People have died for less. It must be a horrible way to go.

Chapter 5

THE GRASMOOR HORSESHOE

Grasmoor is a superlative mountain seen to great advantage from the West Cumberland coast where, further south, Sellafield fronts on to the Irish Sea.

Before you break into a shudder at the dreaded word, I might say that, from my own experience, Whitehaven up the coast can be as dangerous a spot. There are frequent fall-outs in the town centre on a Friday night and I'm not being entirely flippant. As a recipient of a blow from a pool cue in the Land of the Marrers ('All right, Marrer?' they say as they pick you up and dust you down after a fracas by the green baize), I might be qualified to judge. A plaque in the Paul Jones Tavern says 'I do not wish to have command of any ship that does not sail fast for I intend to go in "Harm's Way",' and it pays to remember this in West Cumbria. It also sums up my first visit to Grasmoor.

On the road beyond Whitehaven, past the big Nissan garage and the British Leyland plant which manu-

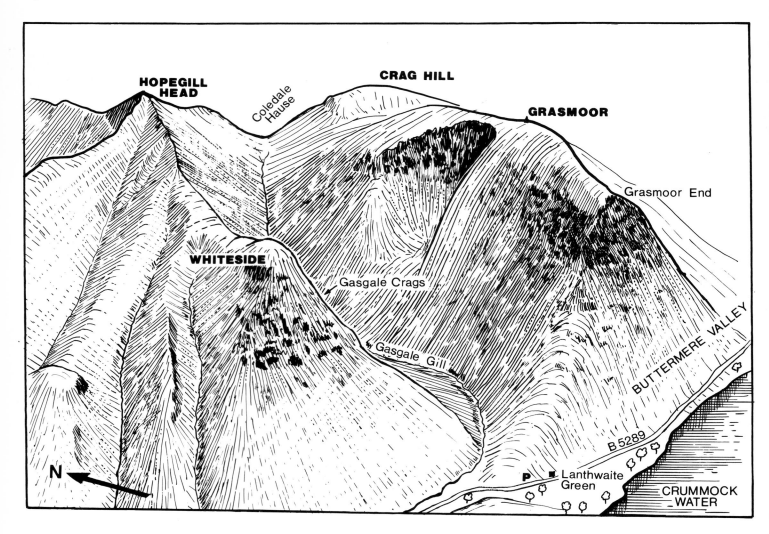

Grasmoor's north-west aspect seen to good advantage from Lanthwaite Green.

factures buses, is Oily Johnnies Pub. Grasmoor fairly leaps into view from this vantage point, dwarfing other Lake District giants. Surely it can't be just because of the heady brew served here? A great axe-head profile soars up into the sky which, with its linking horse-shoe over Hopegill Head and Whiteside, will take you four or five hours to cir-cumnavigate. When you do go round it, remember those words of John Paul Jones, the privateer who set fire to boats in Whitehaven harbour in 1788 after making a name for himself in the American War of Independence. Again I speak from experience – of Grasmoor, that is.

The Grasmoor cirque is in fact a highly satisfying challenge for the hillwalkers requiring a rugged and challenging morning or afternoon. A compact horseshoe overlooking the road-side at the entrance to Butter-mere, it is its position that makes it. Grasmoor dominates the skyline for many miles, a wild and isolated outpost bristling with shattered crags and steeply banked scree and open to the westerlies roaring in from the Irish sea.

I first encountered Grasmoor as a schoolboy on a cycling holiday. It looked as big as the North face of the Eiger across the bright green strip of Lanth-waite Green where the ice cream van stands in summer, bordering the road from Cockermouth to Buttermere – huge, forbidding and compelling. How we succeeded can perhaps best be judged by the subsequent dialogue.

'We'll just have to take it by surprise next time,' said Dan, 'Come a different way. Do Grasmoor from another direc-tion and we can be up it before it sees us'. What he really meant was 'Before we see it'. Because his comments herald-ed an ignominious defeat in our bold venture. Really we had been beaten before we began, but the idea refused to go away, and it remained an objective for the following year: to climb Gras-moor by its north-west shoulder.

A few months later we again set out for the north-west route up Grasmoor. Again the long bike ride. Again a breeze and frost, although this time the sun was shining fitfully. 'It's going to be cold, mate,' was Dan's only comment. For the next five minutes we got ready in silence. Then Dan said, 'Why don't

An airy perch on the descent down Whiteside's ridge to Lanthwaite Green.

we climb that one instead?' He pointed to the adjacent peak of Whiteside. 'It looks a lot easier. That way we'll be able to walk round more easily to the top of Grasmoor from the far side'. 'Not go up the front of Grasmoor you mean?' I asked. 'You know what happened last time,' he said, blowing on his fingers, 'It's even colder today'. I heard myself say OK, Whiteside it was then, though 'I felt anything but OK.

'On the other hand . . .' said Dan. Again the silence. It remained un-broken as we crossed Lanthwaite Green, not in the direction of Gras-moor but towards the peak to its left, and separated from it by the rift of Gascale Gill; we were each deep in our own conflicting thoughts.

A path led us to the glassy waters of Liza Beck. I turned to look at Grasmoor up there to my right just as Dan, who was in the way, turned to glance at me. 'Should we?' he said, nodding to his right. 'Chance it?' I asked. He nodded. 'Let's keep going in that case,' he said. He reckoned that we could join the path we had followed the last time until we had been defeated by the steep scree and rocks. 'We're approaching from the side this time,' he said, 'So it won't look so bad'. But still, look bad it did, I'm afraid, as once again we met the scree.

All the disquiet and qualms of our first meeting flooded back as we bent under our sacks and began the ascent up the steep bank of shifting pebbles. This time, however, we discovered the faintest of tracks threading a route through the shifting stones. Even today it is little more than a succession of well-pounded footprints but using them makes all the difference and provides a firm footing.

The scree slopes finally led us to our point of defeat on our previous visit, a nick in the broken crags overlooking a tremendous view of fellsides plummet-ing into the fields below. We passed through this 'turnstile', clambering on up to a small shoulder 1,000ft above

Whiteside viewed from Lanthwaite Green.

Crummock Water, glistening below, and spared no more glances downhill.

'It's like a bad dream,' said Dan as we clung, often literally as handholds were offered on the bristling outcrops we had to pass as the path weaved up through a gallery of steep crags, seemingly on the edge of space. At a second shoulder, perched even more airily above the distant valley below, we began to enjoy this scrambling up a staircase of rocky slabs, rather than trying to keep our balance on the icy path.

Grasmoor End is not the summit of Grasmoor, although it looks it from below. You have to go further along the summit ridge for that. However, it does have dramatic views: down the end of the mountain, into the lake and with most of the hillside invisible below. This awesome aspect is in direct contrast with the rest of the skyline, being a delightful grassy ridge around to Whiteside via Coledale Hause and across the head of Gascale Gill's yawning throat.

There are, however, two other unusual viewpoints along the way. First, from the ridge beyond Grasmoor itself, Dan and I looked on unbelievingly as the mist drew back from the opposite skyline to show the pleated form of Gascale Crags as if a curtain had been swept aside. Then, having circumnavigated the ridge along its sharp heathery crest from Hopegill Head, we stood on the very brink of those same accordion-like precipices and gazed back at the forbidding north-west face of Grasmoor, gouged out as if by a monster scoop of the type used in the Lanthwaite Green ice-cream van on those hot summer days.

At least this is how I think of it now whenever I climb Grasmoor or see its distant shape from other hills in Cumbria. But there was no ice-cream that day as we descended, laughing and shouting with joy, the frosted path down Whiteside.

Chapter 6

THE BUTTERMERE SKYLINE

Buttermere, as the Normans found to their cost when they were ambushed by the English in a savage battle amidst these mountains, is incomparably placed among wild and formidable scenery. The dalehead remained a mountain stronghold long after the Conquest and whatever stood it in good stead then still holds fast today.

Its sentinels are Red Pike, High Stile, High Crag and Haystacks on one side, with Fleetwith Pike, Dale Head, Hindscarth and Robinson on the other. For our purposes, however, let's take the ridge from Red Pike to Haystacks and around to Fleetwith Pike – a magical horizon that can both invigorate and intimidate. Nor has it lost anything over the centuries in its air of impregnability as rain sweeps across the horizon and

black clouds spiral and rotor above the lake.

Of all the fells in the Lake District that the late Alfred Wainwright has documented in his famous guidebooks, it was on the Buttermere skyline that he requested his ashes to be scattered after he passed on. Wainwright is a byword among hillwalkers, and his choice of Haystacks as his final resting

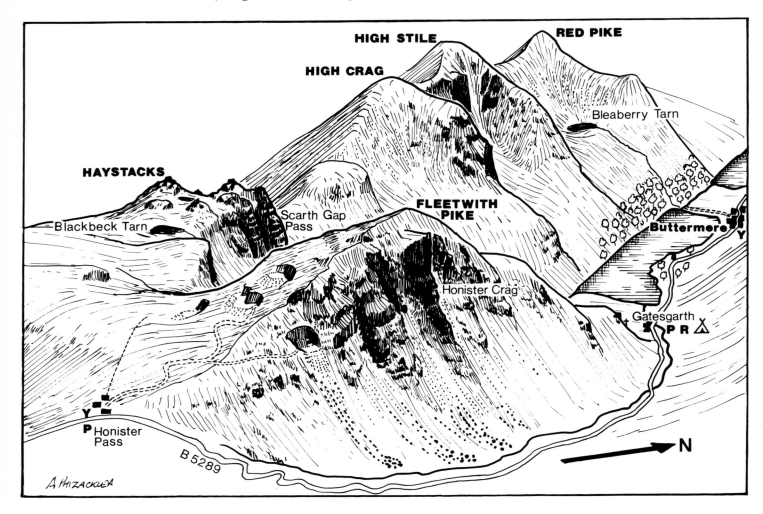

place speaks volumes for the transcendent beauty of these mountains. Yet Cockermouth mountain rescue team is frequently called out to this very place.

Haystacks, which towers above the meadows of Gatescarth Farm at the head of the valley like something from a historic painting by E.T. Compton or Elijah Wilson, is one of the most insidious places of all in having a fatal seductive appeal. Nor is Haystacks alone in this; other places along this great ridge walk can pose a risk. Given unexpected mist or blizzard, and a side of the Buttermere skyline emerges as different as Dr Jekyll from Mr Hyde.

The metamorphosis that occurs can be frightening to the expert and tyro alike. This is why I suggest starting from the Fish Hotel at the bottom end of the lake and doing the walk in an anti-clockwise direction.

As you stand on the foot-bridge across the outlet river from the jade green depths of Buttermere, senses dulled perhaps by city life come alive. Water slaps on the shingle. Ahead, the hillside is cloaked with rustling woods. Down through it tumbles one of the three Sourmilk Ghylls in Lakeland – a waterslide churning white from the

Honister Crag, the steep face of Fleetwith Pike, plunges down to Honister Pass and is viewed from the slopes of Dale Head.

hidden basin of Bleaberry Combe overhead.

Inveterate mountain goats will be drawn to the invigorating scramble up the leafy banks of Sourmilk Ghyll. A fizz in the air tickles the nostrils like a glass of Eno's Fruit Salts. The foliage is lacquered to a gloss with flying spray. Just one more Black Spot where accidents happen, Sourmilk Ghyll should be approached with caution by climbers

intent on scrambling up its very bed. There comes a point high up these waterfalls where it is easy to come unstuck. A fall is always serious here, and has all too frequently proved fatal.

During hard winters, Sourmilk Ghyll freezes solid from the very top right down to the outlet of the lake. In February 1984, for instance, three days of bitterly cold gales followed up by three weeks of hard frosts created a climber's dream.

A procession of Ice Warriors took up its challenge like an invading army. With an ice-axe in each hand, crampons clipped to their plastic boots and bubbling with glee at such unusual conditions, many achieved a route they will always remember – clawing a way up this silvery thread above the silent woods and fields below.

The crucial pitch was like something from *Psycho*. Water thundered behind a translucent shower curtain of icicles hanging vertically overhead. It was into this frail-looking drapery that you had to reach high with first one axe point, then the other – the front points of your crampons biting into the ice as well – and stab your way to the top.

Most people in the normal course of

The North (Ennerdale) Face of Great Gable seen backlit from Haystacks.

events prefer the reconstructed path which branches off up the hillside to the left of Sourmilk Ghyll. It climbs steeply through tall conifers to the open fellside above. Yet others experience a change of heart below this mountainside and walk instead around the lake.

Buttermere's skyline walk may not seem in the same league, technically speaking, as scaling a Sourmilk Ghyll, bottled solid by the freezing cold, but – and it is a big but – before you suspend yourself from what is in effect a shower curtain (made from ice), you should at least accept that it may well collapse as it did in the film when Anthony Perkins attacked the woman in the shower with his knife. On the heights of Red Pike and beyond, however, you are prey to a different risk.

Taken in by the splendour of the views as you clamber up the final slopes of pink scree and shale, and above the bowl of the combe below with its lovely little tarn surrounded by rocks and heather, it is human to lose all sense of reason. Especially as, once on top of Red Pike itself, a line of old fence posts guides you along the ridge.

Once, while walking from Red Pike to Fleetwith, I met a man approaching

High Crag as it appears from the end of Haystacks above Scarth Gap.

from the *other* direction who asked me how far he had to go to reach Haystacks. And this was on a clear, although windy day. The winds, in fact, had done for him. A persistent buffeting by strong gusts is all it takes if you are unfit or inexperienced. It becomes exhausting to fight them, to brace yourself ready for the next onslaught. You become punchy and capable of doing irrational things.

This man had in fact turned round

somewhere along the ridge without realizing it. With his tear ducts streaming – it does not need a wind to bring tears to your eyes on mountains, just jogging downhill will do it – he had not even noticed his about-turn. Proceeding as though nothing had happened, he had begun walking back in the direction from which he'd originally come.

No wonder, then, that lives are lost on skylines like the Buttermere. If you walk eastwards knowing there are crags to the left beneath the ridge but that the right-hand flanks are cragless – as is more or less the case in the instance of Buttermere's skyline – then inadvertently turn around and walk back westwards, you put yourself in real danger!

The risk comes if a blizzard – or whatever – forces you down before you reach the end of the ridge. You know, say, that there are crags in Birkness Combe, to the left. You decide to descend to the right into Ennerdale, which is bordered less dangerously by scree and pine trees. Imagine the outcome, then, if you had previously turned around without realizing and were heading back to the west where the right becomes the left and vice versa. It can happen.

Red Pike is one of the best viewpoints

Innominate Tarn on the Haystacks with Pillar Fell on the distant skyline.

in Lakeland: from seawards to the Isle of Man and across the Solway to Scotland, and back into the heart of the Lake District where the Great Gable rises above its neighbouring hills like the top of Frankenstein's monster's head. And it is in the direction of Great Gable and the plethora of other Lakeland monsters pushing upwards into the sky to left and right that this gorgeous skyline heads.

Firstly, there is the delight that never fades of looking into Bleaberry Combe to the left and across to Pillar Rock, high on the flanks of mighty Pillar mountain across the tank of Ennerdale to the right. Things get even better. Birkness Combe, to the left and beyond the next eminence of High Stile but before you reach the one beyond that of High Crag, is a magnificent mountain bowl. Grey Crag, a series of steep rock buttresses, nestles in its bosom. And Eagle Crag looks stupendously forbidding as befits its name.

Suddenly, the ground falls dramatically away beneath your feet. This time you have not strayed into danger. There is no avoiding the descent now plummeting away into the depths below. It is the only way you can go, down the scree of High Crag – a Big Dipper of a hillside.

High Crag is the kind of place where those nervous of steep places hesitate, and even stall. Stripped to the bone by the passage of countless pairs of boots, the scree is thin on the ground. Mostly you have to descend the ironhard slopes now swept clear of scree which is far more dangerous. It is easy to lose your balance on such treacherous footing, but it is still possible to piece together

smaller chutes of small stones which will carry you down like an escalator once you apply your weight, until you see another stream of pebbles into which you can safely transfer.

The scree finally spills down on to grassy slopes that continue for some way. Though the angle is still steep, things finally level out as you descend into a saddle. All that remains is a further ascent of shorter duration followed by a stretch of delightfully rugged skyline before you reach the brink of the notch in the hills formed by Scarth Gap. The ancient pass from Buttermere to Ennerdale provides a welcome escape route down the rocky path, descending diagonally back across High Crag to the head of the lake.

Leaving the glistening depths of Buttermere behind you, the next cluster of peaks along the skyline beyond Scarth Gap are the assorted heights of Haystacks, looming rugged and intriguingly ahead, and through which you must navigate your way.

A path, so well worn that unfortunately it is beginning to look like a motorway, passes through the assortment of sugarloafs, crags, bluffs and tiny, shining tarns. Fortunately, however, there is no need to follow this. Haystacks covers a substantial amount of terrain through which it is possible to find your own special way. This is a mysterious and fascinating journey so long as you keep a leftwards-bias to your route, but remember the peregrine lives here, a bird not famous for its choice of hospitable nesting sites. There are many crags on Haystacks. Trending too far left would bring you to their brink, so exercise a happy medium, a

target being to reach Innominate Tarn, then Blackbeck Tarn, before continuing around the head of the valley and which involves some ascent.

There are magnificent views down the length of Buttermere, with Crummock Water twinkling in the distance. The juxtaposition of the two lakes connected by a river forms a north-west passage that is splendid to canoe. Your lofty vantage point might be from the top of one of the rocky tors jutting through the bilberries on the lip of the headwall falling sheer below into Warnscale Bottom or it might be glimpsed from the path twisting its way through heathery slopes fringing bright green bogs. Either way it is sublime.

A descent from Green Crag down to the banks of the beck destined to cascade down into Warnscale Bottom, and surrounded by a quagmire during the rains, brings you out opposite the path climbing up the open grassy slopes of Fleetwith Pike. These slopes may look gentle, but they bring you to the most spectacular of summits.

Dropping away into nothingness beneath your feet, the mountain wall of Honister Crag falls away into immensity to the north-east, accentuating the panoramas not only across the gulf beyond to Dale Head but in every direction.

This void accompanies the footpath down into Buttermere, always gaping hungrily there on the right, while to the left yawns the crag-rimmed emptiness of Warnscale Bottom. It is a knife-edge, this descent, famous for its dangerous beauty and dropping into the pastoral heaven of the meadows around Gatescarth Farm.

Chapter 7

THE GREAT MOSEDALE HORSESHOE

The Great Mosedale Horseshoe is one of the most sublime skylines in the British Isles. The adjectives 'divine', 'celestial' and 'heavenly' have also recurred constantly in descriptions of its ridge. No other great sweeping mountain crest – precipitous, rugged and grand – so distils the essence of Lakeland mountains at their best over such a relatively small space. It has always been recognized as so.

In the nineteenth century, Wasdale Head – of which Mosedale is an offshoot – was seen as the natural centre of the Cumbria mountains. It has even been called the English Zermatt. George Seatree, a well-known climber of the time, described it thus in the *Penrith Observer,* 1906:

The rugged peaks, Yewbarrow, Kirkfell, Pillar Mountain, Great Gable, Scawfell Pike, Scawfell and the Screes form a sublime group around a narrow and secluded dale head. The pillars, pinnacles, arêtes, ledges, the ghylls, gullies, couloirs and chimneys of those stern guardians of the little valley afford ample scope for weeks of climbing and exploration.'

The Great Mosedale Horseshoe reflects this mountainous grandeur with a strenuous route. It follows in the footsteps of the pioneers, taking you through the hinterland of crags that

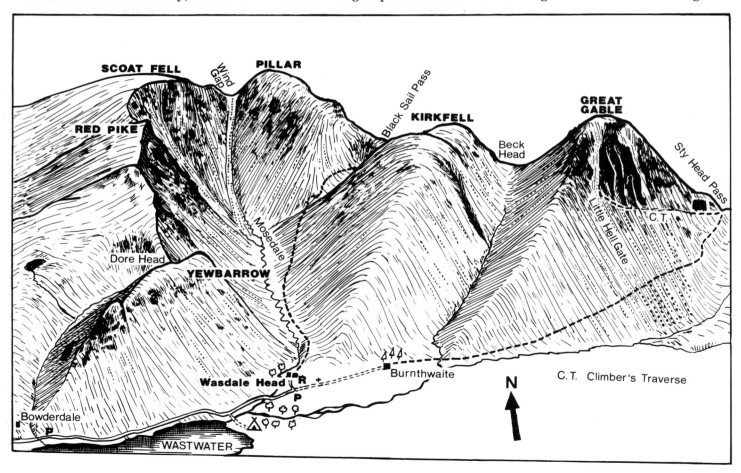

Pillar Rock, approachable by the High Level path as a variation along the Mosedale Horseshoe, is seen here sunlit on its north-east flanks.

Climbers ascending Napes Needle (the birthplace of British rock climbing), the highlight of the Gable Traverse.

are steeped with British climbing history, then on to some of the most rugged skylines in the country. Although you can escape at various cols along the way, these notches in the skyline harbour peaks in between which can, in inclement conditions, become formidable. The skyline should not be attempted unless you are fit, experienced, can use a map and compass and are accustomed to mountain scrambling. If this should raise an eyebrow among those who know that the Wasdale hills require no scrambling other than the occasional short rock step, then that is because with this way I have incorporated the Climber's Traverse on Great Gable. Yes, the very same route which skirts the base of Napes Needle . . .

For over 100 years, the Needle has been a target for just about every aspir-

ing rock climber, drawn by its stark and thrusting silhouette, rising incongruously from England's green and pleasant land. It is a shape more akin to the Alps where savage granite teeth soar

up like space rockets from the snow and ice of Mont Blanc above Chamonix. So what better way to pay it a visit than during the ascent of Great Gable, the first peak of our skyline?

This can be done logically by tracing the route across the base of the cliffs. From there, the Victorian pioneers made their exploratory forays, a process that took some considerable time. For many years the crags of the Lake District were only considered worth climbing in winter as a substitute for the Alps, and rock climbing as an independent sport did not exist, although one or two crags had been noted by the Alpinists as possibly worthy of future exploration. Yet things were to change.

In 1886, a Trinity student, Walter Parry Haskett-Smith, was to grasp the coffin-shaped top of Napes Needle and, although he made other new ascents, this climb stands as the beginning of British rock climbing. Haskett-Smith's ascent was unique in that he had to climb down; normally, rock climbing in this country is completed by walking away from the top of the crag over grass and scree. There was also something else: he climbed it on his own.

The enormity of Haskett-Smith's solo ascent is likely to strike home when you, too, reach the platform at its foot. Like Felix the Cat, the Needle stands alone, is swathed on all sides by thin air and a cloud passing from the left will be obscured behind it for a moment, before reappearing to the right. But this could also apply to other pinnacles and towers among this lunarscape of crag, like the Sphinx Rock, the Shark's Fin, Hell Gate Pillar and the Arrowhead of Arrowhead Ridge. The place is a riot of sharp, steep and foreboding edges, with names like Cutlass, Scimitar and Sabre.

The start to your day begins from the Wasdale Head Inn where the early explorers would stay after arriving by train at Seascale, fifteen miles away on the coast. A lane leads from the rear of the hotel towards Kirkfell, over cobbles and between hawthorn and holly trees. It passes by a glassy beck and dry stone walls so thick that they might have been intended for the fortifications of a castle. Where the lane forks, you take the right-hand branch which heads towards Great Gable and past the foot of Gavel Neese, which is a grassy mountain ridge that can be likened to a very steep edge of the Great Pyramid of Gizeh.

The way ahead up Sty Head Pass is rocky and seems never to end, yet the incline that it cuts across the mountain is gentle, allowing you time to take in the Napes Crags, now looming so directly above that they might be the Sword of Damocles suspended overhead. Or perhaps several such swords, so sharp and knife-edged do they appear from below. The Needle is extremely difficult to identify from this angle, however, and it requires the trained eye to pick it out from here. Gradually the Napes are lost to view as you gain height and round a shoulder of the mountain. The angle relents, the slopes level out and you reach the stretcher box on Sty Head col.

This is a wild and beautiful place, but only on the foulest day is it likely to be lonely. The summit of Sty Head, in fact, is a Piccadilly Circus of our mountains, accommodating parties from so many different directions who have to pass it on their way while moving from one distant valley over to the next or from one peak to another. By far the most people who arrive here, however, are bound for the top of Great Gable by the ordinary tourist route, and there is no mistaking its well-hammered trail up the great broad back of the mountain ahead as you relax for a few well-earned moments on this mountain paradise complete with rippling tarn. If you have any doubts about negotiating the Climber's Traverse, now is the time to consider changing direction by following the tourist route up Great Gable instead.

The route to the Climber's Traverse doubles back from the stretcher box to swing diagonally up across the mountainside above the way you have already come. The first landmark is Kern Knotts Crag – a monolithic face surrounded by boulders and overlooking the footpath, which is now a trail of polished footscrapes across slabs and blocks of grey, rough rock. Beyond Kern Knotts, the track is easy to follow as it climbs steadily across the rugged flank of the mountain, mostly on rock and scree, through the heart of wonderful scenery.

Presently – with Piers Ghyll, Ling-

The summit of Great Gable peeping above Kirkfell.

Children descending Little Scoat Fell's rocky summit.

mell and the Scafells just across the valley and sliding into ever more tantalizing perspectives as you gain height – the path is interrupted by the landslide of Great Hell Gate screes plunging down Great Gable's south-western flank. And beyond it? Your destination: the Napes Crags, those prominent arêtes that rise from a great rock promontory and across which the Climber's Traverse threads its tenuous way. First, however, you must cross the scree, then continue traversing beneath the base of the buttresses and spires looming still some way above. Quite soon you will see Napes Needle jutting out against the sky, like a monster forklift truck with its load wound up to the top.

If you intend doing the Climber's Traverse proper (it is still possible to avoid it by continuing along this lower footpath that passes well beneath the crags until you reach the screes of Little Hell Gate, more of which later), this is the point where it begins. You must

look for the tiny track that leads steeply upwards over grass and rock to the base of the Needle, which is now above you. Firstly, go round to the right of the Needle and up a slanting groove behind it like a half-opened book. Then, squeezing between the Needle to the left and the crag on which it perches to the right, step through to the other side and arrive at the tiny rock platform from where intending summiteers begin their climb.

The manoeuvre is known as Threading the Needle, and it is delightful. The climbing is easy, being on good rock and with large holds, but it does feel steep. There is also the feeling of commitment that heightens the excitement. The top of this groove is like a narrow crevasse and almost like the eye of a needle but with the tip of the top broken off so it is open to the sky. It is the view through the 'eye' that proves so stunning – the steep and unbroken mountain slopes of Kirkfell look absolutely majestic. Silhouetted against the edge

of the Napes Crags is the Sphinx Rock, another striking pinnacle with an undeniable impact, while far below lie the fields of Wasdale Head.

The platform below the base of the Needle is polished rock, and is the size of a postage stamp. Above, springs a wall of light grey and brown rock, speckled with green lichen, cold to touch and fragmented with a million tiny crystals. There seem to be no handholds other than the deep crack that Haskett-Smith first shinned up; it all looks immensely intimidating. However, for those Traverse-bound, the way now is in the opposite direction, by a steep scramble on down into the bed of Needle Gully below, then up again on the far side to the Dress Circle (so-named because of the view it affords of the Needle). Your way now is towards the Sphinx Rock, a traverse achieved by moving up, down and across (and at one point squeezing through another crevasse) towards it – along wherever the most obvious line takes you. It is an absorbing trip until you finally reach the notch between Sphinx Rock and Sphinx Ridge with its superb views of the Needle. A short descent beyond this continues the traverse on towards the next scree fan of Little Hell Gate.

This can be climbed all the way at its right-hand extremity where you will find reasonably solid footing. However, a broken ridge over-looking Little Hell Gate is a finer scramble up to the neck of the mountain where the two Hell Gates meet on a roof-tree that leads towards the summit of Great Gable. Lead you 'towards' yes, but not actually 'to', because the grey bulk of Westmorland Crags forms a blockade that forces you to the left. Only a final barrier remains: the rocky barren summit slopes that stretch on, it seems, without end.

Set in a boulder-field near the summit cairn, you will find the war memorial tablet of the Fell & Rock Climbing Club. Dedicated in 1924, it is the venue every year of a poignant Remembrance Day Service. The tablet is actually a

A distant Yewbarrow is viewed on the descent from Red Pike.

relief map of the ridges and valleys surrounding your lofty eyrie, and it is along the finest of these that your route now continues. Cast in bronze immediately before your eyes, it is forged from volcanic rock just the merest glance away, leading down into Beck Head col by splintered scree and rock, and then up to the broad undulating top – with its twin summits – of Kirkfell. Follow the fence posts along this flattish crest, taking care on the drop down on to Black Sail Pass. The fence gives an approximate guide to the rather indeterminate path, but there are crags, and everywhere the terrain is a chaotic jumble of broken stone.

Black Sail Pass offers an escape route into Mosedale on one side and Ennerdale on the other. Ahead, however, the great ridge between the two valleys strides inexorably to the top of Pillar, passing Looking Stead and offering a superbly mountainous skyline with several steep sections along the way. It is from below the first steep section, incidentally, that you will see a well-worn track veering around to the right-hand side of the ridge and down. This is the famous High-Level Route to Pillar Rock, one of Britain's great rock climbing haunts, a superb sight but one unfortunately missed by travellers along the ridge who pass well above this cathedral of rock.

Accompanying your sojourn along the skyline and on the far side of lonely, forested Ennerdale, are the summits in glorious procession of the Buttermere Skyline – from Red Pike to Haystacks – until, finally, on top of Pillar, your route twists abruptly away. Scoat Fell is the next objective, via Wind Gap (another escape route into the head of Mosedale down lengthy, knee-jarring screes) and Black Crag and a rugged course of broken rocks and boulders.

Scoat Fell is a splendid launching pad for a short diversion north to the diminutive summit of Steeple and its wonderful views, but the line of the horseshoe now continues in the opposite direction along the serrated escarpment of Red Pike. A well-trodden path crosses the western slopes beneath this summit, and it is quite possible, thanks to its option, to complete the long and easy descent into the col of Dore Head without having actually topped-out on the mountain.

Dore Head has a legendary scree run, now stripped to the bone, and a skeleton compared with its former days where your boots sank into gravel that came over the ankles. This has always been a popular way to finish a round of Mosedale, although many people now favour the slower but safer descent to the valley by the path zigzagging down to one side. However, if you are still feeling strong, the ascent of Yewbarrow will bring your traverse to a really magnificent climax, up the precipitous front of Stirrup Crag, which looks such an insurmountable barrier of rock. This is a perfectly acceptable but thrilling scramble for anyone with a head for heights, followed by the narrow keel of a summit ridge along to the top of Yewbarrow with its glorious views of Wastwater, the Screes, Burnmoor Tarn and back around the mountains cradling beautiful Wasdale Head.

The descent is down the southern end of Yewbarrow and back to the lakeside. This is the dizzily steep ridge that catches the eye from the valley. It makes a great finish to the day – with one proviso: crags cut off the descent with hazardous suddenness. To be safe, you should ensure that after you have passed the unmistakeable gash of the Great Door, your chosen path descends the hillside to the right and continues diagonally down in that direction, before detouring back to the crest of the ridge and down to the lake shore at its toe.

Chapter 8
THE WOOLPACK ROUND

The Woolpack Round is the jewel in the crown of Lakeland skyline walks. Not only will it bring you full circle around a great bowl of hills and constantly varying terrain, but this is a traverse over the highest peaks in the country, offering views that are acknowledged by artists and photographers as peerless. Added to this is the spice of danger, for the Woolpack Round is akin to those Scottish mountains where rock climbing is required, and only the capable should attempt it in its entirety along the very crest. Even then, preferably in good conditions.

Both Scafell Pike, which at 3,210ft is the tallest mountain in the country, and neighbouring giant Scafell (which rhymes with 'awful') are part and package of its wild and uncompromising circuit. So too are other Lake District fells that approach the magical altitude of 3,000ft: Great End, Esk Pike, Bowfell and Crinkle Crags. Precipitous eminences all, these are peaks riven by the elements into a notched and twisted skyline with compelling appeal. Scafell, for example, is the one Cumbrian mountain that is strictly out-of-bounds to those groups of Outward Bound students

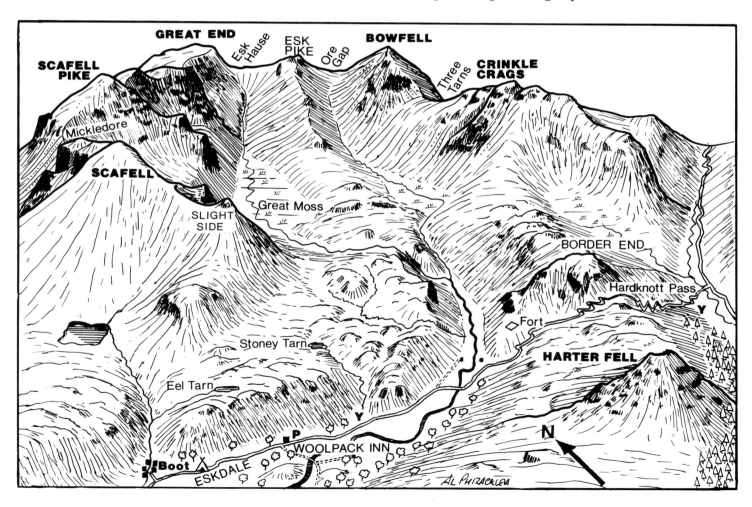

taking part on their final and unaccompanied shakedown expedition. For over half its circumference, the mountain is ringed by towering crags that barricade the way, just one chink in their armour providing a possible route along the very crest of the ridge.

To traverse the Woolpack Round, you should be a competent rock climber so that you can tackle the *bête noire* of Scafell – the steep and slippery chain of rock steps known as Broad Stand. Its first recorded conquest was a descent possibly in the early nineteenth century by Samuel Taylor Coleridge – yes, he of *The Ancient Mariner* and *Kubla Khan*. By his own admission, Coleridge was no climber. Yet Broad Stand is a scene of many of today's accidents on Scafell.

Although Broad Stand can be bypassed, the detours take the edge off what is essentially a major skyline expedition. They also require detailed route finding which becomes worrying in misty weather just when you are likely to be feeling the strain. However, having experienced a little rock climbing is no qualification for Broad Stand. You need to have led rock climbs of at least 'severe' standard to cope capably without a rope on this unforgiving piece of rock. Therefore, if you are uncomfortable in less than clement conditions and highly exposed places, it would be wiser to avoid this most sporting of Lakeland's skylines until you have gained more experience.

The beauty of this mountain circuit is that its hub is a comfortable hostelry,

long a focal point for the local community and hill-lovers alike. Even better, it is situated so strategically that it is possible to start out through the front door of Eskdale's Woolpack Inn and return by the back with the whole time in between spent on the hills.

If we imagine a traditional start from the Woolpack, then – picking up the packed lunch and thermos and stepping outside the front door – the first objective is seen across the road. The distinctive shape of Harter Fell is a stirring challenge, its sharply triangular shape visible from many points in the Lake District. So this first leg of our great traverse climbs Harter and then follows a promontory of enchanted terrain to join the cirque of the highest peaks at Crinkle Crags.

The Scafells from Border End.

Very different from the big hills like Bowfell and Scafell, this introductory promenade is all the more entrancing because of its Cinderella charm. No great mountains these – Harter Fell, Border End, Hard Knott and Yew Bank – but they have a beauty that is unique. The route crests an undulating grassy backbone with rocky summits on countless bluffs and banks of heather and bracken and bilberries too. Tiny pools are landlocked by rocky beaches, large boulders are painted red on their undersides by smitt from sheltering sheep and there are occasional swamps for the unwary which tremble and wobble at your approaching footfalls like basins of green jelly.

The ascent of Harter then begins just across the road from the Woolpack, down the track to Penny Hill Farm and up the slopes above the wooded banks of the River Esk. The views of Eskdale spread out below – the big tidy fields of the dale-head farms and, on all sides, mountains large and small. As the slopes steepen ahead, the track jinks this way and that between the isolated outcrops and knolls that mark much of the way ahead to Crinkle Crags.

The first leg of the subsequent high-level magical mystery tour to Crinkles from the summit of Harter is the descent to the top of Hardknott Pass. This is one of the steepest roads in Europe. Rocks littering the surface tell of innumerable cars that have stalled on the ascent (their wheels requiring to be chocked to prevent them sliding over a ravine). Such is the position of Hardknott that the Romans chose its flanks on which to build a commanding fort amid its craggy slopes, and it is above this that you now pick a way up the path that leads to a belvedere on the edge of Border End.

The late W.A.Poucher, that doyen of mountain photography, described the scenery from here as unsurpassable. Directly across the gulf of upper Eskdale is a panoramic view of the Woolpack Round, this wicked upheaval of mountains, now seen so intimately that the Scafells look sufficiently close to reach out and touch. But it is the bulk of Scafell itself which, with the plunge of crags denoting Broad Stand, will now remain in the corner of your eye like something you are afraid to rub as you continue your sojourn along the lonely and intriguing ridge between Eskdale on the one side and Mosedale on the other, before eventually climbing steeply on to Crinkles.

Crinkle Crags rise and fall through the sky like the humps of the Loch Ness Monster. There are four of these and, as each hump seemingly consists of numerous smaller ones, the name seems infuriatingly apt as the many ups and downs involved begin to take their toll. Certainly, a couple I discovered arguing appeared to bear this out. Having walked from the Roman fort on Hardknott with baby and dog, and with the intention of climbing Bowfell, it transpired that the husband, suspecting black ice on the road, had stopped his Range Rover to check. His worst fears had been confirmed when, still wearing the carpet slippers he favoured for driving, he began to pick up speed down the one-in-three incline, before smashing into boulders below.

Now his wife was questioning his judgment again. It was clear she did not like the look of the cliffs ahead, through which the path now seemed to pass by way of an overhanging rock step. As several walkers and dogs higher on the crags began to move downhill towards us, the showers of scree they dislodged exacerbated the problem.

'I'm sure it's all right, dear,' said the man, gingerly peeling dried blood from a gashed chin, 'I mean, this path's like the M25'. At this point I made the mistake of agreeing with him. 'It only looks a bit ferocious,' I added, 'but actually there is a way you can squeeze through a hole inside the crag. It's really easy'. 'Really?' said the woman, 'It looks totally ridiculous. Besides, how will Barnaby and Rufus cope? I think we should go back'.

Knowing what I do now, I know how right she was. What I hadn't realised was that a rockfall had since effectively blocked this 'through' route to all except proficient cavers. The result was that, urged on by my well-meaning encouragement, the husband disappeared into the inner fastness of the crag only to become so inexorably stuck that it took the two of us hauling on his ankles to drag him back into daylight. And with a cacophony of anguised howls as his battered limbs once more engaged the rock in mortal combat.

'Thank you very much,' said the woman, obviously convinced that everything she had heard about people who wear trainers on the hill in winter was true – yes, me (and apparently risky, agreed, but they were fell-running shoes with an excellent grip). 'That's it, Jonathon, you can do whatever you wish, but I have had enough . . .'

I left them to it and clambered on upwards for 30ft, scaling the well-worn rockface to the right of the overhang. Known as the Bad Step, this is the usual way. An old friend, its large and comforting handholds allow you to gain height quickly, and with exhilarating views. My last glimpse before going over the top was of Jonathon with the baby in a papoose on his shoulders, having managed to skirt the crags by going round to the left. Dogged to the end, he was now wearily trying to disengage his dog from the attentions of two pit bull terriers on the brink of the cliffs. Then my path began to descend the far side and soon the vastness of Bowfell loomed ahead.

Just as from the summit of Harter to the Crinkles is a paradise of trackless turf, islands of peat, slopes of ferns and banks of ling, so the skyline from Crinkles to Scafell is an equally consistent journey but of quite a different nature. Here are rocky mountains abounding with craggy buttresses, fields of boulders, and great scree

A walker approaches the Bad Step (in the gully through the crags above him) on Crinkle Crags.

slopes, littered with stones that wobble and clank as they take your weight in passing along the well-trodden and much-cairned way. From the col of Three Tarns to the summit of Bowfell, then down into the col of Ore Gap and on to Esk Pike before descending onto the saddle of Esk Hause – what an incredible trip it is with mountain tops seemingly surrounding you on all sides.

At almost the height of Langdale Pikes, Esk Hause is the hub at the heart of Lakeland. Valleys like Wasdale, Eskdale, Borrowdale, Langdale and the Duddon radiate outwards from Esk Hause like the spokes of a wheel. It is having reached here that, following an interlude of wild turf on this sky-line shelf, the ascent continues again upwards past Great End to encounter

a wilderness of rock once more, as you follow the skyline towards Ill Crag, Broad Crag and Scafell Pike itself.

The cairn on Scafell Pike is as big as a cottage and to be able to sit down here, after the exacting climb from the col below Broad Crag, was home from home. When I reached the summit after my encounter at the Bad Step on Crinkles, the cairn was deserted. The tiny figures I had seen posing on it from as far away as Ill Crag (and each staking their claim for that moment as the highest person in England) had gone down before the sun did. There was a lovely sense of peace, or at least there was until a yellow helicopter flew low overhead.

By then I'd descended into Mickle-dore – that spectacular notch between

Scafell Pike and Scafell – where people were standing around the mountain-rescue box perched on the sharp ridge. 'Rescue,' said one of them before I had time to speak, 'Somebody's fallen off Broad Stand'.

I asked why the chopper was flying away then as you could still make out a small group of people on the flanks of the mountainside above upper Eskdale, and one of them was lying on the scree. 'They've lowered a doctor and now it's clearing off so he'll be able to hear with his stethoscope without the racket,' somebody explained. Minutes later the helicopter returned with a whip-cracking of rotors that almost clipped the crags, fanned the grass flat like a hairdryer and sent several rucksacks tumbling down the scree.

'That's the doctor,' I was told by a girl still wearing her sack and consequently one of the few not to have to go haring down after their belongings. A figure in a blue cardigan was being winched up to the helicopter. 'And there's the crewman who came down with him.' He was next to be tugged up by the cable and with what looked like a roll of carpet beneath an arm. It was the stretcher. Back at the chopper's doors he turned sideways-on to feed it inside and out of sight.

Broad Stand rises almost directly above Mickledore. Sandwiched between two of the greatest cliffs in Britain – the East Buttress of Scafell to the left and Scafell Crag to the right – it forms a natural staircase of slabs and ledges which would be a delight to climb were it not for a particularly steep and awkward wall positioned nastily above a long drop down the hillside below.

While the crux of Broad Stand is no more technical than pulling yourself up out of the deep end of a swimming-pool, in this particular pool there is no water to make you buoyant. With the knowledge that a fall could be fatal, a certain leaden feeling can afflict the limbs unused to vertical places, and prevarication midway up the obstacle allows the blood to drain from upstretched fingers, thus weakening the grip. All this, combined with finding the lower limbs beginning to shake with the effects of 'disco leg', can all too easily lead to a horrendous fall with its tragic consequences.

Above this, Broad Stand continues upwards more easily through a jumble of rock and scree until at last the summit can be seen across an open plateau of turf and stones. However, at this

Bowfell and Crinkle Crags viewed during the approach along the ridge from Border End.

point might I suggest a detour? If you carefully skirt the edge of the north-facing Scafell Crag you will reach the massive rift of Deep Ghyll, a notable feature here being the summit of Scafell Pinnacle and some astounding rock scenery. It is most photogenic.

The descent from Scafell's summit to the back door of the Woolpack is a joy indeed. First, along the easy grassy ridge-path along the top of yet more crags to the top of Slight Side, a southern outlier of the mountain. Then, following the path down the broad ridge leading to bouldery ground and the lonely and unvisited Stony Tarn, you are on beam to continue gently down to

Eel Tarn before descending south to the Woolpack.

It is spacious labyrinthine territory, utterly delightful when the track is found, although it can prove perplexing and time-wasting if your navigation goes wrong. Then, when finally on course, you can let your feet take care of themselves while you enjoy the constantly changing scene. Down, down you drop, mile after mile through the heather, in and out of grassy hollows while the western sky glows golden over a gleam of silver from the sea, and Harter Fell, now once more straight ahead, begins to glow quite luminous in the sunset.

Chapter 9

A LANGDALE HORSESHOE

The two mountains of Pike of Stickle and Harrison Stickle dominate Langdale not so much by their height as their position and distinctive form on the skyline. Rugged and steep-flanked, riven by steep-sided gullies, scree slopes and crags, their hillsides offer harsh and exposed ground of a most precipitous nature. But then Langdale is a *climbing* valley. Like other great venues of the British climber such as Llanberis Pass and Glencoe, you will always find fellwalkers and rock climbers balancing their way along the airiest of tracks or clinging like spiders to the crags, not only on the Langdale Pikes themselves but on a variety of neighbouring peaks besides.

Pavey Ark, Loft Crag, Rosset Pike, Bowfell, Crinkle Crags and Pike O'Blisco – as well as Harrison Stickle and Pike of Stickle – form a cirque around the head of the valley that is impenetrable except by rough, steep tracks. The assorted peaks spring from tranquil pastures in 2,000ft of sudden upthrust so starkly that their outline competes in popularity for calendars, chocolate boxes and jigsaws with those

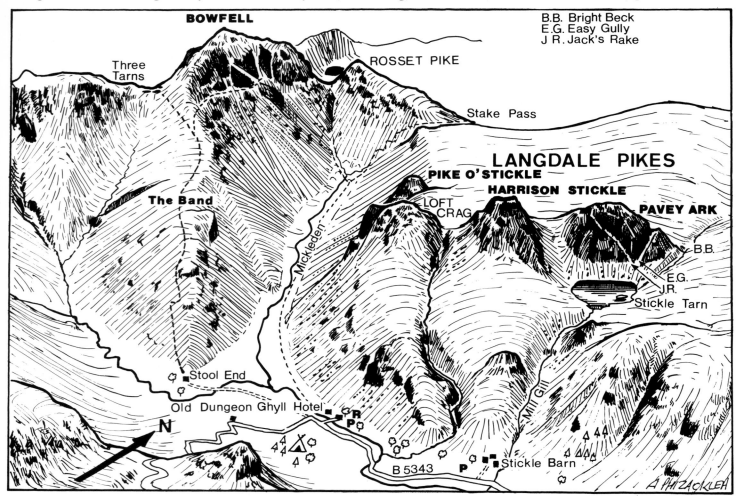

BOWFELL

Three Tarns

ROSSET PIKE

Stake Pass

B.B. Bright Beck
E.G. Easy Gully
J R. Jack's Rake

LANGDALE PIKES

PIKE O'STICKLE

HARRISON STICKLE

LOFT CRAG

PAVEY ARK

B.B.

E.G.
J.R.
Stickle Tarn

The Band

Mickleden

Mill Gill

Stool End

Old Dungeon Ghyll Hotel

N

B 5343

P

Stickle Barn

A PHIZACKLEA

of the tower of London and Edinburgh Castle. To visitors actually in the valley bottom, they present a mountain wall that explains why Langdale has no direct social or economic contact with areas to the north and west. The outlet, instead, is eastwards past Elterwater to Ambleside, and the valley floor is filled with debris left behind by the Ice Age.

Like the towers of Oxford when seen from Boar's Hill or Blackpool Tower from the Fylde Plain, the Langdale Pikes can be easily distinguised far beyond their immediate boundaries, and in particular across the flats where the ice once gouged its inexorable way. While the most celebrated view is from Elterwater Common during the drive up Great Langdale, there are also superb views of the Pikes from Windermere railway station, the Lowood Hotel along the road to Ambleside and even from vantage points as far away as Yorkshire.

The hills you see from this distance are Harrison Stickle, Pavey Ark and Loft Crag with its plummeting sweep of Gimmer Crag. They are, for the moment, all you need to keep within your sights – especially the prominent flat-topped sugarloaf of Harrison Stickle, a splendid space-station *en route* from which to dock with the other summits along your curving orbit.

There is one exception. The mountains on the far side of the valley head – Crinkle Crags and Bowfell – are a part of The Langdale Horseshoe, but they also share the circuit of the greater Woolpack Round. As a result the horseshoe I describe here circumnavigates the valley head by a highly mountainous route but it does – after skirting Bowfell's flanks – descend down its magnificent spur of the Band. However, if you wish to add on the Crinkles and even the summit of Pike o'Blisco to your Langdale round, then you need more power to your elbow.

Harrison Stickle, meanwhile, can be ascended by either of two very

Langdale Pikes from Elterwater Common.

contrasting and worthy routes, one starting from the Old Dungeon Ghyll Hotel at the head of the valley, the other from the New Hotel just down the road. Of the two hotels, the ODG is a traditional climbers' and hill walkers' venue, like the Kingshouse Hotel in Glencoe or the Pen y Gwryd Hotel below Llanberis Pass. It has a fantastic setting, with millions of tons of rock above making its presence felt in the form of crags, great boulders, deeply gashed gullies and rivers of scree.

The fellside directly behind the hotel gives the line of attack by a path that climbs from the back door towards Raven Crag. Beetling and uncompromising, this rock face crouches above the premises, giving a constant source of wonder to the assembled spectators in the car-park below. The rock – orange, grey and pink-hued and soaring to a great overhang – gives perfect climbing and offers many different routes from the easiest, *Holly Tree Traverse*, to the hardest, *Daws Rides a Shovelhead*, which breaches the overhangs above by a mammoth feat of climbing, aided only by the cling of fingers and pull of muscles.

It is by the push of the feet and straightening of the legs that our route

goes, almost within earshot of the climbers on the crag, until, at last, it veers sharply left. The track now begins to rake across the hillside above with a diagonal line that takes you high on the hillside up quite varied terrain.

The first section, across unstable beds of scree, is abrasive, uneven and very broken. However, the path relents into a brief terraced break, offering superb views across the valley to the Band on Bowfell and the great wall of the Crinkles towering above, split as it is with the axe-blows of Hell Ghyll and Crinkle Ghyll. Make the most of this respite, because the path now begins to tackle the hillside above direct with a series of zigzags over more steep terrain.

Originally a climber's track, you will eventually see why as the great grey barrel shape of Gimmer Crag bursts from the fabric of the fellside over to the left. However, it is by the track that continues directly up the fell that your best way lies. Eventually it leads to the trade route from the New Dungeon Ghyll Hotel and brings you out on the col by Loft Crag and, so, near Harrison Stickle.

Great in atmosphere as this method

The Mill Ghyll reclaimed footpath to Stickle Tarn and the Pikes.

of leaving the valley is, what it will not do is bring you directly to the top of Pavey Ark. Indeed, climbing Harrison Stickle by this way means you may well decide to give Pavey a miss anyway as you can now continue along the horseshoe in the opposite direction over more distinctive peaks and without including its summit. Over more distinctive peaks, I might add, than when Pavey Ark is seen from above. This is quite different from when it is viewed from below for, then, Pavey Ark presents one of the biggest and most striking rock faces in the Lake District. And Pavey Ark it is that gives us the alternative route to Harrison Stickle: by breaching its great precipitous defences up Jack's Rake, one of the scrambling high points of a walking holiday.

Jack's Rake climbs diagonally across Pavey Ark like a bandolier. Were there .38 calibre bullets stashed inside it, Jack's Rake could not be treated with more deference by many who attempt it. For there is no mistaking the potential threat of its mighty buttresses, soaring both just above and immediately below this narrow gangway. Sometimes people climbing it can appear to be

handling the rock as if it was a live round just waiting to explode. The route is suspended in a tremendous position and a fall here is generally fatal. I say 'generally' advisedly. This winter a walker fell 320ft from Jack's Rake, but landed in a snowdrift and walked away, rather chastened but unbowed.

Pavey Ark is not visible from the starting point of this walk, that is,

from the New Dungeon Ghyll Hotel car-park, which is a little further back down the valley than the ODG and consequently reached first. Like a robber baron waiting to pounce once you have gained height, and when you are likely to be feeling at your most defenceless, Pavey rises behind the valley skyline. It is hidden completely during the first hour or so of your route, which is along a reclaimed footpath up the right-hand side of Mill Ghyll and a wonderful approach that skirts creaming waterfalls all the way up to the brink of Stickle Tarn.

Immediately across the water from the dam containing the tarn, Pavey Ark rises above a plinth of boulders and scree and with the ramp of Jack's Rake an obvious attraction. For those, however, who feel at the last moment they may lack the nerve and steadiness required, an option is to climb the path by Bright Beck, the inlet stream to Stickle Tarn, and which will lead you to the summit of Pavey Ark by an easy, safe route.

The summit of Pavey Ark is an ocean of rocky slabs and bilberry beds, and has to be crossed to reach the summit cone of Harrison Stickle. Then, after

Pavey Ark overlooking Stickle Tarn, viewed from the dam, Easy Gully (where there are loose boulders), strikes up to the right. Jack's Rake itself is the slanting diagonal ramp up the face to the left.

descending across the great ravine of Dungeon Ghyll, the route continues over Loft Crag, followed by Pike of Stickle, which commands a terrific position over the gulf of Mickleden, that incredibly picturesque valley floor below the Pikes. Descending from its summit the way you first climbed it, a track over Martcrag Moor and gradually down into the col of Stake Pass will lead you to the first point where you can look back down Langdale and begin to traverse across the valley head towards Bowfell.

This broad grassy, undulating ridge makes first for Rosset Pike, then descends to Angle Tarn in the craggy bosom of Bowfell. Nestling below the crags of Hanging Knotts, this is a sombre basin, the scene of a mass pilgrimage as caravans of walkers call here *en route* from Langdale to Wasdale or Borrowdale, or vice versa. If you wish to include the summit of Bowfell in your Langdale Horseshoe, a track follows slopes of grass and scree above the tarn, bending right and left and into the col of Ore Gap, connecting Esk Pike to Bowfell. However, I would not recommend this route in bad weather. The region between Angle Tarn and Ore Gap is fraught with navigational problems as magnetic rocks deflect the compass needle and accidents happen.

Instead of climbing Bowfell, an excellent horseshoe can still be achieved by climbing out of the basin from Angle Tarn to the summit of Rosset Ghyll from where, in inclement conditions, a perfect escape route can be made down the path into Mickleden. And if the weather is good? Then a most interesting variation exists, following the route down Rosset Ghyll a little way, before striking off right across the slopes of Bowfell and following the ancient and tenuous packhorse track until, high above but beneath the summit skyline, you see the tapering pillar of Bowfell Buttress.

It is a long stiff pull up to the base of the great rock nose, which is 400ft

Looking back down Mill Ghyll with Lingmoor – the delightful ridge bordering the far side of Langdale – across the way.

high and an architectural wonder of the mountain. Below the crag, a track crosses scree to the left, to nearby Cambridge Crag where a waterspout from the rock guarantees a cooling drink in the warmest weather. The start of the Climber's Track, this delightful path leads across the mountain by a unique series of swoops and climbs on the edge of space. It is truly memorable, and so, too, is the descent of the Band on to which the Climber's Track impinges, arrowing down to Stool End Farm and the meadows of Langdale below. All the while you are cradled by the marvellous hills that have contributed so much already to your mountain day.

The Band (Bowfell), the floor of Mickleden and Pike of Stickle highlighted with rays of sunlight.

Chapter 10

THE HELM CRAG HORSESHOE

The skyline around the lonely Greenburn valley sports one of the most unusual silhouettes on British hills. There, on the summit of Helm Crag, stand the Lion and the Lamb from whichever direction you look, and particularly when seen from the valley below. There is more! Here are summit rocks that can change into Howitzers, and Ladies Playing a Grand Piano. There is a view where the same outcrop is Melvyn Tan playing a Beethoven piano sonata on a piano forté and Jerry Lee Lewis playing Great Balls of Fire with his feet (which in view of Helm Crag's volcanic past is an appropriate choice). When Ken Russell wanted a weird mountain setting for his latest film, *The Rainbow,* then Helm Crag provided him with it.

Grasmere locals in the Red Lion bar will tell you that Helm Crag was Mount Vesuvius, although my erstwhile geologist friend Dr Jack Soper of the Department of Earth Sciences, Leeds University, told me the redness of the local rock was due, not to molten

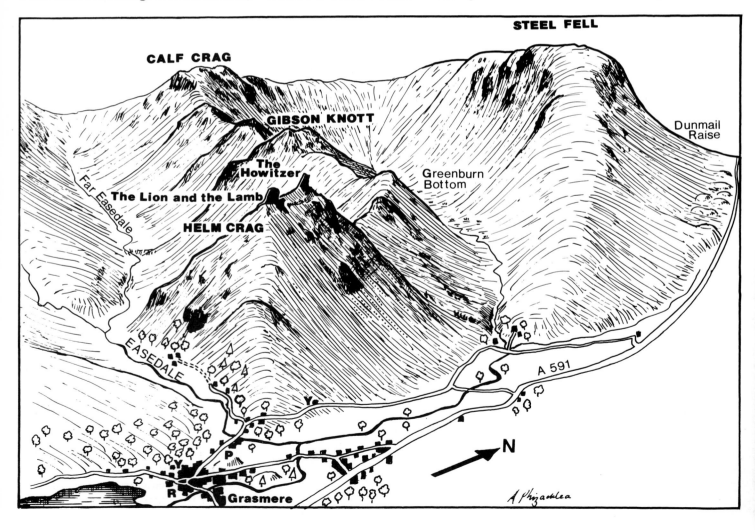

lava fire and brimstone, but to haematite. However, when I asked him some more questions, he said, 'Come off it, Tone. I'm not going to research the book for you. The way that bedrock geology and surface processes continue to produce mountain scenery is a big subject – I might write a book on it myself when I retire'.

Helm Crag does resemble a volcano beetling above the Grasmere Sports show-field, that celebrated bowl in the mountains which is the scene of Lakeland's annual Highland Games. And how it draws visitors from the village which is the home and resting place of William Wordsworth, on a scale comparable with Buckingham Palace or Stonehenge, curious as to what they will find on top.

Helm Crag is, in fact, only one end of the Greenburn Skyline. The other tops, and all very fine they are too, include Gibson Knott, Calf Crag and Steel Fell. However, it is Helm Crag that stands guard over the huddle of cottages, lanes and fields and streets of Grasmere nestling immediately below. It is from Grasmere where we start and finish this walk.

Although the height of the Helm Crag Horseshoe does not surpass 2,000ft, it makes up for it with its ruggedness. Helm Crag, in fact, is less in height at its 1,260ft than the Empire State Building in New York, and the whole of Steel Fell is only 1,800ft or so high, but it has the ambience of a much taller peak, with its steep flanks and sweeping crest. These are just two of the hills along this cirque, but in one way or another it is the same for the other tops too. They all have *something*.

Being rather of a lower altitude than the neighbouring fells, the round of the Greenburn Valley enables a greater number of visitors unversed in fell-walking to traverse its numerous tops and whet their appetite, than do some of the higher mountains. Also, because of their reduced height and the fact they are ringed around by distant leviathans like Helvellyn and Dollywagon Pike, they offer a superb outing with glorious views when their larger colleagues have their tops smothered in cloud or blanketed in heat haze.

My preference for starting this walk is up Helm Crag first, then along to the head of the Greenburn Valley and back over Steel Fell. It is for the very good reason that the best skyline routes generally ascend the steepest parts but descend the gentler slopes, rather than vice versa. When you eventually come to descend Steel Fell, for example, the way down is a delightful avenue between the ferns.

The road to Easedale begins from nearby Heaton Cooper's Studio in the Grasmere village centre. Beyond unfenced meadows, a rough track powers up wooded slopes that have once been quarried. Crags peep through hanging gardens of mosses and wild flowers with a crimson blush that remind you of the cottages in Grasmere. They also have this maroonish tinge, caused by the haematite or iron oxide. A little of it, apparently, goes a long way in staining rocks red.

The path twists this way and that the higher you ascend Helm Crag, breaching steep open slopes of grassy beauty that are literally breathtaking. Quite near the summit you will find yourself in a position to stray a little further right and look down on to the television aerials and satellite dishes of the houses far below. Beyond this and in an upwards direction, the secret of the chameleon-like qualities of the Lion and Lamb rocks awaits.

Breasting the summit ridge, a crag dwarfing a pinnacle below immediately confronts you. Yes, it is the Lion and the Lamb. Yet walk on several score more yards and there is another crag crouching over another boulder perched on the edge of space – *another* Lion and Lamb. Between the two silhouettes (this last one is also known as the Howitzer or the Lady at the Piano), they offer a never-ending variety of silhouettes to be seen from below. From the Lion above the showfield that lounges on the ground like the ones outside New York Public Library, to the other Lion (or Howitzer) overlooking the A591 road over Dunmail Raise and seated bolt upright like the lions guarding Nelson's Column, they are a certain conversation piece.

Were this just an ascent of Helm

Steel Fell, sunlit – the backdrop of Helm Crag seen from the Swan Hotel, Grasmere.

Approaching the Lion on Helm Crag.

Crag, then the hordes drawn to its summit by the Lion and the Lamb would make it unpalatable for those preferring solitude. Yet what a narrow view! There is immense pleasure to be had traversing the Helm Crag Horseshoe. One of these delights is the contrast of being one moment among the hub of humanity, which it can indeed resemble on any day during the school holidays when the Howitzer is the scene of eager children desperately trying to launch themselves up the polished footholds of its gleaming barrel (to the equally insistent cries of 'Dominic, come down at once, *and* you, Arabella, do you hear!') and the next being transported into total tranquillity as you descend the steep end of

Helm Crag beyond the rock fang that gives rise to so many family quarrels. Besides, climb Helm Crag before breakfast or in the evening and you will be unlucky if you see a soul.

Your arrival in the col separating Helm Crag from the lengthy ridge of Gibson Knott is the start of something not only wild and beautiful but literally out on a limb – literally, because this pearl of a ridge between Greenburn and Far Easedale resembles an arm or a leg along which you, Gulliver-like, must travel.

It is a skyline crest of hollows and knolls, craggy protuberences and unexpected ponds, with heather and bracken growing in seasonal profusion. Below to your left is the lonely valley

Temperature inversion – a regular occurrence here in the early morning – over Grasmere and from the slopes of Steel Fell.

The silhouette of Helm Crag's famous summit rocks, the Lion itself.

of Far Easedale with the great buttress of Deer Bield Crag stark on its opposite slopes. While to the right is the trench of Greenburn, around the head of which, after you have passed Gibson Knott, then Calf Crag (another leg of rugged and undulating ridge), your route now swings. Eastwards to the right and around the head of the Greenburn valley.

This is a tract of complete wilderness, boggy and hummocky, which requires care in misty conditions. It would be easy to stray further westwards under the impression you were making for Steel Fell when in fact you were striking towards a region of no man's land defending distant Borrowdale from those who approach it from Grasmere.

Steel Fell occupies the opposite side of Greenburn from the ridge you have just accomplished. It presents a splendid, although taxing, ascent for the initiation into fellwalking. Long, gradual slopes, with the additional help of fence posts signposting the way ahead in mist, lead on to a summit from which a riot of peaks is seen on a good day, from Great Gable to Coniston Old Man and far beyond.

All that remains is the descent to the south-east down the nose of Steel Fell, finally bringing you safely into the mouth of the Greenburn Valley, with Grasmere just a short walk away. It was sad that Jack Soper refused to help me with the three additional queries I had asked him about the local rocks, but he also said something which made me laugh: 'There are more skylines in the Lakes than in Norfolk because there is less sky'. I'll certainly drink to that. And so might you too on successfully completing an enjoyable circuit of the Greenburn Valley which would appear to prove this point.

Chapter 11

THE KENTMERE HORSESHOE

The Kentmere Horseshoe is the first major skyline of Lake District hills which travellers from the south encounter. It used to be said that Staveley, the community at the entrance to Kentmere, was the first village the Lakesbound motorist went through after leaving Hyde Park Corner. Now, Staveley has been bypassed and the main street which proved such a bottle-neck has become an open avenue to the secluded valley beyond, not to mention the glorious coronet of mountains which guard it.

The peaks of Yoke, Ill Bell, Froswick, Thornthwaite Crag, Mardale Ill Bell, Harter Fell and Kentmere Pike cradle the delightful valley head in a firm embrace, offering a high-level walk that is priceless. The going underfoot is turf, and is firm and springy with only the occasional intrusion of rock or scree. In every direction, from shining sea to distant mountains, the views absorb a panorama fit for kings.

Lonely, undulating and compelling, the fells of the Kentmere Horseshoe are not to be taken lightly. Bleak, empty valleys flank them on either side. There are crags and shattered, precipitous

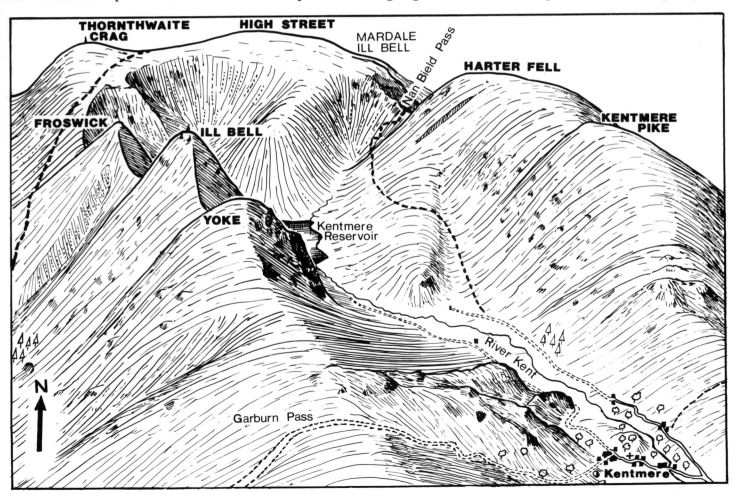

places below the skyline ridge. Indeed, this exciting backbone of high ground can quickly undergo a harsh about-face when the skies darken and the mists swirl and you realize only too well that help is far away. It is the kind of place where at such times – and in certain moods – your mind can play tricks, imagining any number of things, from the certainty that you are walking in the wrong direction to the 'someone' whom you imagine is following so close-ly behind that prickles race up your spine.

Professor Norman Collie experienced a similar feeling on Ben Macdhui in 1891 when, certain he was being fol-lowed by the sound of footsteps, he was 'seized with an intolerable fright' and ran his hardest down the mountain. His experience was to be confirmed by other eminent mountaineers who had also encountered the 'Grey Man'. The hills of the Kentmere Horseshoe are similar in their wilderness aspect to the Cairngorm uplands where Ben Macdui reigns as the highest moun-tain, and it was during my first traverse of Kentmere's skyline that I was re-minded about all this.

I had arrived in Staveley straight from the motorway, the last stop being Hyde Park Corner. Three days in London's West End had given me a surfeit of city life. I could take no more. My hangover – courtesy of the French Pub and the Colony Club and myself – had long since evaporated, but there remained a depression and dissatisfaction that craved to be expunged. My Lake District cottage was still some miles away and I knew it would be cold and cheerless without the warmth of its coal fire. As soon as I saw the hills beyond Staveley receding into the wintery distance my heart skipped a beat. I knew what I must do: detour by Staveley and drive on up the Kentmere valley.

My first presentiment of something unusual happened on Garburn Pass. I whirled around, sure that someone was

Pools after rain on the summit of Garburn Pass.

not only right behind me but matching my every stride. Of course, the lane was empty, as it had been since I had started half an hour previously from the car-park near Kentmere village church. But as I continued up the stony track I began to hear someone calling my name from the fellside. At least it sounded like my name.

It was difficult to pinpoint its source. The wind was rising, distorting the sound, and visibility was murky. Per-haps it was a hill farmer bringing down his flock and shouting to his dogs. But, on second thoughts, how could it be? Any sheep living on these exposed heights would have been brought down into the shelter of the valley long before. Possibly the noise was in my head. A remnant from the French pub, maybe, where I had incurred the legendary wrath of writer Jeffrey Bernard (later to be the subject of the successful West End play *Jeffrey Bernard is Unwell*) by knocking his glass of vodka over – not once but twice.

On top of Garburn Pass I turned around for one last look into Kentmere before branching rightwards along the ridge, and the long, sweeping slopes of its first fell, Yoke. Lovely, lonely Kent-mere, birthplace of Alfred Wainwright's guidebooks, first published by West-morland county librarian, Henry Mar-shall, from his Low Bridge, Kentmere address and – incidentally – my first employer. 'H.M.', as he was affection-ately known, became keen on rock climbing while I was still a library assistant. Every Thursday afternoon we would go out on the crags and how enjoyable it was. By then his son Roger was at grammar school, and showing an interest in climbing too, an enthu-siasm he was to foster with a vengeance, proving a daring and bold climber who, sadly, was to die on Everest at the age of forty-six, on his second solo attempt. (He had previously climbed Kanchen-junga alone.)

Standing there on top of Garburn, the memories began to flicker back in increasing numbers: Roger, of 'Roger the Dodger' fame, bouldering on the valley's numerous outcrops below, his exploits legendary among his many climbing friends. Roger would have been equally at home in the bizarre ambience of the French Pub or the Colony Club (another acquired taste), eager to try anything new. While he was working as a journalist in Vancouver, we had gone on a pub crawl so high-spirited and noisy that we were surprised we survived unscathed – monumental hangovers apart.

A drystone wall follows along the crest of Yoke for some way and I continued alongside this, protected by its shelter from the by-now strong westerly wind, save where it poured through the occasional wall gap with such unabated fury that once it lifted me off my feet. Yet even here I sensed a presence nearby. I found myself repeatedly pausing in mid-stride and glancing uneasily back along the top of the wall to check if anybody who may have been following me on its other side was surreptitiously peeping over the top to watch my progress up the hill. I pulled myself up short. What *was* I expecting? To see Roger's shock of flaxen hair

ducking out of sight as I looked around? 'Get a grip!' I told myself. Yet it was the kind of trick he might have played, trailing me for some way and then, with a great laugh, surprising me when I least expected it.

It was during one such moment that, glancing over my shoulder, my eyes met the bulk of Red Screes. Red Screes, the guardian of Kirkstone Pass, looking from this distance like the east wall of a great Alpine peak. If until now I had become obsessed with ghosts and spectral beings, there had been a time, several years before, on Red Screes when I had almost become a ghost myself – stretchered from below the frozen waterfall on the mountain down where I had disgraced myself by falling (a climber dreads being considered incompetent far more than broken limbs). I had found myself looking up into the circle of familiar faces gazing down at me, while I cringed with embarrassment. The faces belonged to members of the local mountain-rescue team. Did I owe any of them a fiver? Had I borrowed someone's Strimmer and not returned it? Now they had me at their mercy! But what great care they had exercised in retrieving me from the mountain.

High on Yoke, no longer with the protection of the wall which stops well short of the summit, the wind increased its speed with a severity that plucked the loose, billowing nylon of my cagoule and produced a rattle like the sound of a stick scraped hard across a sheet of corrugated iron. It also blew me over again. Progress now depended on my remaining at a standstill during the worst gusts, just waiting for the next lull. Escape seemed out of the question. To the right, just over the edge, lay the precipitous mountainside of Rainsborrow Crag; to the left, slopes did indeed lead down to Troutbeck but I would be facing directly into the teeth of the gale. Besides, there was my car in Kentmere still to consider.

Beyond the expansive dome of Yoke, I approached the summit of Ill Bell with some trepidation, keeping well back from the edge. Danger came to a head beyond the cairns marking the top. It was not feasible to strike from this point straight for the next peak, Froswick, because of the drop into Over Cove. Just as I braced myself against the wind on the path which curls around in a detour, I heard another shout. It stopped me in my tracks. There was not a soul in sight. Yet it had seemed remarkably near, and almost like someone was closing up on me from behind and trying desperately to attract my attention so they could catch up.

Once on Froswick I clambered down the far side, then up again towards the beacon on top of Thornthwaite Crag – the next landmark on the horseshoe. By now I was feeling the strain, always glancing behind just in case a distant figure hurried into view, and weak from lack of breakfast. Just as the slopes began to level off, a narrow path branched off to the right to contour airily around the head of the valley, and cutting off some of the distance I would otherwise have had to cover. Eventually – but only after a further battle with treacherous gusts – I reached the trig

Froswick and Ill Bell from Troutbeck.

point on Mardale Ill Bell (with its aerial views of Blea Water and Small Water below), the next stop being Nan Bield Pass. The steep and rocky descent was at last in the lee of the westerly. I reached the safety of the Nan Bield col and collapsed there against its walled shelter.

As I reclined there, trying to get my breath, I felt a slab of something hard in the top of my rucksack. Chocolate! Feverishly, I foraged inside and discovered only – to my chagrin – my pocket tape recorder. Then I saw something else. The 'play' button had been accidentally depressed. Could that be the answer to the shouts? Suddenly it all came together with remarkable clarity. The last time I had used the recorder was on Catbells in a similar high wind, trying desperately to record salient details by a series of yells, before the struggle to make myself heard against the elements became all too much and I had retired the recorder to the rucksack.

I clicked the button to the 'off' position and returned the tape recorder to my sack. From then on, the shouting ceased,

my strength gradually returned, and the sun came out. Boosted on by the wind – now pushing me on like a portable jet-engine in a power pack on my back – I was transported up the steep zigzags to the top of Harter Fell with remarkably little effort, and with memorable views whenever I glanced behind me towards the bulk of High Street, black and huge above.

The remaining ridge walk back to Kentmere over Kentmere Pike gave a superb view across the valley towards the skyline of Yoke, Ill Bell and Froswick, each peak rising and falling in delightful swoops above the rippling waters of Kentmere Reservoir far below. From every quarter, great views bombarded me as I traversed the gentle gradient with its final taxing incline to the top of Kentmere Pike, surrounded by the distant tops of Skiddaw, the Scafells, Morecambe Bay, Ingleborough, the Northern Pennines and Blencathra. Sapped by hunger and weary with fatigue, my most gruelling part of the journey came on the final climb up Kentmere Pike from Brown How. The descent to the track between

Yoke from the Troutbeck side of Garburn Pass.

Kentmere and Sadgill in Longsleddale, and then by cart track back to the village, proved even more tiring still. I had to push myself to reach the car. Once in the comfort of the driving seat it took me fifteen minutes before I could summon the energy to twist the ignition key.

The following month I felt the familiar tingle of gooseflesh down my neck again as I remembered the tape recorder and retrieved it from the sack to check its batteries. As I slid the plastic cover aside I had a sudden premonition I would find no batteries inside anyway, and that my experiences on Yoke and Ill Bell would still go unexplained. But the batteries were there after all, although, and quite unconsciously, I still found myself looking behind me over one shoulder.

Kentmere Horseshoe from the track leaving the valley for Sadgill.

Chapter 12
THE RIGGINDALE HORSESHOE

I have always regretted the fact that the unhappiest part of my life was spent a few miles away from Riggindale, and I never visited it. Perhaps it was as well. The recriminations and angst of an unhappy marriage that reverberated through my head could well have had a self-destructive influence in that lonely, magnificent valley and finished me off for good, no doubt I emphasize from a *guilty conscience*. For Riggindale is that kind of place. The kind of place where dark deeds in the name of history have been committed in the past and where a mysterious brooding quality prevails. In the hit movie *Withnail and I* the two visit Riggindale and it drives them almost to the brink of distraction.

Not that the Riggindale in George Harrison's film bears resemblance to the Riggindale that you or I will find.

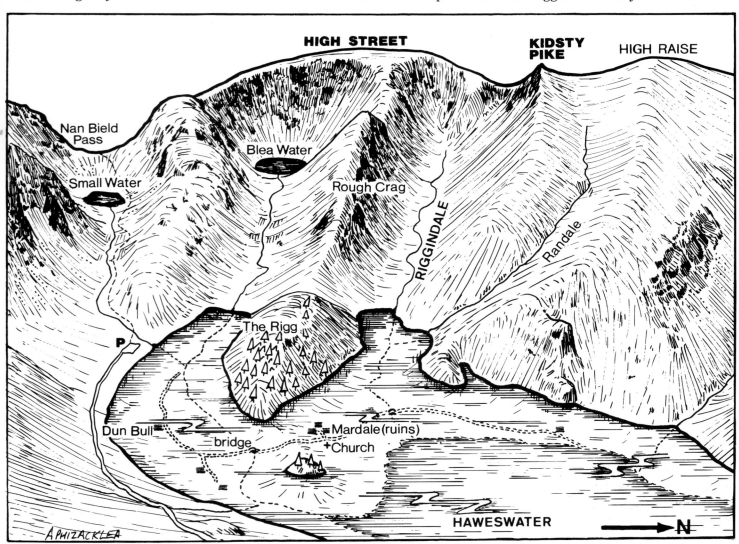

The Riggindale Horseshoe viewed from the Old Corpse Road across Haweswater.

In the film there is a pub, but the pub for Riggindale is under several leagues of water. In the film, too, there are other habitations, while Riggindale actually is totally uninhabited, thanks to the ministrations of the Manchester Waterworks Department who, on damming Haweswater for supplying that great city with its liquid supply, also bereaved the dale head of any living soul.

What does remain the same, however, is the view of glorious mountains. There is a moment in the film when Withnail – he who drinks lighter fuel and who has motored up north from Chelsea's King's Road in the swinging Sixties up-ending a bottle of Scotch at the wheel of an old Jaguar with one wiper blade missing and headlight out – draws back the bedroom curtains, bleary-eyed and hungover. There, framed in the window, is the Rigg, almost as if it were sailing up the Lake. This is one of the magical moments a visitor to these parts receives, rain or shine.

Such is the beauty of this scene, seen fleetingly in the film, and the only shot of Lake District *per se*, that it still remains with you. There is no need for the use of artificial stimulants to create a high with this kind of scenery. It is matchless. Even more so is to walk around the Riggindale Horseshoe. Both will give you a high in quite a different vein.

Riggindale, in fact, is one of the remotest parts of Lakeland, precipitous and rugged in its furthest recesses and captured between two ridges of some character. Its cirque over Rough Crag and Long Stile on to the summit of High Street, then back down the adjoining ridge from Kidsty Pike to the ruins of Riggindale Farm is not only compelling because it reaches into the most desolate parts of Cumbria, but because it starts from them too. The head of lonely Mardale has long been flooded and converted into a Manchester reservoir, but is none the less beautiful and wild for all that. It will take you from three to five hours and, as Haweswater is the highest lake in England, starting from its shores will allow you almost 700ft credit in altitude. On top of this, the journey to Riggindale is a wonder in itself.

The Rigg it is that draws the eye

Sunshine and snow on Kidsty

Bridges and waterfalls: the view looking from the lake shore back up towards the Haweswater road and just across the water from The Rigg.

after your trip through deepest West-morland. Almost at the dale head, with its mountain walls closing in and the lake of Haweswater hiding sunken be-hind the battlement-type Manchester Waterworks walls, the road winds its way down a steep hill. Suddenly, around a bend, appears an island in the lake, an upthrust of rock and fir trees and shaped like a heart. So boat-like is this prominence, for the Rigg it is, that you might be tempted to believe that you are about to be rammed as its pointed bows spear towards you.

Immediately behind the woods of the Rigg – for the island is in fact a peninsula – the skyline of Rough Crag bursts upwards into view, climbing steeply in the distant direction of High Street and adding to the general effect of mountain grandeur. Riggindale is the deep, secluded valley to the right of Rough Crag and hemmed in by the adjoining ridge from Kidsty Pike that runs almost down to the water's edge some way beyond.

The road continues to twist its way towards the head of Mardale and stops finally at a cul-de-sac car-park. From here, a two-mile trip just above the water's edge will bring you back to the grassy swards behind the Rigg before turning away from its heady scents of fir cones and pine needles to begin the ascent up Rough Crag.

During a dry summer, the level of the water in Haweswater sinks to such a degree that it is possible to park your car on the hill from where you first see the Rigg, and descend the steep fellside beneath and walk through the ruins of Mardale Green – a direct route across the bed of the lake to the neck of land behind the Rigg. It is a poignant trip with just one detail from the past still remaining intact: a tiny hump-backed bridge you cross which marks the route from what was once the tiny church to the Corpse Road over the fells to Shap. When the rains come, and this Atlantis of Lakeland disappears once more, perhaps not, as I said, 'leagues' under water but certainly a good few feet.

The footpath, once you begin ascending Rough Crag above the tree-tops of the Rigg, keeps to the left of a drystone wall that proceeds along the crest of the skyline and marks the brink of extensive broken crags plummeting down into Riggindale far below. The ridge runs on and on, leaving you isolated on a heavenly mountain crest between the sombre tarn of Blea Water and its exceedingly rugged combe on one side, and Riggindale, wild Riggindale, on the other.

The Rough Crag ridge presently dips into a saddle, only to steepen dramatically as it climbs up Long Stile on to the massive backbone of High Street, which

Looking down along the ridge from Rough Crag.

crosses its path in a north-south direction. This is the place where it is easiest to stray in mist, via a subsidiary ridge leading west on to the Martindale fells. Kidsty Pike, however, Riggindale's sentinel, seen from as far away as the M6 motorway thirty miles to the east, lies an easy walk away around the valley head and the east.

Kidsty Pike has a distinctive sharp-cut outline because its ramparts actually plummet into the head of Riggindale – something not to be emulated by going too near the edge where more broken crags abound.

Having topped-out on the summit of Kidsty, you are faced with delightful grassy slopes leading down and along the opposite side of Riggindale from the one from which you climbed. And it shows: the views from Kidsty Howes across to the mendacious silhouette of High Stile and Rough Crag are magnificent, especially when it appears soot black as the sun goes down. The return path into the mouth of the dale – and back to the Rigg – is gentle and sublime, a fitting conclusion to your sojourn around this wonderful, secret place.

Chapter 13

THE ULLSWATER WATERSHED SKYLINE

The Lake District, that riotous upheaval of peaks in the north-west corner of England, is split down the middle by the A591 road from Keswick to Windermere, conveniently separating east from west. Although the western Lakes capture most of the celebrated mountains like Great Gable, Langdale Pikes and the Scafells, it is the eastern fells which contain by far the longest horseshoe in this book, namely the crest of the Ullswater watershed. It is staggering.

Covering a spine of continuously high ground for thirty-three miles and including over 8,000ft of climbing in its airy course, this walk offers an ideal two-day expedition with a high-level camp or bivouac *en route,* or even – if you prefer – what is sometimes advertised as the highest-altitude hotel accommodation in Britain for the night.

Alternatively, it can be traversed within an action-packed twenty-four hours of non-stop walking (it actually took me sixteen hours).

The crest of this lonely, desolate and beautiful horizon achieves all this by taking in the length of High Street, ostensibly as the Romans travelled it from Pooley Bridge in the north to Troutbeck in the south, but in this instance actually starting from Askham

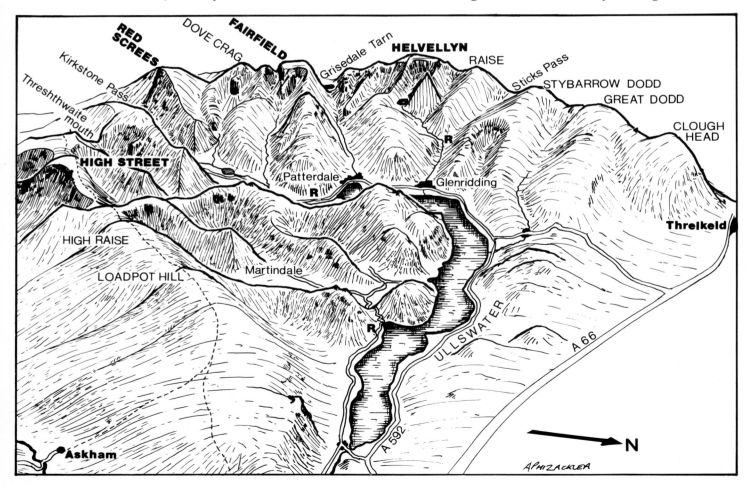

and then going almost the whole way before swinging off round westwards. On it goes over Caudale Moor and Raven's Edge to arrive at the Kirkstone Inn on the summit of Kirkstone Pass, at 1,500ft. So far so good, and how good the going has been along this most divine of ridges. An ascent up the precipitous east wall of Red Screes by the airiest of mountain paths is the next gem along the way, followed by a further westwards trip along captivating tops to the summit of Fairfield, thence steeply down to the peak-locked waters of Grisedale Tarn (and a viable camp or bivvy site). Finally, the ridge climbs on northwards over the stupendous chain of Dollywagon Pike, Helvellyn and the Dodds to finish at long last down the slopes of Clough Head at Threlkeld.

It is an incredible journey and one that will leave a lasting impression on those who rise to its wild and haunting challenge. It penetrates the loneliest fells where lost crag-rimmed valleys were once thickly forested and the domain of brigands and outlaws. Now they are the domain of the golden eagle, fell pony, fox and buzzard, and of roe-deer and red-deer too – herds of them can be glimpsed in the dale heads below as you stride along the mighty escarpment above.

Embracing a considerable interior of tributary hills, valleys, ridges and tarns, as well as the considerable length of England's second longest lake, the circumnavigation of the Ullswater watershed can leave you very much out on a limb if things go wrong or conditions worsen. However, there are numerous escape routes, providing you have taken two things into consideration: one is that you are happy with map and compass in bad weather; the other that you consider traversing the route in a clockwise direction, this being the safest way to tackle any obstacles that may arise. Ascending the difficulties concerned – like that east wall of Red Screes – is much more

preferable to finding you have to descend steep rocks and scree with trecherous crags in the vicinity and in darkness or mist.

An added bonus of this route is that both its start and finish verge on the A66, a major trunk road along which buses run, allowing for convenient transport back towards where your car was originally parked. This road also allows reasonable chances of a lift for those who are hitch-hiking back. Of course, there are taxis only a telephone call away too.

High Street from Loadpot Hill to Thornthwaite Crag

High Street is a showcase of the Lake District National Park, having a thoroughfare of highlights along the way every bit as exhilarating to the hillwalker as goals like Marks & Spencers, Debenhams, Ratners, Rumbelows, Dixons, Top Shop, C & A and Chelsea Girl would be to the Saturday shopper in a High Street. However, *this* High Street calls for an expenditure of hard physical effort.

Loadpot Hill, Wether Hill, High Raise, Rampsgill Head – these are the counterparts of Woolworths and W.H.Smiths for the eager shopper on this route. They have a character that is unique to these isolated eastern Lakeland fells. Being approximately as high as the Langdale Pikes, they require a withdrawal from the cheque book of your energy reserves, which you hope will not leave you too spent.

From the moment you leave the village green of Askham and take the path that rakes up over Moor Divock on the blind side of the High Street range, you may even wonder if you are heading towards something that is more than you bargained for when the ground is slippery and the feet require that extra purchasing power as the wind blows unobstructed across the great whale back ridge. Far below your path, plunge craggy coves so deep you cannot glimpse their base.

I say the blind side because until you breast the summit of Arthur's Pike you can have no idea of the breathtaking beauty of the view along Ullswater on the hitherto unseen western side of High Street, or of the distant

Beams of sunlight approach Threshthwaite Mouth as they move along the Ullswater Watershed Skyline.

vista of the Helvellyn arm of the skyline that you will eventually traverse. When all this finally appears as you crest the ridge, the view is sudden. However, it is not until you then top-out on the slopes of Loadpot Hill, the next summit along the way and the first major peak of the route, that you can look south along the immediate backbone of the High Street ridge and savour the enjoyment to come.

So wild can it prove up here, even when the sun is shining and the valley fields are dappled with racing cloud-shadows, that the prevailing wind can build up ice on the squared mesh of the wire fence running along the ridge to such a depth that it can resemble a continous wine-rack, stretching on southwards into the distance.

Arriving on each summit, only to 'tick it off' and move on to the next requires a certain mental expenditure too when the clouds begin to gather and doubts begin to surface. You may need reserves just not forthcoming from the energy fund as the increasing wildness of the scene nibbles away at your resolve. Too bad, then, when the only equivalents of cashpoints along this High Street are not to be found at the

A fence and wall mark the passage of a rare thoroughfare on the skyline of High Street.

Midland Bank or Nat West but at the windows presented by the escape routes down into the valleys of the Martindale fells to the east. In both instances you will eventually reach roads, but the long walk back is likely to make more inroads on your energy resources – possibly already verging on bankruptcy if you just did not have the essential wherewithal to complete the traverse of High Street.

For this eventuality to have to happen, conditions do not have to be desperate. The out-on-a-limbness of great backbones like High Street can adversely affect people by their sheer presence alone. You have been warned. It was at the southern extremity of High Street, along the Kentmere Horseshoe – which, for our purpose is a quite separate tour from this sojourn along High Street – that I was to experience an unnervingness of the mind that almost had me beside myself with uneasiness and worry. It is the mind that quickly falls prey to the desolation and bleakness of barren mountain ranges and which can tax your progress, if you are not ready for them, long before physical exhaustion. It must always have been the same.

The actual pavement along which the Roman soldiers traversed High Street is now reduced to a procession of faint ruts and grooves, but the way is unmistakable. The vertebrae of high ground stretches on, unwavering in its directness and grandeur. Fifth Avenue, Prince's Street, the Champs d'Elysses and The Strand could not give a finer arcade, a mall along which you cannot divert until eventually you reach the narrows. Here, for a moment,

The Beacon on Thornthwaite Crag.

after the previous straightness of High Street, the ridge jinks around the abyss of Riggindale, and a tributary ridge leads westwards to enchanting peaks like Rest Dodd and the Nab, and even Angletarn Pikes and beyond. Enchanting is the word; they overlook the hidden, green Martindale valleys – perfection in miniature. Yet, having accomplished its body swerve, High Street continues imperiously on past, embellishing its way with breathtaking glimpses deep into the crag-fast recesses around Blea Water to the east and regaining its former direction and thrust as it climbs towards its highest point and onwards to Thornthwaite Crag beyond.

Walkers on the Ullswater Watershed Skyline approaching Raise to the north from Helvellyn.

Thornthwaite Crag to Grisedale Tarn

Travellers intending only to traverse High Street can make their way down from the Beacon of Thornthwaite Crag – as the Romans did – into Troutbeck. They can even graft the thirteen miles of splendid highway accomplished so far on to the Kentmere Horseshoe or even the Hartsop Dodd Round, if desired. For our purposes, though, the skyline of the Ullswater watershed now swings westward over splendid roller-coaster ridges that initially plunge into the Big Dipper of Threshthwaite Mouth, then climbs steeply out on to the summit of Caudale Moor. From here, the way follows Raven's Edge to arrive at the Kirkstone Pass Inn and with the pink east face of Red Screes rising majestically ahead. This second leg of the Ullswater watershed skyline is eight miles long, and the steep climb up Red Screes, a little to the left of the famous rift of Kilnshaw Chimney, constitutes about halfway. Once on top, an outstanding panorama of views spreads to the west, with retrograde glances giving marvellous views of High Street and the Pennines beyond. Turn back to westwards again, and there is the

bulk of Dove Crag unmistakably ahead, black and bold, jutting from the mountain of the same name and signposting the way ahead over its crest, and above more wondrous valley scenery until – finishing along the short section of the Fairfield Horseshoe, including Hart Crag – you reach the summit of Fairfield. The descent to Grisedale Tarn is steep and rocky with lots of scree. It is by no means obvious at first as the hillside is convex. In mist you need to take care and use a compass bearing to keep you on course.

The Dodds Ridge from Grisedale Tarn to Clough Head

The skyline of the Dodds ridge looks as if it is racing through the sky, inexorably, like the carriages of some great train, such as the Starlight Express, pulled by a mighty locomotive.

The switchback procession of hills ahead certainly reminded me, at any rate, of Sir Edward Elgar's musical as I began my traverse under a canopy of galaxy-spangled heavens and over the tops of Dollywagon Pike, Nethermost

Pike, Helvellyn, Raise, Stybarrow Dodd, Watson's Dodd, Great Dodd and Clough Head. This stupendous train of hills not only forms the north-south barrier of the Lake District, but also makes its biggest single mass of high ground. In good weather, with suffcient snow cover, it proves a wonderfully rewarding area for the ski mountaineer.

However, the occasion I mention was not during my traverse of the complete Ullswater watershed skyline, but of an altogether separate high-level excursion, and one typical of this great skyline which can so conveniently be chopped into separate entities, such as the traverse of High Street on its own, or of the Dodds ridge, for a day's walking. In this case I was trying desperately to complete the Dodds ridge in a *morning*.

My alarm clock had brought me to my senses, or rather to a bleary state of consciousness, as I would have been considered by many people to have been in any but my right senses to consider what I was intending to do on that Christmas morning. The time was half an hour before dawn; everything was pitch black and the air outside cold and raw. I had been invited to Christmas dinner near Keswick. As I live at the other end of the Dodds ridge, what more sensible way could there be then, than to walk the five to seven hours stretch along this skyline between Grasmere and Threlkeld?

How quickly I was to change my mind; 'sensible' seemed the last word to describe this venture – a journey which quickly turned from being an exquisite traverse along a great horizon into several moments of undisguised terror.

It became rapidly obvious that these hills were no counterpart of luxurious Pullman railway coaches after all. Instead of any hint of soft leather upholstery and Tiffany lampshades dispensing pools of softly glowing light as the carriages swayed northwards beneath the stars, the great ungainly shape of Dollywagon Pike loomed ominously above Grisedale Tarn like a

freight train wagon clanking through the night. W.H.Davies wrote grippingly about hitching rides across America on freight trains in *Diary of a Super Tramp*. During his classic account he loses a leg, being inadvertently run over by a wagon wheel. I was almost to lose more.

My trip along the mountains began to resemble the plight of Ernest Borgnine, who plays the evil freight train guard in *Emperor of the North*. He hates the hobos riding the rods (the wagons' suspension unit) and dislodges them with an iron bar dangling on a chain – a flail that ricochets upwards from the railway sleepers, battering any tramp within reach. To do this, he has to balance along the tops of the boxcars themselves. It is from these precarious heights that, as he lowers his deadly payload between two wagons,

he is finally plucked into space by Lee Marvin, king of the hobos, who grabs the bar with his bare hands and jams it in a wheel. Immediately, reeled in with such force, Borgnine is dragged on to the tracks to suffer a gruesome fate. Such was the calamity that faced me shortly after reaching the heights of Dollywagon Pike . . .

I had reached Grisedale Tarn by walking up Tongue Ghyll from the Traveller's Rest pub at Grasmere. The next stop was the summit of Dollywagon Pike and its steep procession of zigzags which rapidly eroded away any preconceived ideas about the melodies of Elgar and an astronautical spin through the galaxies. This was a hard, sweating toil. The wind was keen, the dawning day chillier than ever with the edges of the hills blurred into the greyness above. But one thing was con-

A glimpse of Thirlmere beyond the plantations – a view from the lower slopes of the Ullswater Watershed Skyline.

firmed: from above the level of Grisedale Tarn (almost at 2,000ft), all the snow had been blown from the hills.

Dollywagon Pike forms one side of the basin in which Grisedale Tarn sits, competing as it were with the peaks of Fairfield and St Sunday Crag and Seat Sandal flanking the rest of the amphitheatre. The eastern flanks of Dollywagon Pike have gloriously precipitous slopes, disrupted by savage crags and a ruggedly superb mountain aspect. But all this is left behind as the path eases off and strikes due north just below the Thirlmere, or western, side of the summit ridge, with rather the appearance of a catwalk.

The moment that plucked me from my feet came without warning. It arrived all the more suddenly because in every direction the views had held me spellbound. From the path, I gazed down westwards on to the passing scene as it fell behind, each landmark another stage to be ticked off on this magical journey. The summit plateau of Steel Fell, its tiny tarns dulled by the morning gloom, with the ridge of the Helm Crag Horseshoe standing out in relief below, and then glimpses of Thirlmere Lake glimmering between plantations of water-board trees, a magnificent sight among the rugged peaks. To gain even more dramatic views, I had clambered on to the crest of the skyline above, trainers padding now on the swaying, rocking tops of the boxcars of Helvellyn stretching out in procession ahead as this train of hills rolled onwards, their eastern flanks horrifically precipitous beneath the very skyline's rim.

Training shoes on winter's mountains? Fell-running shoes are my favourite for mountains, although I wear plastic mountain boots in winter. That day, however, I had chosen my lightweight Walsh Raids because time was of the essence and the hilltop snow was blown away or so I thought. I had not reckoned on natural mountain drainage freezing solid on the very summit slope and so, insidiously, I had stepped on it before realizing. *WHOOSH!* Without warning I shot down the slope between Helvellyn and Nethermost Pike, the angle of the slope veering me away from the safety of the nearby col between the two mountains. Instead, and rather like the downfall of Ernest Borgnine in the film, I found myself flying through space towards the pines above Thirlmere, hundreds of feet below.

Heart-stopping moments later I was still travelling, fingernails scrabbling at the eggshell of ice speeding me down. CRACK! With a noise like a gunshot I stopped dead. Wobbling, shaken, breathless, I took stock. My feet had lodged on a stone projecting through the ice. The size of a golf ball, it barely supported my weight. I scarcely dared breathe. Overbalance and I would be on my way down again. I was dizzily marooned on a vertiginous slab of ice. An agonizing thought occurred. I remembered how earlier that morning, in the interests of travelling light, I had stopped at the door on my way out and taken my crampons and ice-axe from my rucksack. I would not be needing them, I had reasoned. Not with the hills blown clear of snow and as I was travelling in trainers. *Or had I?* Gingerly I slid the day sack from my back, opening it so gently I might have been shop-lifting. Any sudden movements and I would overbalance. The sack felt amazingly light. And yet — holding my breath, I slid a hand inside. But instead of crampons there was only spare clothing and sandwiches. Hang on . . . I suddenly felt the cold rubber handle of my Barracuda ice-axe in the sack. I was saved.

I was still shaking with relief as I regained the ridge. The summit of Helvellyn was a gentle climb ahead, with Striding Edge standing patiently to the east, looking for all the world like a local line passenger train waiting for our great Freight Train in the Sky to pass by. And so, massively and in-

A fragment of the Dodds skyline overlooks St John's Vale.

exorably, it did. Onwards past the adjacent skyline of Swirral Edge and its plunging drop into Red Tarn below, then over Whiteside Bank and on the summit of Raise beyond. With me, still scrambling along its undulating tops to keep my dinner date. Down from Raise, I crossed Sticks Pass (where to the west on the edge of a wide depression is the hut of the Lakeland Ski Club) and finally faced the rolling, grassy slopes of the Dodds, stretching out ahead like low-loader freight train cars with their huge loads sheeted over, yet bulky beyond belief. Watson's Dodd came first, rounded and humped and 2,770ft high. It was followed in turn by Great Dodd.

From here to Clough Head was ridge walking that was still utterly delightful despite my fatigue, with the little castle of Calfhow Pike, a tiny atoll of rock among an ocean of grass. It is a long, long descent to Threlkeld, but then the Ullswater Watershed Skyline is a long, long skyline. There are few finer in Britain.

Chapter 14

THE FAIRFIELD HORSESHOE

The Fairfield Horseshoe charts a joyful course through the sky behind Ambleside, stringing together a chain of shapely peaks around nearby Rydale. On one side of the curve soar Nab Scar, Heron Pike and Great Rigg; on the other, Low Pike, High Pike, Dove Crag and Hart Crag. At the head of the valley in between is the panoply of Fairfield itself, spread out in magnificent array.

As a horseshoe, Fairfield's famous circuit is worthy of the blacksmith's sweating toil over anvil and forge, with bellows, hammer and tongs, beneath his spreading chestnut tree. And yes, there are horse chestnuts on the foothills, along with sycamores, oaks, rowans, beeches, hawthorns and red-berried hollies galore.

What could be more English than Fairfield? What indeed? Set out

amongst lawns and meadows and pastures old, the Fairfield Horseshoe is part of a national heritage, of England, This England.

However, Fairfield also has an edge, quite apart from the one so obviously waiting to be trodden. Innocent visitors can come to grief on Fairfield, lulled into a false sense of security by its very name. But then it happens. In Central Park, New York City, I fell asleep on

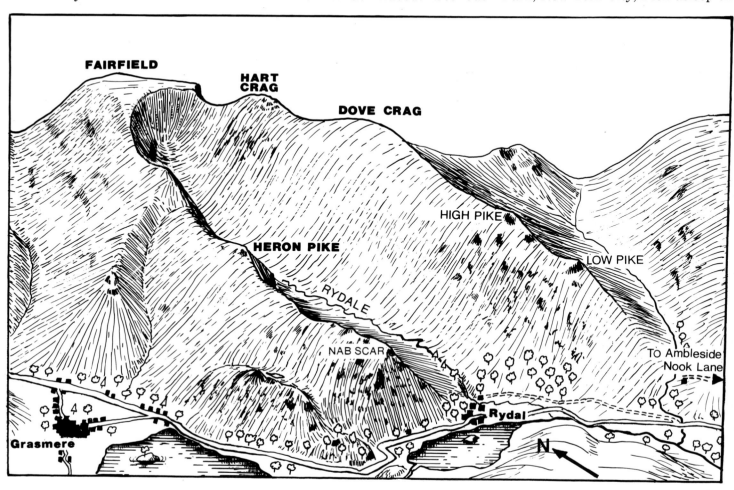

the grass on Strawberry Fields and woke to find my bicycle stolen. So do be careful – not every 'field' promises an idyllic experience. Where, after all, do Liverpool FC play but Anfield?

It is easy to lose your head on Fairfield. Mountain tops leapfrog up behind one another as if jostling for predominance. The hilltop climber is promised one fine summit after another, and with only marginal loss of height between one peak and the next once the main height of the ridge is won by the first climb of the day.

Rydal is my favourite launching pad, just over a mile from Ambleside by a bridle track, and a hamlet so rustic that its inhabitants are still called 'Rydal Crows', and the road between the cottages is a cul-de-sac. Ringed on three sides by hills, here is the Georgian mansion of Rydal Hall, the historic home of William Wordsworth at Rydal Mount and in Dora's Field there is a blaze of golden daffodils each spring. Above all this looms Nab Scar.

The track leaving Rydal for the heights of Nab Scar is steep, so steep, in fact, that it breaks into zigzags immediately on leaving the hamlet. It continues to gain height with every step, corkscrewing its way up the hill-side to a stile beneath trees where larch fronds hang low and, as you clamber over a stile beneath their foliage, they tickle your face with forest herbal perfumes.

At this point, there is little indication that the track wending ever higher through a maze of outcrops, scree and tangled bracken, will ever reach a glorious mountain crest. Gradually, however, the expanse of fellside ahead begins to diminish, the sky expands and you can begin the enjoyable part of your flight around Rydale, like the air traveller who experiences a lift in spirits after a successful take-off and settles down at last with a large martini as their jet begins to cruise high across the sky.

Streaming out behind you, then, your own personal vapour trails – gaining a little height here, losing it a fraction there – as you follow the rise and fall of the great mountain crest, beginning your atmospheric voyage. Nor is this just whimsy. All living organisms, humans included, waft back a skein of airborne scents ('rafts') on the slightest breeze. These are the microscopic particles continually dropping off our bodies – the scents seized on by the Labradors of SARDA (Search and

'The Great Wall of China' on the High Pike ridge of the Fairfield Horseshoe.

Rescue Dogs Association) with their sensitive noses. As well they might have to if you too – figuratively speaking – encounter the gentleman who snipped through the thick chain securing my Raleigh with a pair of bolt cutters while I dozed in Central Park. And you lose your way on Fairfield Horseshoe.

The path now climbs along a delightful crest, knobbly with craggy pulpits overhanging space above the busy road between Ambleside and Grasmere. These are favourite vantage points for foxes, chewing on the carcases they've carried with them. Yet it is all so close to the bustle of twentieth century life that you feel you could abseil from such a pulpit like a spider on a thread and drop in through the sun roof of the Mercedes, backed-up in the traffic far below.

A distant view of the head of Fairfield Horseshoe from near Heron Pike.

Hillwalkers on the Fairfield Horseshoe, approaching Heron Pike.

From the summit of Nab Scar, the vaunted scene of lakes and tarn, flashing like gems in the folds of the hills, creates a fine south-western aspect. View this as the sun goes down and these reflections provide a kaleidescope of bright red light from Rydal Water and Grasmere below your airy perch, away to Windermere, Coniston Water and Esthwaite Water beyond.

Flanking the skyline on the opposite side, and as you continue north to Heron Pike, the Rydale Valley is a different world away, isolated and empty, a study in the greens of its grass, the grey of the scree and the pink ribbons of shale weaving in between. Then suddenly there is a moment of potential drama.

Deep in the gulf of Rydale, like the white flecks of interference on a television screen, speed a band of pigeons racing homeward with rapid wingbeats to their lofts along the industrial coastline of West Cumbria. They have

already flown hundreds of miles from Belgium or France where they were released at the start of their race, but you would never know looking at their jinking, swerving progress through the valley. But how they are tempting fate.

This area of Lakeland has one of the highest densities of peregrine falcons in the world, and you wonder whether you are about to see the screaming 180mph dive from sky-high as this raptor slams into one of the fluttering specks in the back of the neck before airlifting it in the iron grip of its talons back to the crags below? Relics of such kills litter the Rydale screes, the tiny legs and feet, still clamped with the numbered rings used by pigeon fanciers for identification.

As the white shoal flickers into the distance, and you find yourself breathing again, do you perhaps feel a slight unease about your own sur-

vival? Are those spots of rain you felt on your cheek, and is the wind beginning to rise?

Doubts escalate when, after descending easily from Heron Pike, the skyline rises steeply ahead to the summit of Great Rigg. It is not unlike balancing along the vast fuselage of a Boeing 747 Jumbo-Jet that is nosing sharply up into the clouds, especially as the neighbouring horizons of Helvellyn and Dollywagon Pike begin to float alongside the higher you ascend. For a moment, you feel the ground sway beneath your feet and find yourself craving the shelter of the pressurized cabin below as you breast the summit in strong gusts.

There is another switchback descent, then after the climb to its extensive summit plateau, Fairfield finally arrives. As this is grassy, flat and ludicrously littered with many cairns, new fears arise. Clouds are now beginning to roll across the plateau, a barren waste that merges with a fresh complex of hills and valleys. How will you find the way?

The northern flanks of Fairfield and adjoining peaks – those you are about to overlook, given a break in the overcast – are wild, precipitous and chaotic badlands of crags and coves, quite unlike the grassy stairway you have so far traversed.

The col between Fairfield and Hart Crag is notoriously tricky in mist. Facing south-east and deceptively adjacent to the beaten track, it is underpinned by the vast, plunging wall of rock known as Scrubby Crag. And it is not the only one. Rock faces proliferate below the edges of the tops overlooking Deepdale and it pays to be very careful. People have been killed here.

The safest course is to keep to the path as you descend into the col below Hart Crag. Trying to escape from the ridge down Link Cove – the wild, steep valley immediately below Scrubby Scrag – is risky unless the weather is good. Misjudge where the crags are and you can fall through an open trapdoor in the skyline. Instead, keep to the path along the ridge until you feel the gound begin to rise once more beneath your feet as it mounts towards the top of Hart Crag.

Hart Crag is made hazardous in mist by its north face, a crag streaked white with quartz that gives the impression of eternal ice. However, once safely past Hart Crag, you continue south-easterly down a slope of well-scarred, clanking rocks. Then – as the ground begins to slope upwards to Dove Crag – a drystone wall signposts the way ahead from the depression between the two tops.

The remaining skyline now proceeds along the opposite edge of Rydale from the one by which you first climbed Fairfield. Unlike that trip along an empty, open mountain crest, this return route is waymarked by this structure which follows faithfully every undulation along its crest like the Great Wall of China. Only occasionally do you need to stray away from it, an example being on Low Pike where the path veers down to the left to avoid steep rocks.

Those who follow the skyline wall every inch of the way will find a rock step suddenly appears on the descent from Low Pike. It is a steep little pitch, requiring caution. It also arrives just when you think the walk is virtually over, but it can be avoided, as I said, to the left by a steep path.

The fleshpots of Ambleside lie ahead, beyond the ridge of Low Pike, and resembling an airport at dusk when seen from the flight deck of a big jet about to land. Glittering lights flank the main thoroughfare of Lake Road arrowing out ahead like a runway on its way to Waterhead, but the touchdown at Nook End Farm is much closer at hand, and with it, the final taxiing (on foot, of course) along Nook Lane to the comforts of the bar of Golden Rule Hotel.

The Fairfield Horseshoe strides into the distance high above Ambleside.

Chapter 15

THE DEEPDALE ROUND

'The Deepdale Round is *really* good. Have you done it?' asked Chris Bonington as we arrived in the car-park of the Brotherswater Inn.

'It's just up there. Along the ridge above Dovedale, on to Fairfield, then around Deepdale and down the St Sunday Crag ridge. It's great!' He did not receive a reply because my mind was in effect elsewhere. I had seen something that made me sick at heart. The car belonging to the woman I thought I loved was parked nearby. On the back seat I saw the jacket of a climber I knew, a friend in fact. I had vaguely suspected something. But now, my faint misgivings would seem confirmed. I hoped my feelings didn't show.

'You've gone quiet,' said Chris, 'What's up?' But he too became preoccupied. For the tracks of the two people leading from the car were going in exactly the same way through the snow as ours. As we proceeded on into the heart of wild and wonderful Dovedale, the two pairs of bootprints were always just ahead of us. 'Whoever they are, they

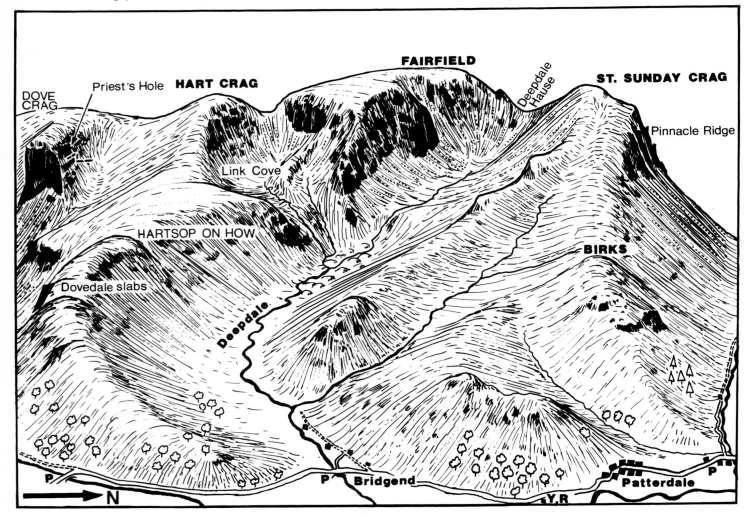

Looking beyond the early morning mist towards St Sunday Crag from Striding Edge, Helvellyn.

have tiny feet,' remarked Chris, 'I hope the buggers aren't going to Dove. There isn't enough ice at the moment for two teams on Inaccessible.' I still did not reply, depressed beyond belief and awaiting with dread what telltale story the prints in the snow would suddenly reveal. It was not until we had passed beneath Dovedale Slabs, and had finally reached the head of the valley below the beetling precipice of Dove Crag that the footprints continued on towards the summit of the ridge above as we turned off in the direction of the crag to attempt our climb, a frozen waterfall. It was *then* I knew where my real anxieties lay. The overwhelming relief that flooded through me in the wake of black despair spoke of my *real* priorities. We would have the ice to

ourselves after all, a river of it un-marred by previous climbers. When next I saw the two of them, I could not have been more pleased, but then thanks to an amazing lead by Chris and just before he went to climb Ever-est, we had made the first winter ascent that year of Inaccessible Gully on Dove Crag.

We all have memories on hills that can be painful as well as joyous, nor can the hills always exorcize the bleak-ness within us at the time. However, hills can sometimes put things into perspective. The actual Deepdale Round, one arm of which traverses the hillside above where Chris Bonington and I had approached Dove Crag and where you – if you had indeed been traversing it that day – could have

looked down on our ant-like progress like a fly on the wall. I mention Dove-dale in particular because it offers a unique approach to the Deepdale Round, if you happen to be a climber. If you do not, though, and are quite happy walking period, there is an excellent alternative for you too. Both routes are superb.

The Deepdale Round actually goes over the peaks of Hartsop-above-How, Hart Crag, Fairfield, Cofa Pike, St Sunday Crag, Gavel Pike and back down into Deepdale, around which it has traversed. I prefer to traverse the hills in this order just mentioned, the clockwise way round, because not only is it more convenient, generally speak-ing, and the views continuously mag-nificent from this aspect but, as I say, there is this fascinating approach up to the top of the ridge if you begin from Dovedale, the valley we had breached on our way to Dove Crag and one of the finest English mountain valleys imaginable.

The Fell and Rock Climbing Club of the English Lake District is a considerable mouthful, but it is the senior climbing club of the Lakes (like the Climber's Club is of North Wales and the Scottish Mountaineering Club belongs to the Highlands and Islands). The FRCC publishes rock climbing guidebooks, and grades routes of quality with a star system, three stars being the ultimate accolade. Walk from the Brotherswater Inn, through the adjacent camp site and up Dovedale, and when you finally reach the gate leading to the open fellside, with the beautiful sheet of Dovedale Slabs (otherwise known as Gill Crag) overhead, you will know that directly above is a two-star 'V. Diff' which can be soloed by proficient climbers or ascended with a rope

Dovedale borders the Hartsop on How skyline, with Dove Crag predominant at its head.

Dawn breaks on the head of Dovedale and the Hartsop on How ridge, seen from near the Kirkstone Pass road.

by those less capable. As a rock climb it is a joy: up a steep little face below the right-hand end of the crag to a grass ledge (Birdcage Walk), then up the centre of the 100ft slab above, up to a tiny pinnacle on the ridge called the Perch.

If you have no interest in actually climbing rocks, however, you can reach the summit of Hartsop-above-How (and the nearby Perch) much more easily by climbing the skyline from its very toe and near to where your transport is parked, the most convenient car-park being at Bridgend just beyond Brotherswater, from where a short walk takes you to a gate leading to a path up the wooded fellside.

The ridge gains height gradually, and develops into an undulating grassy spine separating two glorious dales, with a bird's eye view into each that compares with the finest amongst British hills. Immediately to the south of Dovedale with the stupendous bastion of Dove Crag dwarfing the head of the valley and with, perched above it, the gaping mouth of the Priest's Hole inviting passers-by to bivouac dizzily within its lofty recess. And the valley to the north? Why, this is Deepdale, of course. As Deepdale terminates in the magnificence of Link Cove, hanging

high on the northern flanks of Fairfield and enclosed by the shattered front of Hart Crag, the precipices of Scrubby Crag and the terminal ramparts of Greenhow End, the reward of this glorious panorama confronts you during much of the way to Hart Crag. And beyond? From Hart Crag to Fairfield you encounter a section of the Fairfield Horseshoe which is dangerous in mist. It is indeed wise to remember that this leg of the Deepdale Round skirts the vicinity of yawning cliffs only yards from the tread of your boots.

Leaving Fairfield down its north-facing slopes, and after despatching bristly Cofa Pike, barring your way like a gendarme, prepare yourself for more delightful ridge walking as you descend into the col of Deepdale Hause. The climb up to St Sunday Crag is pleasant and easy, the connection with neighbouring Gavel Pike then routing you back down into Deepdale by its delightful eastern ridge. There is another two-star rock climb, incidentally, a 'Diff' called Pinnacle Ridge, just below the summit of St Sunday Crag, but it is out of sight, poised above Grisedale's endless scree slopes and difficult to locate. It is best left for another day and an approach from below.

Chapter 16

HELVELLYN BY STRIDING AND SWIRRAL EDGES

Striding Edge is a skyline that for sheer popularity attracts the numbers approaching those you find on the Snowdon Horseshoe, yet it has no café on top, no mountain railway to whisk down the walking wounded and no immediate roadside accessibility. However, Striding Edge attracts its clientele by dint of its enthralling silhouette, despite being a lowlier brother in terms of height. Yet who can resist its wicked mile-long stiletto lancing out from the most central Lakeland mountain of over 3,000ft? Who indeed?

What of Swirral Edge then? We hear so much of Striding Edge but Swirral Edge, its complementary neighbour, is rarely mentioned in the same breath. In the second breath, possibly, but isn't Swirral Edge, despite its brevity, wonderful too? Let no one underestimate its quality. In certain conditions it can prove taxing and hazardous. Helvellyn, then, is fortunate to have both Striding

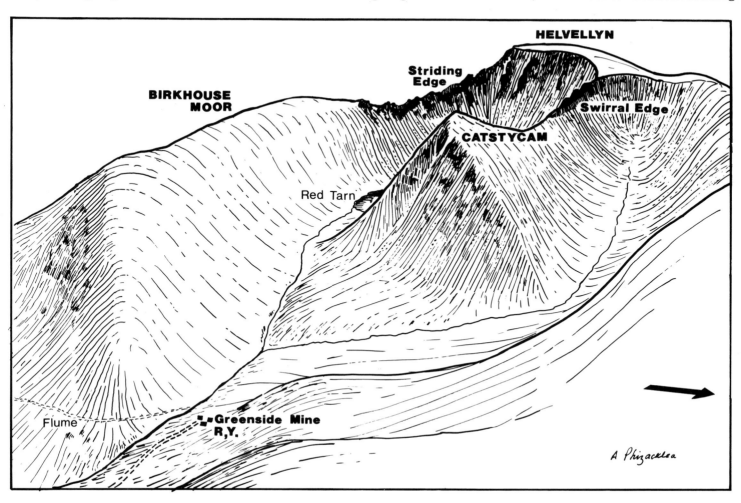

Catstycam is the first mountain encountered on the approach from Greenside Mine.

along the stream (now Red Tarn Beck) bulks the triangular peak of Catstycam that dominates your approach to Hellvelyn and which must now be skirted to its left up the track to Red Tarn and from where Striding and Swirral Edge enfold you deep between their jagged skylines.

It was nearly midnight on the evening of a New Year's Day when Edward Cross and I reached Red Tarn with our breath pluming into the frosty air. As the News at Ten had beamed out to TV sets behind the cottage windows that blazed through the velvety black night, we had beamed too as we embarked on what our friends considered an ill-conceived venture: this nocturnal attempt on Helvellyn's Edges. We had completed the traverse several times before, although, it must be said, always in broad daylight.

Above, a Boeing 747 boomed across a sky so chilled that the engines' roar reverberated down with an intensity to have sent sheep hobbling across the fellside. Our progress on the walk up to the tarn, 'Deep,' as Wordsworth wrote, 'in the bosom of Helvellyn' had been fraught with slips and slides. Moonlight so brilliant it cast shadows on the snow illuminated the scores of footprints paddled in the soft snow of the previous afternoon by passing hill goers. Now everything underfoot was a frozen, ridged and treacherous surface.

Beyond Red Tarn, the east face of Helvellyn blocked the way with icefalls shrouding its crags and a huge cornice fringing the face like a headband. Then a faint glug-glug hinted at water somewhere beneath the ice on which we moved. Thoroughly alarmed, we suddenly realized that we had mistakenly strayed a considerable way on to the frozen depths of Red Tarn. Dark blobs flew below the surface whenever air pockets altered shape under the pressure of a boot. Giggling insanely, we began to retrace our steps back across the ice which now creaked and flexed

and Swirral Edges to provide it with such a great and famous circuit.

The very popularity of Striding and Swirral Edges can give a misleading picture. To watch the multitudes of matchstick figures during weekends and Bank Holidays, progressing along their naked crest gives entirely the wrong impression. Such sights happen invariably on days when the weather is amenable – yes, even when raining or foggy, perhaps, as these conditions are still relatively amenable by mountain standards – yet come the onset of storms and blizzards, and Striding Edge, not to mention Swirral, become mantraps where adults, children and the family dog have been injured or even killed.

To encounter the members of a respected north Yorkshire mountaineering club having to abseil for their lives during such an occasion hints at just how this magical traverse can turn

nasty given inclement conditions. And wasn't it descending Striding Edge's final chimney where a Lakeland mountain guide fell to injure himself on the rocks below? These are but two of a catalogue of calamities that have befallen people here during the last century. This is not a skyline to be underestimated.

My favourite approach is to aim for Striding Edge first. A popular start is from Patterdale and the Grisedale valley, via the slopes of Birkhouse Moor, but car-parking proves a problem here as the road is narrow. However, a large car-park at nearby Glenridding offers an alternative choice of start: up the side of Glenridding Beck to where, from Miresbeck, your route cuts delightfully rightwards across the fellside along a flume to the old mine workings at Greenside (Youth Hostel and National Park bothy) on the opposite side of the waterfalls. Ahead, as you continue

like a giant aircraft wing in turbulent air. The ice sank a little, water rapidly flooding its surface as I tried to close my mind to the possibility of crashing through into the depths. Deep water trips a twitch factor in me far in excess of the fear of falling and the few steps back towards solid ground took an eternity.

As the souls aboard another Jumbo Jet ploughing across the heavens 35,000ft above sipped their beverages from plastic beakers, we tried to forget the respective pints we had each consumed before the pull of the climb had brought us precipitately out on the pub, into our gear and up to here. Now – with crampons at last clipped, Petzl headlamps clicked (and then just as quickly extinguished when we realized the moonlight was bright as a searchlight) and ice-axes at the ready – we began the diagonal climb up the icy ramparts above to the start of Striding Edge proper.

On this midwinter's evening, when the cold air made it painful to inhale sharply with the mouth open, the ridge ahead looked as insubstantial as balancing a way along a tree trunk floating amidst a logjam. However, instead of dark swirling water surrounding the narrows of the precarious way ahead, it was the shadowy blackness of the night lapping against the ridge's walls. It was across this void that progress would have to be made like lumberjacks by stabbing our crampon points into the verglassed timber and balancing against the anticipated roll not so much of that imaginary log but of a crampon point that suddenly skates off smooth bare rock. 'OK?' queried Edward, checking I was ready as we then began to scrunch our way forward, crampon points screeching occasionally whenever they scraped across the rock before locating a purchase to support the weight teetering above.

The alternative to traversing the crest is to follow the line of a path approximately 50ft below and on the Red Tarn flanks. We kept to the profile of the ridge itself, however, as we found our crampons generally gave a locktight grip. Up, down and along we scratched and grated with mittened fists as axes dangled by their slings from the wrists and clanged against the rock like tubular bells. At one point, a dizzily exposed strip of rock as airy as walking the plank led us above the ocean of blackness below.

However, it was the descents that gave the most trouble until we became accustomed to circling around like a dog about to lie down in its basket. Then facing in to the icily sugared rock, we lowered our respective weights from one handhold to the next as we backed our way downwards. The Stygian gloom of the chimney marking the end of Striding Edge was the most awkward of all as we could only feel for the footholds with our front points and then trust that what appeared so indistinct from above was adequate.

Ahead at last rose the steep and intimidating sweep of the summit slopes. Normally poised with unstable scree and boulders and over-looking a pitiless drop into the depths of Red Tarn the ground was now hard as iron. However, our crampon points bit and gouged their way home with each thud of the boot. At last Helvellyn's summit plateau came down to meet us with a pneumatic hiss as we finally stepped up on to its table-top. It sounded like a pneumatic hiss but was actually a final exhalation from my lungs as a moment's respite lay ahead.

Across a draping of crisp white tablecloth, the silhouettes of mountains and the eerie glow from the sodium street lights of distant cities and towns mingled in an unforgettable panorama. Heaped along the skyline were summits like Great Gable, Scafell Pike, Grasmoor and Blencathra, while deep within those sleeping communities were their own Lakelandia of Glenridding Walks, Fairfield Lanes and Helvellyn Closes.

Striding Edge in retrospect when looking back from Helvellyn.

I had a moment's intense longing to be wrapped up in bed down among fleshpots like Scawfell Crescent (sic) in Seascale or Bowfell Avenue in Morecombe or Skiddaw View in Penrith. To be perfectly accurate we could not actually see Seascale (nor its neighbouring cooling towers of Sellafield) because of the mountain ranges intervening between us and the West Cumberland coast but what we could see was crystal clear. Ahead, beyond the concrete trig point and further along the headband of cornice fringing the terrific plunge of crags falling to the shores of Red Tarn far below, Edward had paused. I heard him say, 'It looks hellish!' and the alarm bells rang. Now I remembered that finding the exact spot to descend on to Swirral was never easy especially if you missed a small cairn marking the way, let alone when snowdrifts smothered everything and a bulging cornice concealed any likely descent.

'After you' we both said simultaneously, eyeing steps cut by ice-axes in the snow the previous day and which, as they vanished into the void below, showed signs of having been kicked to death by those who had passed this way before. 'No, *after* you,' said Edward, gesturing into the abyss. 'No, after *you,*' I replied, looking anxiously that mile ahead to where Catstycam soared, almost to the height on which we stood undecided. Until, that is, Edward began to back down the slope, hooking the pick of his ice-axe into the roundness of the cornice and glancing anxiously down past his heels to where

Swirral Edge curved below like a cable of the Golden Gate bridge towards that shimmering satellite of Catstycam.

Communication between us ceased as Edward bent to his task far above the silent corrie below. 'Strewth,' he gasped as he lurched bodily downwards before his ice-axe abruptly stopped him short. Then there was a moment's silence. 'Phew,' he said at last, 'that was close'. With a final admonition to watch the footholds because one had just given way beneath his weight, he disappeared. Only the thuds from his axe, growing fainter as he continued descending, hinted at his progress. Finally his call of 'Down' told me it was time to follow.

Swirral Edge, below the point where I, thankfully, at last rejoined my partner, is still formidable. Its exposed crest is similar, although considerably briefer, than Striding Edge: a series of icy grooves tipping you downwards in succession and requiring you to think and think again as you balance your way down towards the refuge of the col below Catstycam. Gradually, the angle eases and, by keeping right above Red Tarn, a path is reached which offers a convenient descent for those returning to Patterdale by Birkhouse Moor.

However, for true Swirral Edgers there is no other way than strenuously onward and up to the summit of Catstycam. 'Taking your crampons off, then?' asked Edward as we finally topped-out

A walker negotiates the famous raised pavement of rock cresting Striding Edge, so popular with photographers.

Gale force wind flings spray from the surface of Red Tarn below the north-east face of Helvellyn.

on the tiny summit and cast sideways glances across the ocean of space dividing us from Striding Edge; its densely black silhouette, etched in ghostly moonlight, now seemingly another world away. 'Yes,' I said, and then 'Yes!' again. Our progress now became the stuff of laughter and baying at the moon, and a reckless series of glissades down snow runnels dropping from the easily-angled east shoulder to Red Tarn Beck and Greenside mines.

As another airliner blasted the night with its noise, abnormally loud through the pitilessly cold air (and those souls aboard tucked into baked ham and Italian red) we passed a pub that was still open. It was 3 a.m. in the morning and we could have been excused for celebrating. Unbelieving we looked at each other and howled and whooped again as Edward pressed his foot to the floor and we fishtailed down the village street towards Kirkstone Pass.

Part Two

Scotland

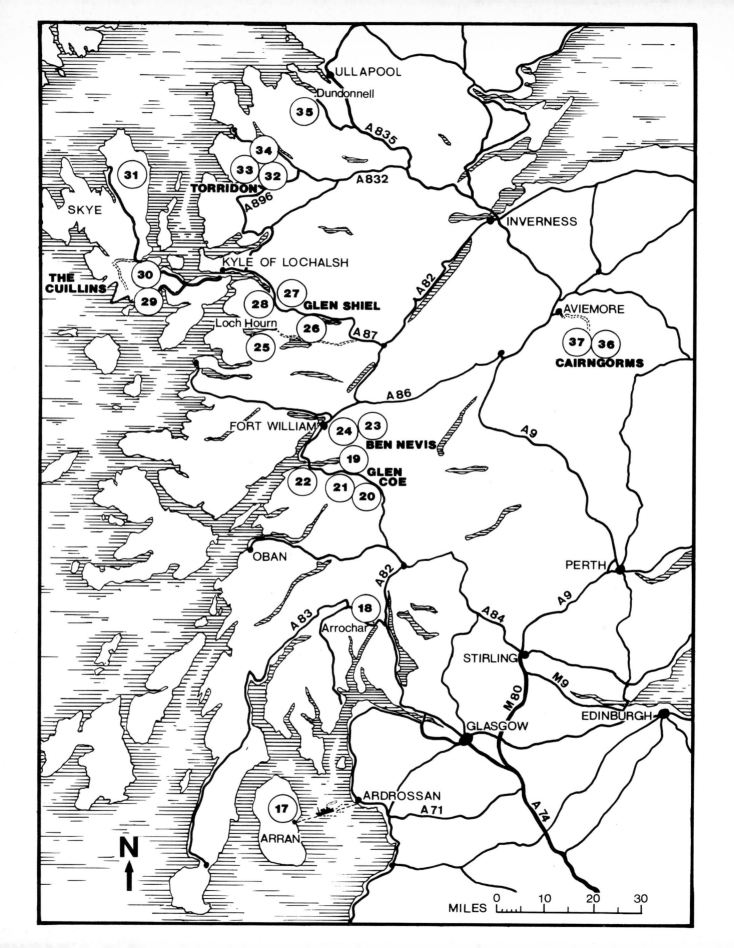

Chapter 17

THE GLEN ROSA SKYLINE

The Isle of Arran looks like a rugby ball knocked loose at the moment of impact from beneath a player's arm. It also reminds me of colliding with the commander of a nuclear submarine at his fraughtest moment. Arran's celestial ruck of mountains surrounding Glen Rosa – Beinn Nuis, Beinn Tarsuinn, A'Chir, Cir Mhor and Goat Fell – also have their impact.

The mountains of Arran, despite being less than 3,000ft in height, are amongst the most spectacular granite peaks in Scotland. The James Bond film *The Spy Who Loved Me* highlights Arran's magic skyline in its opening scenes, juxtaposing it against the rugged features of 007, Roger Moore himself. And yes, I did charge into Connery's double, Cdr Jock McLees

RN at his periscope as he drove HMS Churchill up from the depths towards the surface of the Straits of Gibraltar. But for his forbearance I might have been lashed to a Tigerfish torpedo and fired into oblivion.

Submariners will tell you that there are no passengers on a submarine. Let one loose and see what happens. Commissioned by a woman's magazine

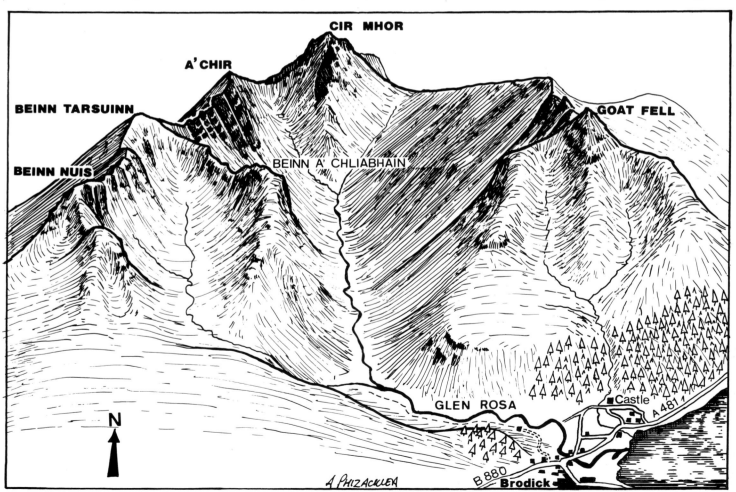

to write on the life of a submariner, I had begun the voyage in the shadow of the Sleeping Warrior, the name given to Arran's profile of hills seen from the Ayrshire coast and which so resembles a slumbering giant. Although I had not then visited Arran, I could not get those hills out of my mind for every one of the four or five days we thrust southwards deep beneath the Atlantic and its tumultuous seas.

The brawny arm hugging the rugby ball of Arran to that Ayrshire coast is the Kintyre peninsula, thus surrounding Arran not only by the waters of the Firth of Clyde but by an outer ring of land that cocoons it effectively on all sides, save the south from which direction the black seal shape of the submarines slip in and out of this massive inland bay on their various missions.

It was not until I boarded Churchill that all my doubts resurfaced. I did not want to go. Not with Arran's slumbering giant so near. Not with those sandy beaches, crystal burns, green pools and acres of superb upthrusting rock calling me across the water.

How wimpish could you be! Here I was embarking on an all-expenses paid trip under the ocean like something from Jules Verne, and I was stalling. Nor were we even going to war when I might have a cause for cold feet, the Falklands say, where Churchill's twin, HMS Conqueror had sunk the Admiral Belgrano. Yet the pull of the mountains was inexorably strong, their soot-black silhouette beckoning through squalls of hail. Even as we sailed south, initially on the surface of the sea, and I was sent on to the bridge on top of the conning tower to cure my seasickness, I saw them slide slowly and hauntingly out of sight beyond the submarine's wake, which was, I had been told, several miles long and as wide as a twenty-lane motorway.

Green with motion sickness, I put my head over the side to vomit into the sea below. It was like looking down one of those precipices in Arran I had heard

Beinn Nuis and the ridge beyond framed by overhanging boughs of trees during the approach up Glen Rosa.

so much about, like the *mauvais pas* on the A'Chir Ridge perhaps, as the 5,000-ton vessel churned the distant ocean a boiling white in the semi-darkness. The handle of something large and lightweight was thrust into my hand. 'The bucket, man! Use the bucket!' roared the officer of the watch gesticulating. 'Periscope lenses are behind you. You will splatter the glass.'

It was another ten years before I set foot on Arran, to take the photographs for this book along the exquisite traverse around the serrated outline of rugged peaks guarding Glen Rosa, the first glen you reach after leaving the steamer at Brodick and so amazingly accessible to visitors on foot.

It was the end of my photographic sojourn of May 1989, in the Highlands and Islands, when the air was like wine and the hills were clothed with purple and gold. I had driven south the night before, after climbing Ladhar Bheinn, sleeping *en route* under the railway bridge at Bridge of Orchy. I made my way next morning through Glasgow to catch the noon ferry from Ardrossan. As soon as the gangway was connected to the quay at Brodick I was down it, and hurrying through the

streets of the town and alongside the seafront beyond.

It was so invigorating having this freedom of movement amongst such

The waters of the Garbh Allt race down their granite slabs below Beinn Nuis.

heavenly surroundings. I thought back to a decade previously, to the swell of a cold metallic sea and the wintery squalls across the hills. What I was experiencing now was that very thing I had been yearning for those years before when I reluctantly descended into the submarine through a hatch so small that my lifejacket, which I had over-inflated in case I fell into the sea on boarding Churchill, had jammed and I was stuck fast, legs kicking, on my ignominious entry into the submariner's world. It had taken three submariners to pull and push me through, banging my funny bone and pulling a wellington boot off in the process.

It does not have to be a submarine to take us away from where our hearts would otherwise be, just the daily toil of advancing years, injury, marriage, having kids, sustaining illness and injury, or whatever will do it – there are hundreds of Churchills in our daily lives. However, now I was free as air, and drawing closer to Glen Rosa every moment.

The view ahead of Cir Mhor during the approach up Glen Rosa.

Having passed the sandy beaches in a northerly direction along the A481, and then the golf course where a distant Goat Fell – the highest peak on the island – looms beyond the fairways, I had taken the turn-off to the left to Glen Rosa shortly afterwards. The initial walk along a narrow country road came next, followed by a rough track, and with the prospect ahead of the mountains closing in around the glen beyond.

Just before the Garbh Allt Bridge, and a water pipe crossing Glen Rosa Water, a path branches off leftwards up the flanks of the Mad Burn. There are, in fact, tracks on both sides of this fantastic watercourse; its deep pools, waterslides and general menacing ambience in times of spate turning this hillside perambulation into a thing of excitement and terror. The paths are soggy, often comprising ledges of overhanging peat. When wet, this sags down under your weight, threatening to collapse at any moment and giving just the insecurity needed for a sporting trip.

I didn't care. The path – and I had pursued the one following the left-hand bank of the river – was water-logged and treacherous. Even as I stepped forward, great pieces of it sank almost to the verge of breaking point, but the sound of the falls, the smell of the peat and the movement of the clouds across the sky pushed me upwards regardless. Finally cresting the path on to the moorland terrain stretching ahead and up to Beinn Nuis in the imminent distance, brought me back to reality. It was further than it looked. However, gradually, the summit – and beyond some monstrous granite boulders – finally arrived.

The ridge strikes northwards from this peak with the main path keeping well to the left of the horizon's crest, avoiding numerous granite tors and the brink of the plunging crags presenting a potential danger along this rim over Coire a'Bhradain. The eastern side of the skyline is impressive, but so are the views whichever of the varied routes along the ridge you take, and especially westerly towards Kintyre and Islay and the Paps of Jura beyond. As the sky now began to darken and clouds brushed several distant peaks, I donned my cagoule ready for the worst.

Beinn Tarsuinn was next, a delectable peak with several tops when seen peeping over one or other of those same granite tors, jutting upwards like weathered castles. It gave a hint of the climbing to come along the A'Chir ridge with yet more mountains of a similar nature in the distance beyond, sharp-backed and razor-edged, all springing mendaciously into view.

The descent from Beinn Tarsuinn is steep and easy going all the way into the A'Chir col, so long as you avoid becoming trapped on the grey, rough and speckled-with-crystals granite slabs that clad the nose of the crest – advice that needs perpetually repeating. Beinn Tarsuinn is also, it is worth mentioning, the place where you can, in the face of worsening weather, approaching ferry times or whatever terminate the full horseshoe and substitute it with a shorter yet still useful round, by descending steeply down the path to the subsidiary ridge of Beinn a'Chliabhain, which provides a shorter option back to the head of the Mad Burn and a worthy escape route. This can be difficult in winter with the prospect of plunging drops below and the going underfoot quite technical. Also, because of the crags imminent in the area, you need good navigation, particularly in descending from Beinn Tarsinn and connecting up with this tributary ridge.

However, it was on the subsequent climb from the A'Chir col and after descending Beinn Tarsuinn, that the excitement began. It was during the still strenuous climb up the increasing sharpness of the all-rock ridge to A'Chir, its summit a large block which is a sporting mantelshelf move to sur-

Sunlight on the granite boulders of Beinn Nuis.

mount (and even more so to descend), that the sky assumed that vivid orange associated with the greatest levels of risk on mountains – a thunderstorm. Yes, there were distant peals of thunder too. Such was the magnetic appeal of this ridge, and the fact I knew I was here, I decided to press on and continue climbing.

The light was disconcerting, like the ending of the world. It reminded me of something nagging at my brain. But it was not until over half a mile further north along this crucial part of the horseshoe, and the part which separates the climbers from the walkers (and I mention this not in an elitist way but simply to point out that a well-worn path to the left of the ridge bypasses the very crest along which I was now

bumbling my way into unaccountable difficulties) that I suddenly realized where exactly I was – *Le Mauvais Pas!* – and also what it was about that weird orange sky, now outlining the magnificent outline of the next peak, Cir Mhor ahead.

During my voyage on HMS Churchill, I had been told to switch my torch off in the control room, the nerve-centre of the submarine. This at the time was in black lighting so the periscope would work at night. It takes twenty minutes for the eyes to adjust fully from daylight to darkness, but only five minutes from red light. Red lighting is used then in submarines from sunset to dawn. My problem: I had ordinary glass in my flashlight while everyone else had red glass in theirs. It sounded like

the story of my life.

I knew there was an abrupt rock step on the ridge down a well-scratched variation to the left which I avoided. Then came a gash in the ridge across which I strode. Shortly after this came another sudden notch in the ridge which took some working out. Past I went, eventually, to the right, by a steep, awkward step before following a turf ledge which became an exposed channel across the rock face with a chimney below.

This rim of the skyline was hard granite, sharp with crystals and delightfully rough. Abundant in the Alps and glorious to climb upon, it was still disconcerting without a rope as a backup and the prospect of a daunting fall if I slipped. By no means all the rock was covered with holds.

As I prospected the descent down the chimney with the notch beckoning below, grasping a couple of minute hand-holds while lowering myself down, the early hours of the day when HMS Churchill arrived in Gibraltar came back to mind with embarrassing clarity.

We had still been under the sea four days after leaving the Firth of Clyde, but were nearing the end of the voyage. My quarters had been a sleeping-bag on top of the torpedoes, racked like carpet-factory samples in the fore-end. I relaxed by watching videos in the ward room, which was as big as a small caravan. I had first arrived there just as Churchill canted and my ensuing flight down one side of the table mowed down two officers and the steward pouring coffee. 'Welcome aboard,' Cdr McLees had said, drinking his coffee from a big DON'T FORGET WHO'S THE BOSS mug (a gift from his wife). On the final evening that I was to spend on board, the video was *The Spy Who Loved Me*. And there was the silhouette of the Sleeping Warrior stretched out above Arran's lovely isle! Spellbound I watched, just waiting for Goat Fell, A'Chir, Cir Mhor and the rest to return to the screen. The film over, I went out into the Control Room on my way back to bed down on the torpedoes, the only way there was to go.

The Control Room was in darkness, thick curtains sealing its exits. It was also full of people, like a crowded bar in a power cut. I felt for a handrail I knew was above to guide me through the throng at such busy times and pushed

my way forward. One person in my way refused to budge and so I tried to squeeze past. However, rather than giving way under pressure, he started back-pedalling towards me, making me retreat in some confusion as by then I had stood on several people's toes and I could hear the grunts and exclamations as my size 12s sought them out at random. My eyes could now take in the back of a head directly in front of me, the shoulders and arms attached to it being occupied in lugging the heavy periscope around by its handlebars. I had been trying to bundle Churchill's CO out of the way. 'Please do not stand on me,' was all he said, his eyes on the eye-pieces but those in the back of his head eyeballing me too. 'If you can see, come through, but do not stand on me.' Paralysed by the enormity of what I had done, my legs turned to jelly and I could not move. Blind still, just below the depth it takes a periscope to break the surface, a submarine is unpleasantly vulnerable to the keels of deep-draught supertankers slicing deep into the water, and there were busy shipping lanes directly overhead. 'Will someone get that lunatic out of here,' said a voice and someone took pity on me and helped me through the darkness and beyond that crowded cell where computers glowed like kitchen cooker hot-plates – as did my face.

'Please do not stand on me!' It was as if the granite had spoken. The footholds were non-existent. I felt in danger of suddenly having to jump, yet it would be all too easy to misjudge such a flying

leap and fall crashing into the corrie below. I *have* climbed a long time, however, and it was only with that experience, and by more luck than good management that I finally managed to locate the holds and slither down into the gap.

The rest of the ridge was still superb, followed by the summit of Chir Mhor with its breadth of views over the Firth of Clyde and the wilderness of distant hills beyond. The descent by the path is extremely steep, with some scrambling on leaving the summit as you descend into the tremendous sweep of The Saddle, a landmark amongst Arran's complex of mountains and also an escape route down into Glen Rosa. Would I need to take it in? The glaringly orange skies persisted but the thunderclaps were fading into the far distance. I continued on around the crest.

The climb up to Goat Fell – now across the far side of Glen Rosa – terminates steeply in a sharp ridge with a rocky, exposed skyline. In the first part, a succession of chimneys and grooves required much care. I felt the past days' efforts taking their toll. Following this, a succession of small granite tors finally led to the vantage point of the summit itself, overlooking Brodick and with more incredible views in the stormy lighting of the sky, as wearily I took stock. Down the east ridge, I staggered, the path eventually leading across a shallow corrie and boggily down towards the trees screening Brodick castle. I had arrived back at Brodick, some eight hours later.

Chapter 18
THE COBBLER

The Cobbler was the second mountain I photographed for this book as a freelance writer living in a state of penury through every fault of my own (the hard times a writer experiences are usually self-inflicted), and writing the book on a shoestring. There, within the boundaries of Glasgow all but, is a mountain that could be Alpine in aspect. Perhaps it is no coincidence that the village nestling below The Cobbler – Arrochar – is twinned with a Bavarian counterpart, nor that the group of hills over which The Cobbler reigns supreme (if not in stature then certainly in grandeur), and which are recognized for their steepness and rugged character, are known as the Arrochar Alps. This then was definitely a Scottish mountain to include in the book, even at the expense of a more remote giant of the far north. Like An Teallach, which I have included, but which brought me to the brink of despair on my very first Scottish outing.

The Cobbler's grotesque skyline would not be out of place in outlandish places like the Grosse Mühlsturzhorn in the Berchtesgaden Alps, the rugged playground of great mountaineers like Hermann Buhl. Poised above Loch Lomond's neighbouring hills, this has

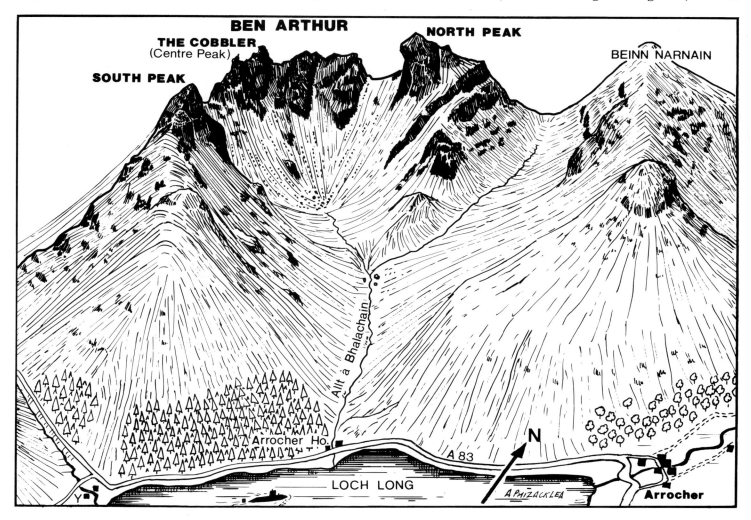

The summit of The Cobbler (Centre Peak) with Ben Lomond beyond.

the level of any self-respecting Munro. And taking, over its three distinct summits (two of them calling for scrambling skill of some order, although the third, a monstrous overhanging prow, requires no more than a walk), three to five hours to circumnavigate.

Yet I could not have made a better choice, although Quinag, Stack Polly, Suilven and Slioch are presumably fantastic peaks, and one day, perhaps, I will tread their remote heights, and I look forward to it greatly. The furthest north I did reach was mighty An Teallach (I had to make it a day trip of 600 miles with shared petrol and it rained) and even its memory is no more vivid than that of The Cobbler, and its Arrochar Alps – proof that it does not require great height to make a grand mountain. Munroists who shirk at climbing Skye's Innaccessible Pinnacle in Skye, in fact, may also fail to surmount The Cobbler.

Riddled with self-doubts, then, during the glorious May in 1989 when I planned with luck to take all my Scottish pictures in one go, I arrived in Arrochar. May is supposed to be the best month in the Highlands but would it live up to its reputation?

Would my funds fall short? Would my creditors send in the bailiffs in my absence? Would I fall foul of my old friend Ed Grindley in Fort William and splash all my money in the bars and working men's clubs of Lochaber on a monumental bender? Would the Mini's sub-frame finally give way and dump me on the edge of trackless Knoydart? Would my new-fangled AZ-300 Olympus, fondly residing in what I called the Bozo Bag (named after myself, a thickly padded thing to be worn on a waist belt and for which I was to become grateful for it saved the camera from so many knocks and bangs during that ensuing month) survive? Time would tell.

View The Cobbler across Loch Long from the road descending to the water's edge at Arrochar and it will send a tingle of anticipation up your backbone.

always been a mountain for those who lived in Glasgow on the dole and without transport, yearning to be in the steepest places. So it was, in a similar way, for me, and I live 150 miles to the south. There are peaks in Sutherland and Wester Ross that might as well, as far as my finances were concerned, be in Outer Mongolia. Apart from the cost of petrol and food to sustain me while waiting for good weather, there were the photographic requirements to consider. I could only allow two or three rolls of Fujichrome per skyline, yet I had to include forty-five skylines, all taken by myself to prove I had done the climbs. The prospect of including The Cobbler became doubly attractive as it was so immediately accessible. The only problem was that, by Highlands standards, it was not terribly high – a mere 2,891ft in fact, an altitude below

As the sun pierces mist on the mountain to fleck the purple water with gold, its bizarre skyline peeps above a hillside clothed by trees and which first can be ascended from the shores of the loch by the banks of the Buttermilk Burn. It is an unusual skyline, gnarled and spooky, and The Cobbler is the summit in the middle between the North and South Peaks. Ben Arthur is its real name, for King Arthur is remembered in Scotland as well as the south-western parts of Britain, commanding as he did the Britons from Central Scotland to Cornwall, after the Romans had already built the roads.

The footpath, following the handrail of the Buttermilk Burn, starts from the torpedo testing station on the A83. The Allt a Bhalachain on the map is the burn. It plummets like a thread of mercury down through the trees as you slowly climb alongside to gain height. It is as you do this that the south-east ridge of The Cobbler hoves progressively into view, until the full sweep of grassy slopes rise with increasing roughness to the pincer-ended buttresses of the south and north peaks, encompassing the corrie of The Cobbler, and enclosing in the middle, the Centre Peak and highest point of the mountain.

At this point, following the footpath from the Buttermilk Burn past the old stone howff of the Narnain Boulders (and after falling off several climbing problems on these two immense blocks of rock surrounded by a sea of peat mud), new doubts surfaced once more. I had unfortunately snagged a trainer while choosing to clamber up the boulders in the Buttermilk Burn itself, ripping one of the uppers. These were the same fell-running shoes that were hopefully to serve me on Sgurr nan Gillean, the Four Tops and Liathach.

The Narnain Boulders are mica-schist, a rock that predominates in Central Park, New York City, where after rain its notorious skiddiness is more deadly to the city's rock climbers than the muggers on the sidewalks. A new pair of Walsh mountain trainers costs nearly £50. Never mind New York, I felt Scotland's mountains were mugging me before I had even begun. My heart sank.

Every misgiving seemed exacerbated in the next section of the climb. The footpath grew increasingly muddy once I had crossed the Buttermilk Burn, and my trainers turned to pulp. On the uphill slopes, through the cragginess of the corrie itself, blue sky reflected in the puddles. However, things changed. The going underfoot became rocky and hard. Now the mountain atmosphere was tremendous as the path twisted through scree and crags towards the towering cliffs above. I followed the footpath very steeply into the bealach just left of the North Peak and sat myself down on a rock slab for a breather.

Yet fresh doubts would not leave me. The day had turned out to be brilliant. The soggy going and the beaded marble-like slipperiness of the Narnain Boulders were a thing of the past. Up here it was perfect, with a multitude of peaks on display and a thin scattering of snow, although still May, on the shaded western and northern slopes, whilst against the vivid blue backdrop reared the beak of the North Peak. But how could I photograph this terrific rock scenery athwart the skyline without someone in the frame? And not only The Cobbler, but the other great Scottish peaks to come? They say he who travels fastest travels alone, but I began to regret my lack of a companion able to pose as a model for my camera.

Disconsolate, I scrambled to the top of the North Peak with its immaculate views of Beinn Narnain and Beinn Ime, and across the corrie to Centre Peak, the true top of the mountain. Descending back into the bealach, I continued southwards up and along the ridge. This is a straightforward skyline saunter over rocky slabs and boulders but I was always conscious of the crags to the left, plunging into the corrie below. The rock tower of the Centre Peak – The Cobbler itself – proved a thrillingly airy excursion, but I needed someone else in my viewfinder to give it life.

I was just considering the hazardous option of leaving my camera on a rock, setting the delayed timing device and clambering as quickly as possible back up to its summit in time to be in the picture when a dot appeared toiling up the south ridge from the col below the South Peak. A climber! But would he pose for a picture? Then a few yards below, he sat down and began to unwrap his sandwiches. Biting back my impatience I waited in a fever of suspense for him to finish. The light would go! He would never agree! I was getting cold! Eventually he shouldered his pack and began to climb towards me. Would he, I was able to ask at last, pose for a picture on top of The Cobbler?

Not only would he gladly do this, he agreed, but he would pose for several.

A hilltop climber tops out on the summit of the Cobbler's North peak.

The overhangs of the North Peak with climbers on the classic Recess Route.

A rock climber who had hung up his rope after an unfortunate brush with the Thearlaich-Dubh Gap on the Skye Ridge, he still displayed all the self-possession of old, climbing on to the bulging north face of the pinnacle, and then disappearing suddenly from view, to reappear as if by magic on the south face. Again, he disappeared. The next time reappearing finally on top.

It was, we agreed shouting, an exposed scramble. First, the tight wriggle through the window passing through the heart of the Cobbler, which landed you awkwardly on a slanting shelf above a yawning drop, then the traverse along the ledge, to the final delicate move back left and up on to the flat summit block. 'Can I ask you one more favour?' I asked hesitantly after he had descended the difficulties and re-emerged through the keyhole. Would he agree to be photographed on the North Peak? 'No problem,' he said.

Together we retraced my previous steps along the skyline towards the North Peak, descending into the col below its prow. I pointed out the scramble up to the summit around its back and my new-found friend took it. Soon he was silhouetted on top, a pin-prick in the camera viewfinder. The effect was hopeless, the yawning drop below him lost. Until I remembered the automatic zoom facility . . .

I pressed the rocker switch, heard the motor wind out the lens to a 105mm and there miraculously he now stood, larger than life, poised above thin air and on the edge of space – *almost*. 'On, on! Go on!' I yelled, 'I want you on the very edge'.

Cautiously, he prodded forward with his stick like a blind man feeling the way, and also, I'm sure, convinced that he was in the hands of a maniac. For a moment, I thought all was lost as he teetered on the brink of the abyss above. I had gone too far. I had once shouted similar directions to a former wife backing a car, and she had hit another vehicle. But no, he stayed poised a moment longer.

I was able to take the photograph I wanted the moment before he stepped back, descended and joined me for some relieved laughter. Then he was on his way with my promise to send any shots worth having.

Back I went along the skyline southwards once more and as far as the Centre Peak, then descending through a maze of large boulders to the south-west before climbing a little again to the narrow connecting ridge between the Centre and the South Peak. The steep scramble up to the summit of the South Peak beckoned, an exposed and easy expedition when dry, I discovered, but presumably more difficult during rain, owing to the skiddiness of the highly contorted and folded mica-schist rocks.

I descended back into the col and rejoined the path, which took me down round the base of what now appeared a most formidable South Peak, and between boulders and past a tiny pool nestling like a jewel in a hollow against the crag face. All that remained was to continue round to the south-east ridge along the peaty path, surmount the hump of An-t-Sron and descend delightful slopes to the dam on the Buttermilk Burn. Finally, I retraced my way back down through the trees to the roadside, with every detail of this marvellous day remaining fresh in the mind. Every time I look at the photographs it all comes back.

Chapter 19
THE AONACH EAGACH RIDGE

'Nelson's Column, Greensleeves. You're just the man,' said Edwin Ward Drummond, as he was then called, himself a man destined to climb not only Nelson's Column but also the Statue of Liberty (on which he held a candlelit vigil and kept the police waiting until the morning when he descended and gave himself up), the Embarcadero Center and Grace Cathedral, both in San Francisco.

'We'll climb it together, you and me.' 'No thanks.' 'Why not?' 'This burning ambition of yours, Ed, to make your name register with TV producers and editors and not just the climbing world, where will it end?' 'Incarcerated forever in The Tombs, San Quentin, Sing Sing, Folsom, Alcatraz, Brixton, Pentonville, Wormwood Scrubs,' he said with foresight (Marylebone police station, a gaol

in Manhattan and the Hall of Justice in San Francisco were the places where he was actually kept on hold) 'you name it'.

Nor would he let it lie. He was going to join Admiral Nelson and fly a 'Barclay's profits for Apartheid's coffins' banner over the city, and I would accompany him. This he decided as we motored north towards Scrabster and

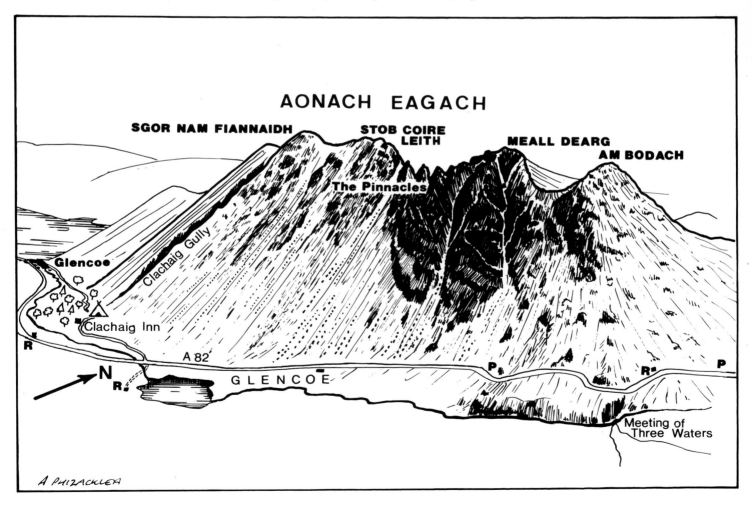

Aonach Eagach from the east, with the Big Fellow silhouetted to give an idea of the scale.

the Orkneys where Ed and his friend Oliver Hill intended making the first ascent of 1,200ft St John's Head on Hoy. I was to cover it for a newspaper. Then Oliver would return to work. And Ed and I would visit the West End, according to him.

'The overhanging bit at the top looks the hardest part – but it's not,' said Ed feeling in his rucksack, 'I've made these clamps to fit the lightning conductor cable. They *work*.' He fished out a couple of gadgets, clicking them in front of my face as I tried to concentrate on the winding road. 'The tricky bit is at the bottom. If the police see us getting a grip on the lightning conductor they'll pull us down before we start.'

'That's all you need.' Ed laughed, 'All *we* need, Greensleeves. You're coming with me. Listen to the plan. We go into Trafalgar Square after midnight carrying a step-ladder. Workmen, right? We prop the ladder up against the

column. Then I climb up it, clamp on and move up out of the way and you follow behind, kicking the ladder down before you climb higher with the clamps.' I still said no.

On the way back south we stopped off in the Cairngorms and climbed a route on the Shelter Stone Crag. Ascent accomplished and continuing south again I was by now enthusiastic about the idea of climbing Nelson's Column, but Ed had lost interest.

'I'll manage the clamps, Ed,' I said. 'Greensleeves, I know you will,' said Ed, 'manage the clamps? Those clamps were made for you! You would be perfect with the clamps. Only thing is I've seen you climb now. I think you might have trouble on the ladder.'

How these words played back inside my head as I looked up the rock face on which I had become imprisoned. It was my first acquaintance with the Aonach Eagach ridge, that switch-

backed and pinnacled show-piece dominating the northern boundary of Glencoe for four uncompromising miles. A serrated skyline towering majestically over a succession of scree slopes and gullies which crucially eliminate all but two points of access and exit, it commits those who embark along its stark crest to an inescapable foray. The thinnest skyline rim in the British Isles and supposedly slimmer even than An Teallach, it includes two Munros – Sgor nam Fiannaidh and Meall Dearg – and is one of the most popular mountain expeditions in Britain.

But how those words re-echoed: 'The only thing is, I've seen you climb now. I think you might have trouble on the ladder.' How right they were! Here I was pawing at the rock, unable to go up or down, and feeling out of my depth and lost. On my own and without a rope, the nearest person, The Big Fellow, was some way above and unaware of my plight.

The step-ladder part of the story is apocryphal, but it has proved a standby for the pub at that certain level of intoxication when the glazed expressions of friends who have heard it before can be missed in my enthusiasm to labour the point again.

Ed Drummond and I did not climb together on that trip, but what I was experiencing that cold Saturday morning on the Aonach Eagach showed me in a far worse light than the one in which I had been trying to show myself for years. This, after all, *was* happening.

I had met The Big Fellow at the start of the ridge, in the course of which I introduced the subject of my beloved rock climbing ('So good I'm surprised it's legal,' I think I said). The Big Fellow, meanwhile, who had the disconcerting Scottish habit of calling me 'Sir?', had no such pretensions. He was a psychiatric nurse at Hartwood Hospital between Glasgow and Edinburgh, the largest of its kind in Britain. A member of the Hartwood Hill Walking Club, he lived for his days out on the Hill and now, in his big boots, all 19 stones of him had floated, just *floated*, up the crux of this particular rock face as though the drop below did not exist. While here I was, stuck on the arête behind him, unable to follow his route.

A tumbling raven barked, freefalling and then recovering to soar high and perform the same trick again, light as a scrap of charred paper whirling above a bonfire, taunting. Waiting for me to fall? The Big Fellow, meanwhile, looked unconcerned, and not without reason. I hadn't made a sound to signal my distress. How could I, desperate as I was to bluff it out? 'Are ye no up yet?' he had asked, popping his head over the top, giving me a cursory glance then disappearing again. 'Just coming, Stewart,' I called, 'just sorting out this wee problem'.

The problem was just one move: a step up a polished crack on small holds required a determined lunge and the prospect of a huge fall if the one rugosity that looked as if it might be a jug was not in fact the superb handhold it appeared. I began to go into a cold sweat. Soloing in trainers wasn't my style. But now I was making excuses; the number of times I had used trainers to solo on rock before!

The ravens had departed. Were these not the one species of bird that actually helped to attract other ravens to feed off their food stocks – the carcasses of dead animals – rather than fighting them off? Perhaps the one that had been overseeing my futile efforts had not returned for the same reason that the raven did not return to Noah's Ark, because presumably it had found carcasses floating in the water on which it could rest and feed? My raven probably discovered a body inside one of the deep gullies seaming the flanks of Aonach Eagach, just one of the numerous victims claimed by the ridge, as The Big Fellow had been at pains to point out.

'Aye, it is a fine morning,' he had said on our first meeting a couple of hours previously, a giant in his late twenties at a guess, who had caught me up on the first peak of Am Bodach as I had paused, framing Bidean nam Bian in my viewfinder across the pass of Glencoe to the south. He was cordiality itself as we introduced ourselves, he being Stewart Govan from Shotts. 'Yes, Sir,' he said, 'I will be glad to go ahead and pose for you on the tops ahead.' And so he did, responding to my yells,

yells that frequently startled other passers-by as I would bawl directions across the abyss to the tiny figure on the next peak, and a 'Sir?' would hang in the air.

This spot is a popular choice for those about to make the east to west traverse, the advantage being that the difficulties are slightly easier going in this direction, and you finish on the doorstep of the Clachaig Hotel, the seventeenth-century inn that – with the Kingshouse Hotel – gives Glencoe two of the most popular meeting places for climbers in Britain.

I had parked the car at the layby near the house called Allt-na-Reigh on the A82 through Glencoe, but there are climbers who prefer parking at the Clachaig, then walking back up the road to the start of the slopes leading to Am Bodach, secure in the knowledge that their transport is waiting when they finish. Either way the road walk is arduous, and lifts are notoriously rare as the traffic speeds through along the straight. A third option may attract you which is exacting and requires you to be fit, but more later.

The path begins very steeply, climbing a ladder of footholds up the luminous green turf which flanks the lower slopes of Glencoe's Pass for so much of the way before it changes into the over-powering scenery of scree and crags above. A dramatic signpost warns you that you should not try to leave this ridge too early; something that you will hear about frequently regarding the Aonach Eagach. So many of the reported deaths in the Highlands are of walkers and of these, many fall foul of bad route finding, of which – like wrongly trying to descend Five Finger gully from the summit of Ben Nevis – mistakenly trying to come off the Aonach Eagach Ridge too early, ranks as a black spot.

The path tacks back and forth across the grassy slopes the higher you climb – at one point below crags to the left, dipping into a hidden canyon before then ascending out on the other side

Stob Coire Leith's eastern prospect of the Aonach Eagach.

Walkers queue to climb the Pinnacles along the ridge.

and tackling a long toil by the side of a small stream through a landscape littered with rocks and scree. There are more crags overhead and to the left, the path swinging around to the right and then back over these to the summit of Am Bodach, and the eastern end of the Aonach Eagach proper.

Shortly after this I had met the Big Fellow and we had gone our separate ways; he going ahead and waiting on the tops of the eminences while I took pictures of his distant silhouette.

The place along the ridge where I found trouble in following in his footsteps happened towards the end of the row of pinnacles and on the narrowest part. By this time we had negotiated such a rise and fall of obelisks, monoliths and gendarmes, and the subsequent notches between them, that I had lost all track of distance.

First, I had attained the crest of the skyline by walking north-westwards and following the edge of the crags to the left of the cairn of Am Bodach. Then the path had dropped suddenly and steeply, requiring a further inspec-

tion as to which way the route actually went. It was not as improbable as it looked. What was rather more awkward was – after making the initial airy descent – a sloping rock ledge that had to be traversed around a fin of rock, with an appalling plunge of space gaping into the openness of the glen below.

Meall Dearg is the next major peak along the ridge and from here Aonach Eagach reaches out ahead, a narrow procession of exposed pinnacles poised at crazy attitudes above the emptiness of the valleys below. The Pinnacles stretched as far as Stob Coire Leith where, according to the map, the ridge widened and the walking would be more straightforward.

A footpath winds its way along the crest of the Pinnacles, taking the line of least resistance and circumnavigating certain problems by the side. At one point on the ridge, about halfway along the narrowest section, a tower of rock appears an insurmountable problem. Then you see the short chimney which solves it, followed by a slender, airy arête some way further on still.

It was at the end of the Pinnacles that I found my *bête noire*, on a steep arête, its holds scratched by crampons and polished by the rubber soles of passing boots. I was not prepared to take the risk of committing myself to a move I could not reverse. Finally, I down-climbed back to the neck of the ridge below, took several deep breaths to calm my nerves, and then escaped to the right where I discovered an easier option in the shape of a chimney. The Big Fellow was sitting with his back to me as I crested the ridge, eating his sandwiches and gazing out to sea. But Stewart, having read this now, you will know the truth, or perhaps you have done all along.

He certainly enlivened the traverse over the Pinnacles with his astute and pithy comments, as he did on the subsequent traverse from Stob Coire Leith and onwards to the end. 'You look terri-

fied. Ye should no be here,' he told a po-faced hillwalker with a Motorola car phone. To a climber of septuagenarian years from Guernsey who approached us from the other direction, and who said he had been hillwalking for sixteen years and so long as the bellows kept going he was okay, TBF gave him this admonition: 'It's light till eight. Hamish (McInnes) sweeps along the ridge at 10 p.m. If he finds ye still here, he'll give ye a parking ticket.'

By contrast, the final stretch of the Aonach Eagach from Stob Coire Leith to Sgor nam Fainnaidh is more pedestrian, but gloriously so and provided with lovely views. A line of fence posts marks the route. It is on reaching the far summit, too, that the further option I mentioned of avoiding a long road walk back to your car if you left it on the park near Allt-na-Reigh can be considered. It is a valid option to return now along the ridge to Am Bodach if you are fit and experienced on the Hill. This is a glorious reciprocating route which eliminates the long, arduous descent to the Clachaig and the tedious walk back along the roadside through Glencoe. If you are fit, strong and experienced it is worth considering.

If you decide to descend as we did, the open corrie south of Fiannaidh offers a safer descent than the one skirting the edge of Clachaig Gully. Safest of all, is to follow the ridge from Fiannaidh west, then west-north-west on to the heather slopes above the old road.

After the narrowness of the ridge – and as a contrast from the views of Bidean nam Bian and its satellites to the south and Ben Nevis and the Mamores to the north to which you will have become accustomed during the course of your traverse – the opening up of the view below comes as a fresh surprise. Down to Glencoe village with Loch Leven and Loch Linnhe presenting a blue foreground to the hills of Ardgour, and with the prospect of a refreshing pint in the Clachaig drawing ever closer as you descend.

Chapter 20

THE BUACHAILLE ETIVE MOR TRAVERSE, WITH CURVED RIDGE

The mountain looms above as you approach The Hut, voices lowered and respect in your every stride. To all intents and purposes you are paying homage to this Scottish giant, the mighty Buachaille Etive Mor, overlord of Rannoch Moor. Also to its glorious adjoining skyline, hidden behind and running a south-westerly course over Stob na Doire, Stob Coire Altruim and Stob na Broige. Inwardly you are quaking for quite another reason, or is it really still perhaps the same one? You know what lies ahead (a seven-hour trip, at least) because of the climbing material you have read but, really, you are still wet behind the ear-rings.

When it comes to the Greater Scheme of Things, you are still a beginner. How it shows is in your not entirely irrational dread both of your first serious ridge walk in winter (which includes a technical ascent up an awesome mountain and with a companion as green as yourself), *and* fearing a chance encounter with the occupants

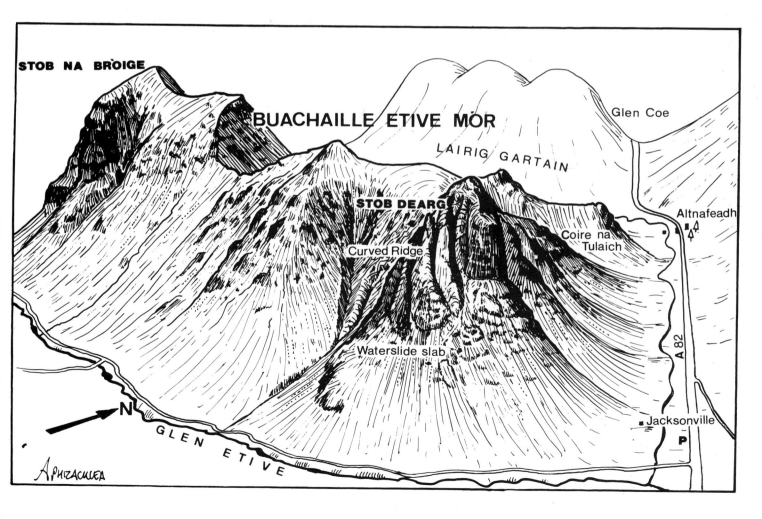

An early May morning view of the Buachaille Etive Mor above Jacksonville.

on the hills as a team). Unsupervised and equipped only with the equipment you own. You *have* tried: double-checking the weather report, noting landmarks like Waterside Slab, memorizing hilltop compass bearings *and* confirming with a phone call to the Kingshouse Hotel that, despite the snow and ice, there is still some lovely pink rock on display. But first you must pass The Hut.

So lowly that its windows peep only just over the boulders of the ancient sheepfank that surrounds it like a fortification, The Hut spells trouble. Its cladding of green roofing felt and black bitumen-painted walls merges it against a hinterland of peat hags and bog. Fortunately there are no signs of life, no smoke from the chimney, no stirrings behind those sightless windows.

Isn't this, you remember, where hikers on the West Highland Way occasionally bivvy mistaking it for just another bothy? And wasn't it here you read in one such account that backpackers woke after midnight to a real-life nightmare? Gazing down on them in the flickering lamplight was a ring of faces, one covered in blood, another shrieking with maniacal laughter as its owner brandished a chainsaw and a third who was eating porridge with his fingers? The Fools ('for Fools rush in where angels fear to tread') were informed that they were trespassing even though much that was said was incomprehensible. On being told they could stay, they picked up their belongings and fled into the night.

In his Scottish Mountaineering Club (SMC) Journal account of 'An Excursion in Scotland', it now comes back to you that American climber Royal Robbins, and his wife Liz, had negotiated stepping stones 'across a creek' at this point with difficulty, only then to be told by SMC doyen Tom Patey they were lucky that the occupants of The Hut had only rained yells at them. It could have been rocks.

of The Hut (which unfortunately you must now pass).

You have both been on rock and winter climbing courses at Plas y Brenin and Glenmore Lodge to acquire the basic skills, but now you are facing your most serious venture yet (even though you have so far survived a year

Now the stepping stones have gone. The width of the burn is as clear as a sheet of clingfilm stretching to where The Hut squats on the far side. Hesitantly you remove your boots and socks, roll up your salopettes and, lacing your boots back on, gingerly wade across the deep and icy current. It is then – after collapsing on the far bank, and desperately hushing any protests about the chill of the water – that you receive the fright of your life. The Hut door flies open and out leaps a figure in vest and underpants like one of the rogues from *Brigadoon*.

The reason he has sprung into view is, it soon becomes evident, not to get at you. At least not immediately. In the time-honoured tradition of bothy dwellers everywhere, he makes for the rear of The Hut and directs a jet of hot steaming urine into the frosty air, in this case towards the Buachaille Etive Mor. However, he might have been wielding a claymore for all those shock waves you are experiencing.

You find yourself shaking as he makes his way back towards The Hut. Holding your breath, you feel for a moment that you have gone unnoticed, suspended in the act of emptying a bootful of water back into the burn.

'Aye,' he says as if to himself in disgust, 'They're always building steppin' stones.' Then with relish he adds, 'An' we're always getting rid.' He slants his eyes at you, 'Steppin' stones!'

There is something about your response that seems to intrigue him because he waits a moment longer. 'Is this Jacksonville?' you ask knowing damned well it is, but the question is offered as a sop to this demon of your imagination. (And how many more like him lurk inside The Hut?) He nods and asks what you are doing the day?

At this innocent query a new panic seizes you. Here you are at the Holy Grail, as it were, of the Creag Dhu Mountaineering Club, the Glaswegian group formed in 1930 and which has been immortalized in legend ever since, the first ascents by its members being legion and no more so than on the Buachaille's great crags. Even Royal Robbins had had it explained to him that the Creag Dhu 'made the New York Vulgarians look like cream puffs in comparison'. So how can you bring yourself to reveal plans on which he is bound to pour scorn?

You may well reluctantly admit to peaks in your career, like having climbed several three-star Severes in

Cornwall and having led Main Wall on Cyrn Las, but you know these will cut no ice in the Ville, as Rab Carrington names it in *Cold Climbs* (Diadem, 1983). But it will have to be dragged out of you before you admit that your intentions now are merely a Mod, and not even a Moderate Mod, but a mod so easy that it is the descent route after climbers have ascended Rannoch Wall. The shame of it makes your cheeks go hot.

So what begins as a mumble where you are hardly able to get the words out, ends with a touch of defiance as you try not to sound apologetic: 'Curved Ridge', you say, and immediately regret it.

There is a moment's silence as he takes this in. Then he lifts his eyes to the Buachaille and says, 'Ah! Curved Ridge. A beautiful route.' He glances at your 11mm rope, the cheap crampons and classic ice-axe buckled on each of your sacks (packed so firmly they look like oxygen cylinders). 'Aye. Grand rock for climbin', and sensible too.' He pauses, looks as if to confirm something inside the two of you and seems satisfied. 'Aye, sensible. Be careful, mind. Curved Ridge has seen people into poly bags before today.'

You cannot believe this. Is he sending you up? These thoughts are reinforced when, no doubt influenced by your chattering teeth as the chill bites deep, he invites you inside The Hut for a brew. If thoughts of a winter ascent of Curved Ridge had delayed sleep the night before, this offer eclipses even those fears. Is this a prank of the Creag Dhu? Is there perhaps a hutful of villains just waiting inside to pounce? Fearfully, you enter the gloom of the 'Ville.

The hut smells of pine needles (or is it telegraph poles?) and the coals of a fire glow red. But it is dry, clean and apart from a rucksack and sleeping-bag on the planked floor, empty. The smell is warm telegraph poles you decide as these in shortened form add a

Snow cornices on the north face of Stob Coire Altruim..

substantial framework to the structure. Everywhere you look, pieces of plastic sheeting or tarpaulin or roofing felt or industrial foam cladding help to block draughts. You sit down on the floor.

You are invited here, you are given to understand as your host puts a blackened brew pan of water on the stove, because of your attitude. It is something that, it is also made plain, is not always evident in certain young climbers today, and you should hold on to it with both hands. You weren't, for instance, like those individuals who having left their GTis in the nearby layby, prance across the stepping-stones in their designer gear with the price tags swinging in the wind, cock-sure that because they can hang on by their eyelashes to the hardest rock climbs in summer, they will be able to do the same to the ice of the Buachaille in midwinter.

'You get boys here, keen as mustard but down on their luck,' he tells you as you wait for the water to boil, 'their

Close-up view of the cornices on Stob Coire Altruim's northern face.

ma's sent them packin' for the weekend with a wee tin of Ambrosia rice pudding, a couple of slices of bread, a tin of beans and a sausage link. They call round here and we whip round and gi' them a feast.'

'Then' he says, 'others arrive with all the clobber. They come in and lay out their pits, surreptitiously nudging our stuff an inch here and an inch there out of the way, and tidying everything just so. An' then when they have it all laid out nice and neat, we ask, "Do ye need any help?" and when they say no we kick them out. Attitude's everything on the hill. In this establishment everyone shares everything. You assume nothing.'

Feelings of guilt surface as you watch the pan begin to boil. 'Would you,' you ask, 'like some lemon tea from our flask instead of using your tea bags?' And he laughs. Apparently biting off several remarks which he then thinks better of he says, 'Aw, boys, no, no. Lemon tea! What are you now, a couple of poofters?'

As you go on to sip his scalding brew from a battered tin mug, he continues. 'Keepin' things simple on the hill is the thing. You're on the right track. Folk make things so complex today when there is nae need. "Why do you wear a Rolex?" they ask me. "Because I *like* wearing a Rolex!" It's as simple as that. "Why do you climb?" they say. "Cos I *want* tae!" Same with people climbin' nowadays some feel too obliged to climb harder than they should, there are so many pressures. Then they get hurt and others should be killed but they're dead lucky.

'You're right to be keyed up, windy even. You're surprised I noticed? Och, I can tell. Fear'll keep you on your toes. You need that on the hill. You did well to choose a climb well down the grades in February; it'll be a lot harder up there with the krabs stickin' to your fingers and the rope freezin' like a wire cable.'

He pauses to sweep embers from the

floor with a yard brush, only a couple of inches of its handle remaining ('The ****s cut bits off for the fire'). Then he says, 'I could see you did na' want to tell me about Curved Ridge. But far better that route than Raven's Gully and you end up in the hands of Hamish and the rescue. You climbed rock all summer, right? Aye, I thought so. So to go for an easy rock climb on a winter hill when you're inexperienced, what could be saner? Time enough later to buy the ice tools and clip-on crampons and purple boots. Anyway, you'll no find Curved Ridge a walkover.'

And neither do you, neither do you. You go outside, walking on air and fall smack on your arse as the soles of your boots hit the icy path. But it's a glorious day. The best, yet. The ascent of Curved Ridge goes like a dream, yet there are places where you need to keep a cool head, where you have to chip ice off the holds and where problems continue all the way to the top. One of these is becoming accustomed to the weird feeling of crampon points grating on bare granite and crunching into the mountainside below your feet, and strange how you'd forgotten this aspect of winter climbing from the course you'd taken only those twelve months previously. Now you climb with new determination. It's not everyday after all that a couple of novices have an audience with a doyen of the Creag Dhu to start the day with – not only on such a great mountain, but on a superb mountain traverse as well.

It is not every day, either, that the Buachaille Etive Mor and those adjoining summits of Stob na Doire, Stob Coire Altruim and Stob na Broige are refrigerated with snow and ice. Nor is it always so cold that, in the words of your newly found mentor, 'You jump outside the bothy in your underpants for a piss and find your socks are stuck fast to the ground.' There are glorious days to be experienced here during the other seasons of the year. For those with hillwalking experience and modest rock climbing ability, the ascent of the Buachaille via Curved Ridge, followed by the traverse of its adjacent skyline, is one of the joys of British mountaineering. In winter, of course, it is a serious mountaineering expedition, requiring fully equipped climbers.

The car-park from where the individuals with their GTis leave their vehicles is tucked away off the side of the A82. It is small and can prove deceptively hard to find when a gigantic articulated lorry laden with logs and with *LUMBER JOCK* lettered on the front has been hot on your tail across Rannoch Moor and you frantically begin to wonder just exactly where it is that you pull into the side. Then Jacksonville appears, tiny below the towering ramparts of the Buachaille. As it draws alongside across the moor, the entrance to the car-park finally appears. A footpath from it leads to the banks of the River Coupall with hopefully the stepping-stones in place.

An alternative approach is by the path which leaves the road for Lagangarbh, the SMC hut directly below the great furrowed scoop of Coire na Tulaich (Lagangarbh Coire), the easiest way to the summit of the Buachaille and certainly its safest descent route, further north from Altnafeadh. After the path has crossed the footbridge over the River Coupall and bypassed the *SMC* hut, it then branches, one fork entering the vast corrie ahead while the other veers left across the hillside and gently rises to meet the Jacksonville path at the Waterslide Slab way up the hillside and beneath the crags of the Buachaille Etive Mor.

Curved Ridge meanwhile has been in view throughout the approach from Jacksonville. It can be found by locating Crowberry Ridge, the central pillar of rock that appears to fall beneath the

Buachaille's summit. This is flanked on its right by Crowberry Gully and on the left by Easy Gully and the tapering scimitar of Curved Ridge forms the left-hand rib of this latter defile. Approaching a lofty 800ft in height, it starts some way below the impressive pink cliff set on the south-east face of Crowberry Ridge, the fabulous Rannoch Wall no less, and ends beneath the base of the Crowberry Tower, the topmost cone of Crowberry Ridge.

To reach your objective, the path turns with the prominent Waterslide Slab on its left, climbing past heather terraces as it skirts the base of the cliffs. Eventually it reaches the foot of Curved Ridge, below the junction of Crowberry Gully and Easy Gully, offering the best start towards its right-hand edge where a procession of holds becomes a magical stairway to the summit. Near the start and around midway the ridge relaxes into a scramble, but after each of these interludes it rears upwards again, really narrowing and steepening on its final flourish towards the Crowberry Tower. At this point you are level with the exposed upper part of Rannoch Wall, seen to sensational advantage here through a camera viewfinder. But by the same token Curved Ridge looks equally marvellous from Rannoch Wall. 'Ah canna believe it,' a climber had shouted down from Agag's Groove, 'what ye're on looks a lot harder than our route'. Perhaps it was the way I was climbing.

However, once at the foot of the Crowberry Tower, and with the vast expanse of Rannoch Moor spread out below so its countless lochans reflect the sun like scattered diamonds, the top is near. Scaling an easy gully to the left of the Tower, you reach the Tower Gap (with the black chasm of Crowberry Gully gaping down to the right) and, after surmounting the mountain's

final step, the summit cairn of Stob Dearg.

Stob Dearg, at 3,345ft, is the Buachaille's highest point and a splendid start to the great skyline cresting on towards the distant summit of Stob na Broige. Rocks and shingle sigh beneath your feet like a seashore of bleached, crushed shells as you make for the next summit. This is Stob na Doire, over a mile along the ridge and, on the rocky descent beyond its summit, a fine vantage point for Stob Coire Altruim, the next peak along the way (angling back to the north, on the skew to the main thrust of the ridge and often preserving a snowfield with beautiful cornice even into May). The path follows just to one side of the rim of the cornice, providing an easy, if energetic route to the trig point on the summit where everything finally levels off. This leaves you with more delightful ridge walking and gentle slopes that lead to the final peak of Stob na Broige and its impressive views down the length of Glen Etive.

The descent favoured by most walkers who complete this ridge is to return along the skyline as far as the col between Stob Coire Altruim and Stob na Doire. Then you drop down lovely green slopes littered with scree fans and small streams into the fastnesses of the Lairig Gartain below. The walk along the floor of this great channel between the hills is only bettered by traversing its slopes at a higher level along any one of the innumerable well-trodden deer-tracks you might choose, and which are characterized by their unerring ability to contour the flanks of the mountains at a constant height. The tracks will guide you all the way round and back to Jacksonville if you so wish and as they did for me, without having to go anywhere near the busy road.

Chapter 21
THE MAIN RIDGE OF BIDEAN NAM BIAN

London Dungeon in Tooley Street made an impression on me in a special way when I visited the city with my daughter. This famous tourist attraction dwells on the horrors of the past, yet I was more horrified by the sights of people sleeping in shop doorways and cardboard boxes, and only too aware that this was where I might end up myself. Hannah, eight years old and oblivious to it all was just full of excitement at the shops, too grown-up now even to want to hold hands on the busy Christmas streets. But in London Dungeon she did. Things must have been bad! By a cave mouth squatted a man, woman and boy, evil-looking in the extreme as they tended a bubbling cauldron inside which a human being was being boiled alive. And this is what the caption said:

'During the reign of James I, Sawney Beane lived with his wife and many children in an enormous cave near the shores of Galloway.

'They supported themselves for twenty-five years by robbing and killing passers by, cutting up their bodies and salting and pickling them.

'Eventually they were discovered and taken to Edinburgh and executed without a trial. The men were castrated and their hands and feet cut off and left to bleed to death and the women burnt in three fires.'

I was reminded of London Dungeon when I stayed the night in a Glencoe bothie called the 'Bendy' before climbing Bidean nam Bian the following day. Both Sawney Beane's lair and the Bendy had a similar ambience when first seen in the dwindling light of day. I entered it with trepidation.

The Bendy, or to give it its full name, the 'Bendy-Bendy', is not your usual bothie, the kind of tumbledown shelter that consists of four walls and a roof set picturesquely in the wilds. Not only is the Bendy near a road; it is actually underneath one, and a busy road at that. The sound of traffic flowing through Glencoe's famous Pass reverberates above and drops of water from beneath the concrete span drip on your sleeping-bag when it rains.

The Bendy, as its name suggests, is a desperate place if you are tall. I had to jack-knife over from the waist and remember not to straighten up suddenly, otherwise my head banged against the ceiling with a percussive effect, bringing tears to my eyes, especially if it happened to be where stalactites hung down like fangs from the pre-stressed concrete. This experience made me see Bidean nam Bian as similar in terms of discomfort, risk and inaccessibility to the bothie that was giving me such a hard time.

Bidean nam Bian, the monarch of Glencoe, is in fact like the Bendy in that it cannot be seen from the main road through Glencoe – well, apart from one or two moments where its summit peeps over the phalanx of great peaks that guard it like sentinels, their precipitous flanks full of a sense of savagery and foreboding. It is also difficult to reach because of the amount of rugged walking and scrambling

Evening sun gilds the pyramidal cone of Stob Coire nam Beith which hides, to its left, the West Top of Bidean. The photograph was taken from the A82, near the Clachaig road-end and looking towards Achnambeithach.

required. The three great cliffs of the Three Sisters guard Bidean well and offer a sight of such glorious perpendicularity to travellers that it is *de rigueur* to photograph and marvel at them.

The main ridge of Bidean nam Bian curves like a boomerang, facing north, and is fronted by what is in effect this giant wishbone of ridges screening its elusive summit to magnificent effect. The vast buttresses of Gearr Aonach and Aonach Dubh sandwich huge corries between them, poised above the distant road. The culminating point of four great ridges, soaring to nine separate summits, Bidean nam Bian looks more like the backcloth for one of history's most notorious blood-baths than where the Massacre of Glencoe actually happened, which is further west along the glen. (And where, in 1692, thirty-eight members of the Clan Macdonald were hacked to death for failing to swear allegiance to William of Orange.)

My night in the Bendy was everything I had feared. As I evacuated it at the first sign of daylight, I almost killed myself in my haste to get away. Descending towards the river booming through the gorge below I had a nasty experience. The knotted rope down which I was obliged to slide to escape at the utmost possible speed parted suddenly, allowing me to crash spine first on to the rocks below and knock my favourite woollen hat flying into the river where I watched helplessly

The North Face of Aonach Dubh (with Ossian's Cave in view). Above, the winter climbing playground of Stob Coire nan Lochan stands guard over one of the highest and most beautiful corries in the central Highlands.

as it floated away. The evening before I had hoped to wake up to the sight of sunlight bathing the Three Sisters in liquid gold. What actually happened was that a concrete stilt, supporting the bridge, got in the way. Also it was misty, the mountains beaded with dense fog, like the film of perspiration that glistened on my forehead.

The Bendy is not only hidden beneath the ceiling of the lofty road bridge but is also perched on the top of a crag. Constructed from breeze-blocks in the gap between the concrete span above and the top of the rock face below, it incorporated three window frames, a door frame, an iron stove and a stove-pipe with several dog-legs in it.

To reach the bothie you must first scramble from the roadside above down to the water's edge beneath the bridge, a somewhat precarious manoeuvre in times of flood as the base of the crag swims in water. Like a popular indoor climbing wall, the footholds on the crag are fiendishly polished and become entertaining when the new arrival is exhausted after a day on the Hill or has been drinking. Of course, there was always the rope hanging from the door lintel to give assistance.

It was in the middle of the night that I heard someone climbing up it towards me. Yet how? I had previously unrolled my sleeping-bag on a slat of old plywood and lain there listening to the thunder of the traffic above and the roaring of the water below, but only after I had first pulled up the rope, like a drawbridge, so that anybody who arrived late would find difficulty in reaching the bothie via the rock climb, known laughingly to climbers as the 'Vee Diff'. I admit that this was not in the traditional spirit of the game where, after struggling up the glen on your last legs, soaked to the skin by driving rain and borne down by a monster pack you finally arrive at the bothie door to be met by a blast of heat from the fire and a friendly welcome from the inhabitants as they

shove up to make space for you. But alone in the confines of the Bendy, I just wanted to survive the night.

What had caused me to grope for my headtorch in the early hours was the sound of curses and the tinkle of breaking glass. As I reached out, my hand encountered the rope, finding it stretched quite taut. I switched on the light to look, dropped it accidently through sheer panic and felt desperately for my penknife so I could cut the rope. If it was not Sawney Beane himself advancing towards me, it was one of his sons.

Shinning up the rope towards me had been a man with greasy hair, several teeth missing and a broken nose. He was clutching a whisky bottle that had broken at the neck and cut him badly. This also added to the difficulties as his feet kept slipping and his grip on the rope was impeded by the bottle – a fact provoking a further stream of blasphemies.

Just as the windows had no glass, the doorway of the Bendy had no door. By the time I found the headtorch and slashed at the rope with the knife, he was at the threshold and lurching towards me. 'Ay've got ye the noo!' he roared, at the same time cracking his head against the stalactites which only seemed to madden him further. At that point I woke up, my heart racing and the dreadful cries still echoing in my head. Everything was silent and faint signs of daylight seeped below the bridge.

Then I saw the rope. It was hanging down the Vee Diff. Had the coils I had placed so carefully on the threshold slithered off in the night? Possibly it had all been real, perhaps I had not imagined anything. Perhaps someone had been climbing up the rope and fallen? But one thing I did know. I would never be able to go back to sleep. I packed quickly, slid down the rope and . . . the rest you know. Well, almost the rest you know. There was an aftermath.

The equivalent of the knotted rope

that had led up to the Bendy and which hangs down from the skyline of Bidean nam Bian might also have soaked up the blood from past history when the MacDonalds were put to the sword, fleeing into the bosom of hills wherever they were able. It is a natural handrail. And I hoped it would take me high from a point just west of Loch Achtriochtan where, just across the A82, a narrow road turns off towards the Clachaig Hotel. Above me was the pyramidal cone of Stob Coire nam Beith, a magnificent lure, with its great buttresses, to the hilltop climber.

Crossing the bridge over the River Coe, I followed the path to the right of the burn that poured down from Coire Nam Beith, the great natural amphitheatre above. How can it be anything but the equivalent of a knotted rope, this path with its waterfall scenery so marvellous it takes the mind off the upward toil quite wonderfully, leading you high into the corrie to the confluence of two streams with relative ease? Rather harder, however, was the pull up steeper slopes of boulders and scree to the south-west to attain the crest of the peak.

If I had found the previous evening's bothie a gruesome experience, that of Bidean was sombre, redolent in its atmosphere of a bewilderment of feuds, conspiracies, kidnappings, murders and wars, the whole turbulent drama stalked by terrible despots like Black Douglases yet illuminated by veins of grand romance like Robert the Bruce and Mary, Queen of Scots. Or perhaps it was my mood following the rigours of the Bendy. Here, as I followed a south-easterly course towards the West Peak of Bidean, and then continued eastwards for more glorious ridge walking right on to the summit, I had never felt higher amongst the wild

The famous view of Gearr Aonach and Aonach Dubh, two of the Three Sisters of Glencoe.

and glorious Highlands, one of the last wildernesses of Europe whose romantic landscapes catch the hearts of so many.

Reluctantly I took my leave of the views of an unparalleled mountain scene that day from the summit of Bidean. It was a world removed away from the busy road far below, now screened from view by the bulk of Stob Coire nan Lochan, which stands guard over its rugged corrie below, one of the highest and most outlandish in the Highlands.

Dropping down from Bidean, I took the easy south-east ridge, still patched with snow frozen hard over its rocky surface, to the pointed summit of Stob Coire Sgreamhach. Then, turning north-east, I followed its skyline along the rim of the Lost Valley below and to the west – a sunken paradise with the

tranquillity of a water meadow, sealed from civilization by huge boulders that had crashed down from the very cliffs I was about to traverse. But only after I had first negotiated the ridge with its exciting scrambling – including one particularly awkward step that requires care in greasy or icy conditions – to the twin peaks of Beinn Fhada. Then I descended eastwards from spot height .811m into the friendly entrance of the Lairig Eilde. Though after such a taxing twenty-four hours – and occasionally wondering if I *had* really slashed at the knotted rope with my knife, cutting it partially and contributing to my fall? – I still took care, just jubilant to have survived the experience of these bleak and inhospitable ranges, the very thing for which the climber craves.

Chapter 22

THE BEINN A'BHEITHIR HORSESHOE

The Peak of the Thunderbolt, Beinn a'Bheithir, and its electrifying crest curving around the peaks of Sgorr Bhan, Sgorr Dhearg and Sgorr Dhonuill, and frequently displaying a hanging wave of snow, dominates the foothills and forest behind Ballachulish when viewed from the lower end of Glencoe. Viewed from either of the summits of Beinn a'Bheithir's twin peaks (and including Sgorr Bhan to make three), the vistas of seascape along the edge of mountainous Lochaber are superlative, a fact that made me frustrated and angry as I failed abjectly not only initially to climb them but even to start to climb them.

It was from the bridge across Loch Leven some years earlier that I had pointed up at the cornice of snow suspended between Sgorr Bhan and Sgorr Dearg. But Mark, my son, was glancing out to sea where skimming straight towards us wingtip-to-wingtip were surely the Red Arrows, but without the customary trails of red, white and blue smoke. Quickly I braked while Mark, then eight, and Chris, my then-wife leapt out of the car. By then the crimson jets had passed beneath us

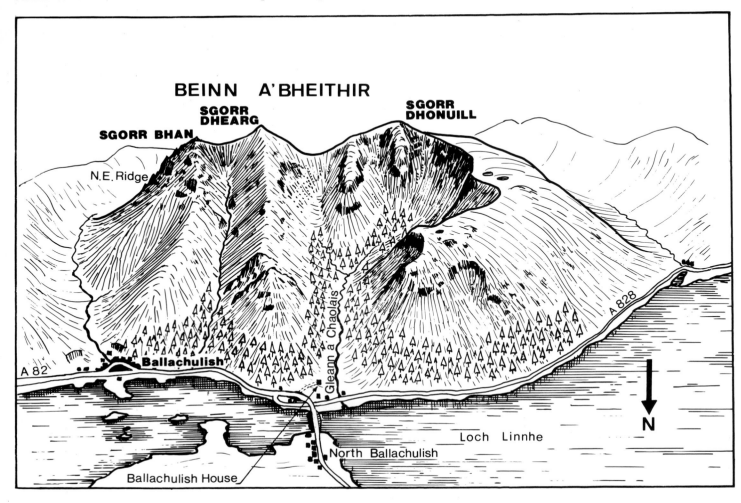

BEINN A'BHEITHIR

SGORR DHEARG

SGORR DHONUILL

SGORR BHAN

N.E. Ridge

A 82

Ballachulish

Gleann a' Chaolais

A 828

Loch Linnhe

N

North Ballachulish

Ballachulish House

with a roar that quivered the metal superstructure of the bridge like a tuning fork and were climbing to avoid the soaring mountain wall of the Mamores at the head of the great sea loch.

The Peak of the Thunderbolt is an evocative name, ball lightning being just the kind of emblem Strike Command pilots might use for their personal insignia. 'The Red Arrows, Mark,' I had shouted, 'the Red Arrows!' 'Gnat trainers, Dad,' said my son, 'they're Gnat trainers'. I have since been told we could both have been right.

Bheithir is pronounced 'Vaire' which rhymes with despair – and so appropriate that lovely morning when things went wrong. By coincidence I felt my failure to get started on this fantastic mountain skyline could be linked with yet another occasion when I was also deafened from close range by numerous jet-engines. Each instance could also be said to have become critical when my headgear was introduced into the proceedings, but the related factor in both cases was not so much the size of my head as my self-destructive streak.

That second occasion I mentioned happened after a jet fighter had buzzed my daughter as she played on the doorstep. She was terrified and clapped her small hands over her ears as the V-winged demon hurtled so suddenly and ferociously over the house that its sound and shadow were like an instant thunderstorm. Did the Royal Air Force have to fly so low? And what was it like to have the responsibility of the pilots who, until we find a better way, are doing their best to help preserve a peace which allows four-year olds to play on their doorsteps in the first place? The RAF arranged a flight so that I might write about the experience. And *She* magazine obliged with a commission. I was to fly in a NATO exercise from RAF Coltishall in Norfolk and as 'passenger' in a Jaguar with two separate cockpits, one sited above the other. Belted into my seat, overlooking

the pilot, I waited twenty minutes in the jet before the pilots emerged from their battle briefing, to accustom me to the slimness of the supersonic plane.

Pilots, rather than pilot, please note, because we were due to fly in battle formation; four Jaguars, taking off in pairs as they thundered down the runway trailing smoke, or that was the intention.

The canopy of my cockpit had been raised on its hinges behind my head to give me a chance of fresh air during the wait, like a large version of a welder's face-mask, and now as we taxied out to the end of the runway my pilot, Sqn Ldr Ian Hall, asked me through the earphones in my helmet, to close it as we had rehearsed earlier that morning. Try as I might, I could not seal the canopy. There was a button to click and levers to pull – something only I could do from the inside – and Ian had previously listened intently to my clunks and clicks as he stood outside the plane on a step-ladder. Now, however, the roar from the Rolls Royce/Turbomeca Adour turbofan engines didn't help. I could no longer hear if the clicks were clicking or the clunks clunking. I saw Ian shake his head

through the canopy just below. 'Try again,' he said, his voice officer-crisp and no-nonsense in the earphones. I knew that speed was of the essence. If our flight was to reach the Scottish Borders and back, every scrap of fuel was essential. How many gallons had I wasted already with this delay? Suddenly it clicked – not the canopy, but *why* I had this problem. My rehearsal in the cockpit had been in my everyday clothing, and bareheaded. Now I was wearing a bonedome of a helmet and it was pushing up against the underside of the canopy, keeping it a fraction from closing. Help! What did I do now? I tried to clunk the lever once more, this time ducking down: success. Ian gave me the thumbs up. Like boy racers we took off, my cheeks as red as Cox's Pippins, the name of the other pilot alongside us coincidentally being called Piers Applegarth, one of those things that stick in the memory because it was such an incredibly rustic name to be handling such an instrument of devastation as opposed to a horse and plough on the Kentish Weald.

The morning I intended traversing Beinn a' Bheithir's immaculate skyline I had another problem related to my

The corniced curve of Sgorr Dhearg from Sgor Bhan.

headgear of the moment. As it also concerned my running out of fuel, I felt I had been there before as the problem was once more caused by my own short-comings.

For a start, to climb a mountain skyline as serious as Beinn a'Bheithir's you need a good breakfast. And I was almost out of paraffin. My trusty Primus – the ultimate jet engine – contained just sufficient I estimated (unlike the RAF Jaguar, there was no control panel of glowing lights and beeping sounds to warn me when it was low) to serve me a vital brew and possibly warm me some muesli if I was lucky. How it roared as I worked the pump! Now for the water. But when I reached out behind me for the one pan I possessed, something warm and wet closed around my thumb. Horrified, I came to an abrupt halt. It was at that moment that memories of what had happened the previous evening began to flood back.

The previous evening I had stopped

Sgorr Dhearg's cornice glimpsed from the roadside near Loch Leven.

for a drink in the Kingshouse Hotel, strategically placed for its tremendous views of the Buachaille Etive Mor rising across the moor and with nothing else to spoil the stunning scene. Into the bar, presided over by Big Ian – he of the Nicholson ilk who soloed Point Five and Zero Gullies on the Ben all those years before, creating a landmark morning in the history of Scottish winter mountaineering – arrived members of the Creag Dhu straight from Jacksonville, wearing the wellington boots in which they had crossed the burn outside the hut.

I suppose it was inevitable, but the water in those same wellies – some of them steel toe-capped as befits their owners' reputations and stamped most appropriately 'Argyll' on the maker's label – was lovingly poured unimpeded from the big rubber boots into various drinks while the rafters rang with laughter.

Nobody objected, least of all me. I was not that tired of living. Even when a fish plopped from one boot into a pint of bitter and Creag Dhu fingers went into the glass to try to revive it not a word was spoken in anger. I just drank the beer as if nothing had happened.

But now with my head throbbing as I groped behind me for the pan, I knew something unpleasant had happened in the night. Then I felt its contents lapping around my thumb. The pan was full of urine.

In the doorway of the tent the Primus was roaring its head off like a micro version of the Jaguar's turbofans. The morning sunlight hurt my head as frantically as I tried to remember the train of events after returning from the pub and also to think what I should do next. During the night I had woken up with my bladder bursting, and, assuming a kneeling position inside the tent, had grabbed the nearest receptacle, my winter climbing helmet. As I sent a jet of steaming urine, splashing and foaming into it, I quickly realized that lightweight stonefall helmets have

four small holes placed at intervals around their circumference to allow for ventilation. Suddenly four streams of liquid, bright amber in my head torch, jetted forth from equidistant points around the helmet – now shaking with the weight in my hand – like something from the Trevi fountains, wetting everything within reach.

So full was I of ale and the waters of the Coupal Burn that I could not stop, and I did not have enough room to evacuate the tent. The waters would have to continue to flow until the level in my bladder had lowered to that certain point when I could exercise some control (at least at my age anyway). So reaching back for the pan in which I cooked I began to piss into this instead, desperately trying not to slop it over the rim.

My sleeping-bag had been back-heeled out of the way during the scuffle when I had first wriggled out of its comforting warmth. But the ground sheet of the tent was now seriously awash at one end. Fortunately this followed a slope in the ground, isolating the flooding from the things that mattered. Finished at last, my muscles screaming with the unaccustomed tension of holding the two increasingly heavy objects at arm's length and without spilling, I set the pan down carefully. Then holding on to the helmet with both hands as one alone was in danger of letting go altogether, I flung it, contents and all, outside into the night. Off it went, bowling down a slope in the camp site where it scored what sounded like a direct hit amongst a nest of pans presumably stacked outside some distant tent and triggering an outcry of outraged voices and yelping dogs.

When I woke again it was bright with sunlight and I had a raging hangover. That was when I lit the Primus and reached behind for the pan, considering that I had forgotten its presence, it was still miraculously full of the amber fluid. 'Miraculously' because

The view along the skyline from Sgorr Dhearg to Sgorr Dhonuill

it had stayed upright by my sleeping-bag while I slept and I was lucky I had not accidently knocked it over. But the smell of urine still hung thickly inside the tent. Reaching out through the tent entrance, I threw the contents of the pan on to the grass.

I might have mopped-up the ground-sheet in the night but I would need to do a lot more. What I did not forsee was that I would have ample time for the restitutional cleaning operations required that same day.

The Primus, meanwhile, was roaring its head off, its fuel atomizing through the vaporizer tube in a fair imitation of those RAF Jaguar Rolls Royce/Turbo-meca Adour turbofans. I had to act fast. Would filling this pan from my water bottle constitute a health risk?

Was urine dangerous? I didn't think so. I certainly couldn't spare any clean water to wash it first. Wiping the pan clean with a sleeve cuff, I spilled the last of my water (drinking water, that is) into the receptacle and lowered it tremblingly with fatigue on to the stove – just as the flame died.

There was no ascent of Beinn a'Bheithir that day. A superb day for photographs was ruined through my fecklessness and ineptitude. This was the most important period of my life, trying to get straight again after a time of self-inflicted depression and failure. I had been given a glorious day for capturing Beinn a'Bheithir on film and had wasted it. I would have to start again, see this as a rest day, and learn. I had already taken photographs

of the Cobbler, the Buachaille, Bidean and Aonach Eagach within four consecutive days so perhaps this time-out was just as well. At least that was how I endeavoured to rationalize it in my misery.

I washed and rinsed the tent thoroughly before driving to Fort William for supplies. Here I had a stroke of luck at last. I managed to see my dearest friend Ed Grindley coming down the street before he saw me, a climber who looks like the Mekon in Dan Dare – with thick spectacles – and whose infectious company was not in my best interests at that moment, not with so many bars in the Fort and all of them open. Quickly I dodged around the solid stone fascia of the Scottish Trustees Savings Bank and as Ed walked on down the street, sublime in his ignorance, I felt a twinge of guilt. But make it up to him I would, I promised, as I continued on in the other direction, trying to recover some semblance of sanity.

The cornice between Sgorr Bhan and Sgorr Dearg was the thing that had gripped my attention that black day, although it was now May and gloriously sunny. Motoring back from Fort William after my lucky escape from Ed, I had kept glancing at its long and perfect wave, high above the traffic crossing Loch Leven. So . . . that had been another day. Now, though only separated from those hours of disaster by less than a day, I arrived below the mountain in the early hours of the morning – it was 4.40 a.m. to be exact – and the weather report was good.

Depression washed away by a spell of sobriety and a good sleep, and the natural progression of things which is said to bring an upswing in the wake of the blues – had not Sir Isaac Newton, Goethe and Bernard Shaw suffered periods of being withdrawn, pensive and sad before respectively working out the laws of motion and gravitation, writing *Faust* and thinking up the story for *Pygmalion?* – I was on my way.

Ballachulish lies back off the main cut and thrust of the traffic pouring through Glencoe and so touristed you might think it was short of only one thing: a MacDonald's concession. Now the morning was keen, and quiet.

From the centre of Ballachulish, behind the Spar shop, the battleaxe edge of the north-east ridge of Sgorr Bhan falls in an unbroken line from its shaft, this being the skyline I hoped to traverse. Spellbound, I could not take my eyes off this tremendous plunging sweep of mountainside, one of the best I saw in the Highlands that May.

I parked by the old school beyond the village, nestling below a more northerly ridge falling in appealing fashion from the heights of Sgorr Bhan. Not as compelling as the north-east ridge, it is dominated by that other skyline which overlooks the approach from Ballachulish in no uncertain manner, rising like a rocket above the Spar supermart and never for a moment relenting as I made my approach towards it up Gleann an Fiodh, the old route to Glen Crenan.

The footpath up Gleann an Fiodh gives a splendidly scenic start. It channelled me gradually higher in a southerly direction before a faint track led rightwards towards the south-west and diagonally up the hillside towards the north-east ridge above. The steepness of this prelude is considerable, the only respite in the climb being narrow terraces of bright green turf, where it was possible to stop and draw breath. The greens of the turf were vivid, like the grass at Ibrox or Wembley when floodlit. It was with mixed feelings that I realized that I was now below the battleaxe, its leading edge directly overhead. The prelude was finally over; the ridge itself was breathtaking.

The initial climb up the ridge was grassy but unrelenting. Presently, outbreaks of rock proferred the most enjoyable kind of scrambling on the black and pink-tinged outcrops, the drop below increasing in a spectacular plunge above the glen so far below. Higher up the ridge, its blade becomes a continuous edge of rock. Certainly it is daunting enough to warn off all but the experienced scrambler. However, there are alternative paths taking easier ground.

The summit lies above scree slopes that top out above the ridge, and a delightful prospect opens up. With supreme views of Bidean nam Bian to the east, the Aonach Eagach and the Pap of Glencoe to the north-east, and the glittering fingers of Loch Leven and Loch Linnhe giving a 'V' for Victory with the massifs of the Mamores and Ben Nevis in between and further north still. Or perhaps, depending on your mood, you might see the twin lochs as offering a 'V' sign, period, and surely the one I had deserved the previous day.

The direction of walking for Beinn a'Bheithir's tremendous ridge however was westwards towards the sea and the prospect of the panoramas out over the Western Isles, blurred like smoke smudges that early morning. I was looking for eagles for, they say, there are always eagles above this part of the Highlands. But next I was descending, eyes down into the saddle below, from where I was subsequently to exit by the lovely curving rim (though keeping to the south side so that my trainers were treading hard ground as opposed to the ageing snow of winter) of the north-facing cornice between Sgorr Bhan and Sgorr Dearg. This is where the hanging wave of snow stays put for so many months, and which is seen to such good advantage from the valley.

A marvellous path leads on down, steeply and with substantial loss of height into the escape hatch of the bealach beyond the summit of Sgorr Dearg, and now above Gleann a'Chaolais. Then I was climbing out again up the rugged, at times narrow, and gratifying spine of Sgorr Dhonuill. Continuing along its crest around the rim of Gleann a'Chaolais and down, at times descending quite rough scrambling and rocky terrain, its path eventually immersed me in dense forest, which proved the trickiest part, before I emerged on the road near Ballachulish House.

Chapter 23
THE RING OF STEALL

The Ring of Steall explodes around the firmament of heavenly peaks created by An Gearanach, An Garbhanach, Stob Coire a'Chairn, Stob Ban, Am Bodach, Sgor an Iubhair, the Devil's Ridge (peaking on the very summit of Stob Choire a'Mhail) and Sgurr a'Mhaim in the Mamores. The very name, the Ring of Steall, evokes a host of images. Not the least being when I visited Notting Hill Carnival and the Caribbean rhythms of the steel drum bands was mimicked by the sound of my skull exploding against the side of a large red bus, slammed there by two gentlemen who had been exhorting the passers-by to pick out which card was the queen from the three playing cards being dealt upside down on a cardboard box in a shop doorway. To cut a long story short, I had suggested to a man putting his money on his choice of card and losing heavily that the game of 'Spot the Lady' was crooked. The two 'onlookers' reacted speedily, one standing on my foot, the other placing an elbow on my chest and shoving me so that I flew backwards, describing a parabolic trajectory across the pavement. The rest you know. But that moment, I

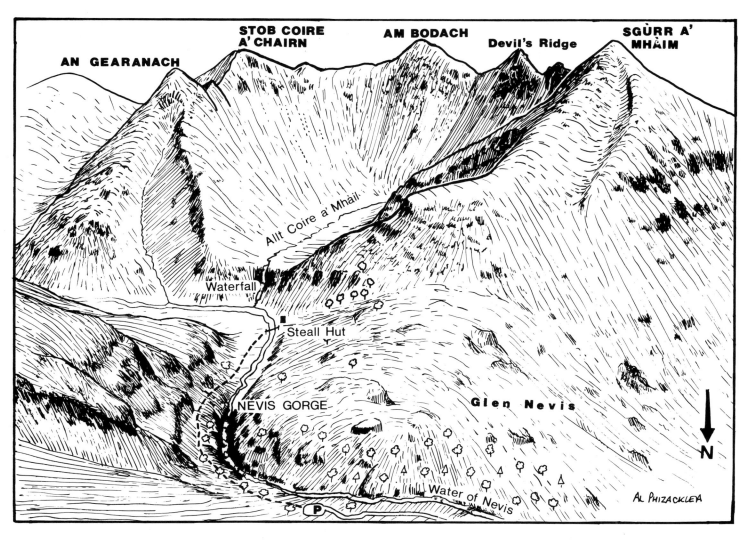

realized later, was one of those clangers you drop in life that you do not repeat again.

Clangers I have dropped in plenty (during national service in the Royal Air Force I was nicknamed Bomber, although I was a typist in the Orderly Room or, as the sergeant would call it when I was typing the weekend leave passes, the 'Disorderly Room'). But the error I had perpetrated the previous day when, during glorious weather, I had failed to try the traverse of Beinn a'Bheithir as a result of circumstances over which I will draw a veil, was criminal.

I had poured away the previous day of golden sunlight beaming on to glorious mountains, mountains moreover on which I was staking myself, my life and my bank account. It was almost too bad to think about, almost like (as Martin Amis replied when asked how he would choose to end his days) dying in the arms of my bank manager.

Now, however, I was buoyant – almost. I had just completed the Beinn a' Bheithir horseshoe by two o'clock in the afternoon. The light on the hills had been iridescent. I had had the most fantastic views over Glencoe, Lochaber and the sea.

The only thing was that it was still a lovely light, a great and perfect day for taking photographs. I began to feel I had mismanaged things yet again, and it gave me a headache. Not only had I squandered the previous day, but now I was wasting the rest of this one as well. Yet how could I redeem myself? What was there to do? And then it came; Why – the Ring of Steall, that was what there was to do. Within easy range of Ballachulish. A highlight of the Mamores, just across Glen Nevis from Britain's highest peak, Ben Nevis. And incorporating in its embrace of the magnificent mountain amphitheatre of Allt Coire a'Mhail, some of Scotland's most exalted mountains.

Did I have the energy? It was a crucial question. Beinn a'Bheithir had been

Along the Ring of Steall, between An Garbhanach and An Gearanach, looking towards Ben Nevis and Carn Mor Dearg.

a most strenuous trip. Would I burn myself out for good by trying the Ring of Steall as well? Was I asking too much?

I sat on the car seat, stretching my legs through the open door and enjoying the sun. Almost on the point of falling asleep, it came back to me with renewed force. I must not waste a further moment of this precious day. The thrill of knowing I might be able to do two ridges in a day, because the evenings did not get dark until later (and anyway, I had my Petzl headlamp with me) mounted.

I swung my legs inside, started the motor and, with my gear still unpacked and unsorted from Beinn a'Bheithir, drove straight from the Ballachulish car-park to Fort William and its inestimable silhouette of the Mamore hills ahead. On I continued, on up Glen Nevis to the furthest car-park. There I paused at the start of the walk through the Nevis Gorge and from where this fantastic circuit of mountains begins.

Glen Nevis is one of Scotland's most accessible glens, tremendously popular and exceedingly beautiful. Following a seven-mile drive through its halcyon vale, the mountain walls steepening with every twist and turn of the road, it terminates in the narrowing of the Nevis Gorge, before continuing along an extensive green strath above an upper Glen Nevis. It was while venturing through the bottleneck of this precipitously magnificent ravine that my thoughts began to darken again.

Trying for two major skylines in a day was all very well, but – I realized – I should have thought of the *following* day too. I would be too shattered for anything else that next day. Once again I would get nothing done. This doubt, however, was replaced by a positive thought. It might rain. Certainly that would allow me a legitimate rest day with nothing wasted.

I stopped for a breath, gazing down through the foliage screening the side of the path to glimpses of silvery-rushing water far below. Booming cataracts squeezed between the converging walls of the defile, fighting to pour through and blocked with gigantic boulders as big as the carriages and locomotive of a train brought down during the collapse of a mighty bridge. The debris, gathered in the bottom of the gorge was straddled by the current as it battled through the slit to reach the quieter waters flowing by the road to Fort William below.

There was a remarkable change as I emerged from the gorge. Huge boulders by the path landmark a transition where you step into another world. The proximity of the slopes and fury of the ravine have been left behind; ahead

was the green sward of upper Glen Nevis, still land-locked between wonderful hills but everything now all openness, tranquillity and light. However disadvantaged and challenged I had felt moments previously, the sight of this, and especially of the flanks of Sgurr a'Mhaim and An Gearanach just across the way – those guardians of the Ring of Steall themselves – picked me up no end. I no longer felt quite so tired and aching. Now I was eager to begin the real climbing.

What really catches the eye at this point is the huge waterfall creaming down the lower slopes of Sgurr a'Mhaim. It is towards this that you make a bee-line, the path leading you to a wire bridge across the wide and deep river.

Then, passing the Steall Hut on the far banks, the path now passes idyllically between birch trees and pines, threading a way towards the increasing thunder of the fall.

Refreshed and exhilarated, I began to enjoy each upward step as the footpath angled more steeply up the slopes of An Gearanach beyond the falls and broke into a succession of wide zig-zags up through the grass and scree. It was a heavenly afternoon, the looks on the faces of people I passed coming down off the Hill after what had obviously proved an ace day, saying everything about their feelings of tired elation.

The downswing to my own good feeling came gradually. It was a return to

The rock caterpillar on the slopes of An Gearanach.

those previous blues – a gnawing feeling that I had erred once more.

The zig-zags approached a steep bank of snow, just beneath the immediate skyline. Thankfully, for I had not brought my axe with me, deep footprints had been hacked out by parties following the same route earlier in the day. But it was as I unconsciously almost reached out and took handfuls of snow to eat while I crossed the exposed traverse that the worries began to bite. I had brought insufficient food with me.

A Mars Bar and pack of Rowntrees jelly was not enough for the cirque ahead. I had let my enthusiasm rule my head. Because I am of that kind of metabolism where I never put on or take off weight, but find I have to eat constantly on the Hill to replenish lost energy, I may have jeopardized my shot at this ridge, possibly collapsing with exhaustion somewhere round its course – a failure to the end. What had I done!

But this self-castigation wasn't going to help, although as I reached the next steep climb from the col in the ridge to the summit of An Garbhanach, I was feeling ravenous and deciding whether or not to eat the Mars Bar then and there, or to cut it into slices.

The ridge levelled out once I'd ploughed on up still further eminences, graced with a cornice on Stob Coire a'Chairn. I tried to concentrate on taking the photographs, for this was what I was finding the most difficult, the mental effort required in the stopping and starting again involved in taking pictures when I was already being taxed by the actual climbing. And was I grateful for the automatic control exerted by the camera's brain! I was not to know then of the darker side of automatic zoom cameras, an experience which I will relate in a later chapter.

So many good shots presented themselves that May evening, the further I padded along in my trainers. While the sun unfortunately came at me over

the rim of the Devils Ridge in the distance across the corrie, I was still able to concentrate in other directions, especially on the superb views of the back of Ben Nevis with its dramatic swoop down into the col between it and the Carn Mor Dearg Arête, that knife blade also looming up into the picture, demanding to be captured whenever I looked due north.

Down, steeply, I went, picking my way from the summit of Stob Coire a' Chairn, down into the col below the steep upsurge of sharpened crest leading to the top, seemingly so far away, of Am Bodach. Scrambling of an easy nature, followed by sheer exhausting and steep climbing of the hands-pressing-down-on-alternate-thighs variety; the exertion was never-ending, the calls on my resources non-stop. The Bozo Bag – the padded thing in which I carried my camera – had by now been slung to one side on its belt, as if to put it out of mind for by now it was a chore to stop and photograph even the most glorious scene.

All I craved was to accomplish the Ring of Steall and return to the comfort of my luxurious down-filled sleeping bag, a piece of expensive equipment that so long as it is always kept immaculately dry is conducive to the deepest sleep. And eat, of course, and eat. Visions of food reeled before my eyes, not the sumptuous repasts you might expect, but things like Big Macs and bacon and egg.

Tinged with further clangers I had dropped, such was my frame of mind in realizing that opportunities were slipping past as the camera remained unused and my lethargy compounded the crime – even though I knew what chances I was wasting.

As I finally crested the summit of Am Bodach, I found a plastic lunchbox by the cairn. In it were two or three biscuits, several segments of an orange and half a peanut butter sandwich. I wolfed them down and was momentarily refreshed, and eager even for the remaining mountain crest cutting

An Gearanach forms the background to the Steall Waterfall.

such a crisp outline ahead, curving around quite blackly now, the part remaining for me to do, shielding the sun completely from its north face.

Perhaps it was the endorphins, the human morphine, we manufacture after extended periods of physical exercise. My pupils were no doubt as tiny as if I had just emerged from an opium parlour. Could this explain my second wind? From Am Bodach the ridge narrows and lifts towards Sgor an Iubhair, then, twists and turns towards the Devils Ridge, with its sharp and exposed edge. Ennervated as though Old Nick were after me himself with his pitchfork and horns, and now with twilight creeping its long fingers along the corrie below as its far slopes caught the last rays of sun, I descended into the gap,

Sunlit skyline snow during a May evening on the Ring of Steall.

passed the slightly awkward block that many will say is the crux of this airiest of sojourns, and then began to climb once more.

The final ascent up on to the summit of Sgurr a'Mhaim was, I knew, one that brought me to the last gasp, all my previous late-found burst of energy now dissipating into such a leaden feeling my knees and legs felt on the point of giving way. As darkness encroached higher up the slopes, threatening to envelope the crest itself, I flung myself on the ground for several minutes respite. The gloaming, however, gave the hint. Get down now while you still have the benefit of the last light of day, said a small voice somewhere in my head. And so I did, tracking down the grassy slopes, winding off the altitude as though a clock in the sky made up of twinkling stars wound off every single metre on my way down like it might on some television game show.

There was just sufficient light to see as I reached the waterfall into upper Glen Nevis and grasped the cables of the wire bridge that twitched and pitched while, exhaustedly, I fought them for a semblance of co-ordination and balance, dreading a moment's indecision which would plunge me into the pool, my camera and film wrecked forever. It was not to be, I succeeded in crossing at the last gasp, reeling down the steps and path of the Nevis gorge with its welcoming thunder from below growing louder and louder the further I descended towards the car-park. At last I staggered on to that very place, the Mini being the only vehicle remaining. Without any thought of driving to Fort William to catch last orders, which even though I might be late, my friend Ed Grindley could always arrange, I did something sensible for once – well, almost sensible.

I pulled out my pit – that costly sleeping-bag full of finest eiderdown – and threw myself on the ground under a starlit canopy of velvety sky. There was both good news and bad news when I woke the following morning. It was raining.

Chapter 24

BEN NEVIS AND THE CARN MOR DEARG ARÊTE

On the summit of Ben Nevis, a man is gesturing with an ice-axe in one fist and something white in the other. His beard is frozen, his helmet of thick black hair also tinselled with frost and only his deep-set eyes sunken behind high cheekbones display an inner glow like the light beyond a furnace door. It could be the Black Douglas himself or the Black Prince or the Black Dog for that, exhorting their followers to deeds of revenge and cruelty. It could be on the other hand an accountant I once knew asking how my figures had been arrived at, or were they just a guess?

'This. . .piece . . .of . . .paper . . .' he bellows into the gale screeching across the summit plateau like a banshee 'Is . . .no . . .effing . . .use . . .to . . .me . . .whatsoever . . .'

The suggestion his demeanour gave

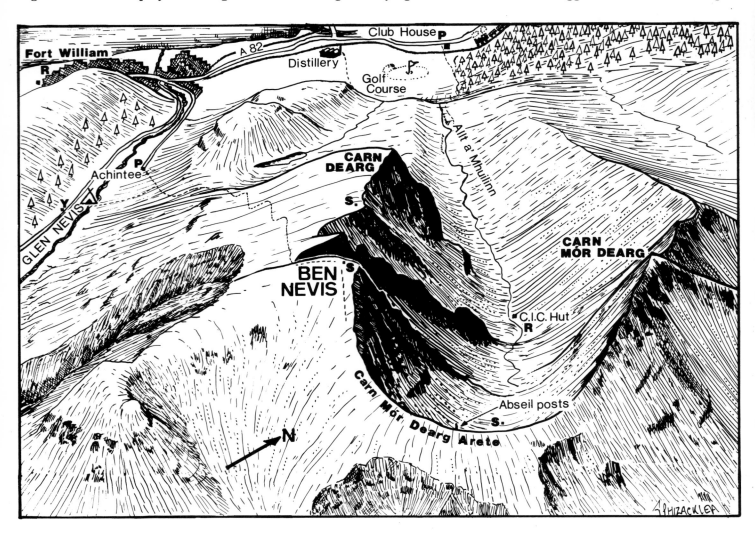

Ben Nevis from near Fort William.

that he was about to break out, axe lashing, at other groups of climbers coiling their ropes and drinking from steaming flasks on the summit after their respective climbs on the north-east face would not be far off the mark. Colin, Gunārs and myself had, in fact, just completed the North-East Buttress in a blinding gale and slashing hail and whirling spindrift. Finally, on the summit plateau, we had crammed the frozen ropes into our sacks and tried to navigate our way down the path to the abseil posts on the Carn Mor Dearg Arête.

This should have been no problem. We were all experienced climbers, all seasoned in mountain navigation (and Colin in fact was the hero of the Nevis 'rescue' mentioned in the Coledale Horseshoe). However, this time we met with no success. Each time we came to

an abrupt halt at a spot where it was clear, it would be dangerous to proceed further. You just could not tell what lay below.

Yet the route we sought should have been attainable, even though plastered with snow and in conditions verging on a white-out. Many climbers that day, to judge by the bootmarks in the snow, had passed that way before and presumably they had also steered by compass. Yet somewhere we kept going wrong. At each impasse, then, and in an increasingly bad humour with each failed attempt, Colin would turn around and we would climb back to the summit and try again.

'This is so effing embarrassing,' he said, glancing out of the corner of his eyes at the other teams of climbers still there and preparing for the descent after their respective climbs on Tower Ridge, Smith's Route, the North-East Buttress or whatever, and whom we had already passed previously

on our own evacuation of the summit. 'Hope there's no one here who knows me.' He pulled his balaclava helmet down and you could imagine the clang of a helmet visor closing.

What had happened was that we had made an elementary error. The previous summer Pete Long, a friend and a climber of some standing, had visited the summit of the Ben and had noted the compass bearings and distances to all the salient features on the summit plateau of the mountain. Knowing these bearings and the number of paces to walk along them before changing course – the yardstick being for 'a man of 6ft, weighing 12 stone, with quite long legs, walking at a comfortable gait with regard to the conditions' – was invaluable, especially as we all fitted that description. Not that that mattered anyway. Whether we had been 7ft tall basketball players or the Seven Dwarfs, with these magic figures it meant we could check the

Climbers on the corniced rim of the north-east face of Ben Nevis.

line of our descent from the summit in a blizzard so much faster than from the map. In fact so sure were we of the efficiency of this new system that we hadn't even brought a map with us. We had, however, overlooked the human element in our plans. We just set our compasses on to the required bearing and began walking. Only gradually did it dawn on us where we were going wrong.

The summit, for the purpose of the diagram that Colin had in his possession, was taken from the stone pedestal on which the emergency bivouac shelter stands on the very summit of Ben Nevis. This, however, was covered by a snowdrift. What we had mistakenly thought was the summit was another larger snowdrift nearby. Once we had located the summit proper, furiously excavating it from the snow with our axes as if digging for buried treasure, all was revealed. Within half an hour we had arrived at the abseil posts.

Ben Nevis, at 4,406ft the highest mountain in the British Isles, has two distinct characters. The popular view is that it is a disappointing mass, and to most people who are content to look at it from a distance, that is a reasonable view. But the climber knows that its northern face is as wild and compelling as anything in the country. Only among the Cuillin mountains of Skye are there vistas as rugged and precipitous. However, the sheer height of the crags on Ben Nevis make this the magnet that climbers are drawn to summer and winter. As we have just seen, even they are not immune from the difficult nature of the terrain.

The truth about Ben Nevis is that it is a difficult mountain to see. From Fort William it is screened by the low-lying slopes of the Hill of Rest; from Banavie the summit of Carn Dearg closes out anything like a view; and even from Glen Nevis the lower slopes completely hide the mountain. From a distance, one may get some impression of the true character of the mountain, notably from the western shores of Loch Linnhe, or from halfway down Loch Eil. A good vantage point, too, is from the railway between Corrour station and Loch Treig. Closer to hand are the views up the hanging corrie of the Allt a'Mhuilinn which can be seen from the vicinity of the golf club and beyond, from the A82 north-east of Fort William.

It seems appropriate then that from the summit of Ben Nevis it is possible to see the town of Inverness where Marks and Spencers has the biggest choice of parkas, cagoules and anoraks outside Oxford Street, and Melven's bookshop is the last cultural outpost before the Arctic Circle. Ben Nevis, in fact, is a world away from your normal British hill, a fact accounting for its high accident rate of those who quickly find they are out of their depth.

Inside another Ben Nevis (but known locally as the Jacobite bar), several songs I selected on the juke box refused to play. Jimmy, muscular and wearing amber glasses ('Like traffic lights, Laddie. Just watch they dinna turn red, ye ken?') returned from the bar with a key, retrieved my money and said it would cost me a half. The half turned out to be a sherry and a whisky. 'D'ye want to carry your head home in a hanky?' he enquired as I began to protest. The altercation involved several bystanders and the police. Later, in the police station – some of us destined for the cells, some for statements and first-aid (like myself) – I glanced into a room empty but for a large relief map of Ben Nevis surrounded by grey tubular chairs. 'What an excellent map,' I said to the sergeant. 'It has to be,' he said, 'the number of people who arrive in Fort William with their companions away up on the hill, injured, and their position to be pinpointed before they succumb to the elements.' Then, as an afterthought he added, 'Try not to bleed on the glass, Sir. It's the devil of a job to remove.'

If anything takes the unwary by surprise on Ben Nevis it is the name the 'Tourist Route' for the route which climbs the inclines of those unexciting slopes. The Tourist Route is in fact quite serious. Initially it was a pony track made for the former summit Observatory (1883–1904), and although it is the easiest and most regularly climbed route, when drifted with snow or hidden in mist and driving rain, it is possible to stray on to the edge of tremendous crags and treacherous gullies. The Observatory ruins are, after all, so close to the edge of the huge crags that a gully directly below – and well known to climbers – is called Gardyloo Gully. 'Gardyloo' is derived from the French warning of *'Gardez l'eau'* as slop-buckets were emptied in Edinburgh streets. It would be yelled from the top of the Ben with gusto, usually. In winter the Chief Bucket Emptier was belayed to a wooden post, and the operation was not without ha-

Looking from the dam at the lower end of the Allt a'Mhuillin glen towards the North-East Buttress and Tower Ridge of Ben Nevis.

zard if a strong up-draught was present. However, in a good south-easterly, the rubbish was simply hurled into the air and carried away by the gale.

Fine weather is crucial. Ben Nevis rises straight from the sea, standing in an isolated position and facing the storm track of North Atlantic hurricanes. Cloud can smother the mountain when the rest of the sky is clear; it averages only two hours of bright sunshine a day. The annual rainfall is nearly 160in. Snow may fall here at any time of year, on the summit plateau and lingering snow forms huge cornices overhanging space at the edge of the mountains. It is worth remembering that it is on the summit and easy slopes where many – including experienced climbers – have

died because of sudden changes in the weather.

The traverse of Ben Nevis and the Carn Mor Dearg Arête is the finest in this book. The stupendousness of the scenery is unrivalled in the British Isles, the giant horseshoe facing north-west providing a contrast between the sheer precipitous bulk of Ben Nevis on one side (and from its best side, the tremendous and complex north-east face) and the elegant, narrow crest of Carn Mor Dearg. Because this *is* the Ben's best side, and its matchless cliffs are seen to such glorious and sustained advantage from the length of Carn Mor Dearg's crest, it is from this direction that I recommend you traverse the cirque. Not only is the Tourist Route

up Ben Nevis uninspiring on the ascent, the descent from the summit down to the abseil posts, as we have seen, has its difficulties, and in poor weather demands knowledgeable compass work. Arriving at the abseil posts from the other direction, from, in fact, the summit of Carn Mor Dearg, means that a change in conditions threatening the ascent of Ben Nevis can be heeded and a timely escape made down steep slopes into the safer recesses of Coire Leis.

Unlike the Tourist Route up the Ben, the ascent of Carn Mor Dearg is less tiresome in aspect, being a varying succession of shallow dimples up the hillside offering idyllic views across the Allt a'Mhuilinn to the starkness of Carn Dearg, with Ben Nevis just beyond.

A view along the Carn Mor Dearg Arête with Sgurr a'Mhaim in the Mamores in the distance.

The Ben Nevis Distillery, and adjoining car-park, is a useful starting point, a track through the yard leading you across the railway to the banks of the Allt Coire an Lochain beyond. This is followed to a bridge which takes you to its north side, and a boggy path follows through scrubland to the rough road and stream dam at the lip of the Mhuilinn glen – and Campbell's Kingdom revisited. (The path from the Golf Club crosses the course to join this route after climbing a twisting boggy route through groves of hazel and silver birch to the dam.)

A path now continues easily to the left of the burn for half a mile or so when the valley begins to narrow, and it is possible to strike left up the rugged hillside past boulders in profusion and follow the easiest line up slopes dimpled with grooves and hollows. Then you reach the broad shoulder of the skyline and eventually the granite screes of the rounded summit ridge.

The rocky summit of Carn Dearg Meadhonach is the first peak along the skyline to be reached. It is a marvellous viewpoint of a panorama that will grow even better the further along the ridge you progress. Not only is the upraised wing of the Carn Mor Dearg Arête itself viewed to superb advantage from this humble beginning, but across the void of the Allt a'Mhuilinn thrusts the great spur of the North-East Buttress falling from the flat summit of Ben Nevis into the corrie below. Tower Ridge stands out as the buttress to its far right, beyond a frequently snow-filled Tower Gully and with the narrows of Gardyloo Gully at its head. These are only part of a scene which is a wonderland of famous climbs on the smooth dark porphyry rock or winter ice, so magnificent that they are one of the finest mountain prospects.

Following a brief descent, there is an easy climb to the twin summits of Carn Mor Dearg, followed by a delightful traverse southwards along the narrow crest of the arête, and with Ben Nevis drawing ever nearer and the vistas of its north face zooming ever larger into view. The scrambling *en route* is easy and can be avoided; the views below are dramatic. As the arête begins to steepen towards the junction with Ben Nevis, the abseil posts offer an escape into Coire Leis down a steep mountainside which can be negotiated without a rope – with care (though in winter an ice-axe and crampons are necessary too).

This escape route into Coire Leis and back down the Allt a'Mhuilinn to Fort William, incidentally, passes the Charles Inglis Clark (CIC) memorial hut, an Alpine base of the SMC below the cliffs. But you will not find sanctuary there – not at least unless it is occupied and your distress is dire. Shuttered and bolted with steel plate, the CIC hut is fortified to withstand the ravages of the Big Red Key; in other words, the red propane cylinders nearby that in the past have been used as battering rams to gain entry.

An abseil post marks the beginning of the final climb in a north-westerly direction up wide slopes and massed with large boulders. A tenuous path weaves through this rugged terrain, frequently covered with snow, to the summit of Ben Nevis itself.

The descent must be taken seriously after the elation of the heady sights below and summit views that can range from Ben Wyvis in the north to the Paps of Jura in the south, including the coast of Ireland 120 miles away and hills clearly on or near the 100 mile circle. Now is the crucial part of your traverse if visibility is at all suspect. Not only is there always a threat from the crags to the north but on the other hand it is possible in mist or darkness to stray too far in the other direction and drop into the accident black spot of Five Finger Gully which borders the descent path to its left.

The way down begins from the summit shelter along the Tourist Route, first in a southerly direction before turning west along the deeply bitten edge of the crags. Cornices still fringe your route through spring and into early summer, their instability notorious. If the weather is good, a wonderful finish is to veer rightwards from the path, descending into a dip in the plateau before climbing out on the far side and – in a north-westerly direction – following the cliff edge and passing the marker post for No.4 Gully, to cross the barren plateau to the summit cairn of Carn Dearg.

The Tourist Route is rejoined by striking south from the emergency bivouac shelter on Carn Dearg. Its steep zig-zags drop steeply down beside the defile of the Red Burn, though by no means should you go the whole way down by this prominent landmark, and care should be exercised as at one point the path crosses the Red Burn and also involves a short stretch of uphill track. Then more level terrain is reached above Lochan Meall an t-Suidhe, which you pass on your left as you descend northwards and eventually down grassy slopes to the Allt a'Mhuilinn dam – and from where you retrace your earlier route from the Fort.

Chapter 25

THE CLASSIC TRAVERSE OF LADHAR BHEINN

'Go by boat to Ladhar Bheinn,' they said, 'Charlie McTavish at Arnisdale will take ye over. A bottle of good whisky, that's all he'll need.' So I drove to Arnisdale and discovered that Mr McTavish would indeed ferry me over for a bottle of the malt, but he wanted another bottle to bring me back.

With my finances stretched to the limit because I had committed myself to doing this book, including spending all the May of '89 in the Highlands, I drove back along the coast to consider it. There is a pub in Glenelg and I found that, like my young daughter Hannah's name, Glenelg is a palin-

drome: 'Everything we do forwards in Glenelg we can do backwards,' said the woman behind the bar. I thought about this with regard to Mr McTavish's offer and his requiring another bottle for the return and – being a Yorkshireman – decided to walk in to the mountain after all. But I did let Mr McTavish know.

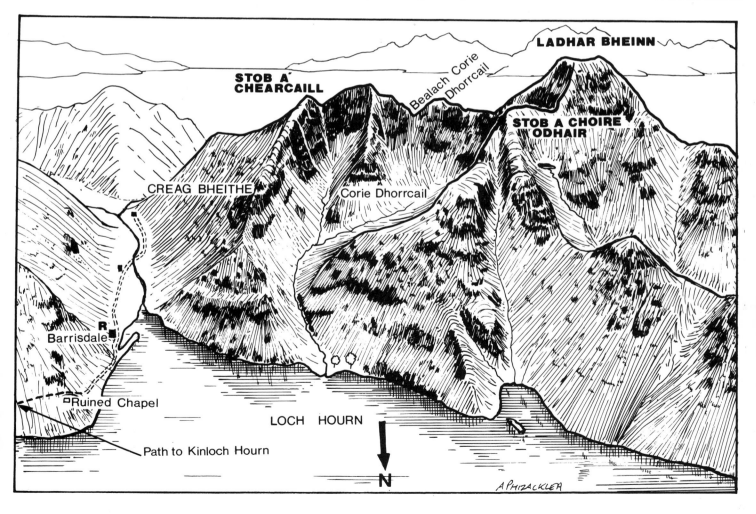

While the bar reverberated to the sound of inflatable power boats offshore, and the landlord timed them with a stop watch through the open door, I considered another option. 'Or you can take a boat from Mallaig,' friends had said. However, I also remembered that while time was of the essence and Ladhar Bheinn is renowned for its remoteness where – other than by sailing – walking is the only way to reach it and then by a most arduous route, that sea crossing from Mallaig was fraught with possibility.

Inside my wallet was a cutting of a magazine article written by one of those friends. Trying to ignore the draughts whistling through the open door, I weighted it down to the table with an ash tray and my glass, bowed my head over it and began to read.

'Hang loose, buddy,' said Hank, the resident Yank, as the boat began to crank over at an improbable angle. Hang loose? With insides bursting

The steep buttress of Stob a'Chearcaill, the superb and committing moment of ridge along the cirque of Ladhar Bheinn.

tight? With bladder bursting? With the roaring in my head? Wasn't this an entry into what could be a very hairy piece of ocean indeed? The Sound of Sleat, no less, and quite capable of unnerving anyone without sea-legs, given a sudden outburst of bad weather?

Why was I here? I dread water, especially deep water. Heights don't bother me but fathoms do. Yet this way had been sold me as the most painless way of reaching the misty skyline of Ladhar Bheinn, the sentinel of Knoydart, Britain's last great untracked wilderness bravely thrusting its blunt-nosed peninsula into the Sound of Sleat, the natural waterway separating Skye from the mainland of which Knoydart was a major part.

I had found a lift around the coast of Knoydart the previous evening. Driving up the coast from Fort William, I had chanced on Hank and his merry crew in a pub on the quayside. Sailing in, of all things, a dipping lug cutter. That's something straight out of Moby Dick. Ladhar Bheinn was on their itinerary for the following day. Did I want to go along?

Was this a golden opportunity I immediately wondered? Or something else? I noted how they laughed when I asked if I could retire to the cabin should the going become rough. Cabin? There was no cabin. There was no engine either – just sails, the colour and shape of old sacking. Fear of drowning battled with greed for the experience. Hence my indecision. I wouldn't get another chance as easily as this. But did I want another chance as easily as this?

I must have done. Next morning I was being ferried out to the cutter via a rubber boat. 'Is this the usual angle?' I asked as we set sail. The sea hissed along the gunwhale. We had tilted like the plastic bucket I'd been given for bailing. Someone laughed, 'We're not out of the harbour yet, mate,' he said.

Visions of not lasting five minutes in the Sound of Sleat before being swamped gave more power to my elbow. I baled that part of the ocean we crossed, which came swilling over the side in cold dollops, like a man possessed. Training for later eventualities.

The weather did indeed worsen, but by then we were sufficiently committed along our route. Then Hank said 'Hang loose' as the water seemed to change. Our shouting and bawling, dipping and hauling, had ceased. We were turning now directly towards the sheet of gunmetal grey that flowed ahead like a great river. The wind blew from the side now, the sails powering us forward, but slowly. Couldn't we pick up speed before things changed for the worse?

'OK,' soothed Hank. He explained that we had caught some tide or other which boded all for the good. 'Keep that bucket swinging.' Savage breakers plunged up and down to left and right. We kept to the strip that swept between and through. The cold, greasy-looking water had eddies evil enough to send us broadside into all the frenzy on either side if we lost momentum.

Sucking sounds along the gunwhale! Everyone looked. Whirlpools as big as windsocks were opening up, like massive bath tubs draining. One – luckily – to the side looked big enough to have us spiralling down its funnel like a Wall of Death rider out of petrol.

They popped up in all directions, similar to the craters which appear in a pan of simmering porridge. 'Keep going!' I found myself urging the weighty old hulk, 'Don't stop now.' That to the wind. The mountains of Knoydart reeled past like a slow-motion film. Behind, the rubber boat was in tow like a leaf on a pond, occasionally disappearing into one of the vortices for a second or two. I gazed at the cinema screen. Watching the dinghy was too suggestive of what might happen to us.

How did *Blow the Wind Southerly* go? Except, I realized, we were going in a northerly direction. I whistled a few bars anyway (I know – a sign of nerves). And THUNK: something flew past to stick quivering in the telegraph pole of a mast. A sheath knife, still loosely connected to Hank's fingers. 'Whistling' he said. 'Oh-uh!' I asked why and he replied that ancient mariners whistled to raise a wind but knew they were summoning dark powers and took a risk. They might whistle up a storm instead. To appease the gods they offered iron if whistling *was* necessary, hence the knife in the mast.

Good thinking, I felt. Sitting on top of those billions of tons of water, squeezing between the land masses of Skye and Knoydart, gave you a let-well-alone feeling all right. The silence was uncanny. We might have been riding the surge of a mighty reservoir which had burst its dam, now pouring through to swallow the plains and cities below.

I felt the others were urging the cutter on too. Lips moved. Nothing was said. The wind kept pressing us on. Then grins began to come – relieved ones. Hank leaned across and retrieved his knife. 'Don't do it again,' he said. We were round the top part of Knoydart and, still keeping near the coast, entering Loch Hourn. Safer now.

The reflection of the boat rode alongside on the water; houses across the water near Glenelg looked close enough to touch. Yet there was no feeling of anti-climax. The place was too serious to say it had been easy. Towering above into the mist, the bulk of Ladhar Bheinn brooded over our entry into the waters it guarded so massively.

That night a west wind blew over Barrisdale. The sea grew wild, and then an incredible sound could be heard through the tent walls. A moaning like the sound of a large piece of wood containing a number of holes might make, when swung around the head of a giant on a length of rope. It was a noise from distant, fathomless dreams of when the

Ladhar Bheinn from near the jetty at Kinloch Hourn.

sea and mountains met, and heard repeatedly in the past, only it didn't quite bother me now. Well, not quite as much.

All in all, I decided, I would walk. I had no more a love of deep water than the writer of that magazine article. Even though I was sure the boatman I hired would be a different proposition from Hank and his merry crew and that his boat might improve on the primitiveness of a dipping lug cutter, the Sound of Sleat would still be the Sound of Sleat, a wild piece of racing sea, given wild weather, to the end.

Distracted, I saw people had come into the bar. Locals by the sound of them. 'Aye, we just came in for the war-r-r-m,' said one rubbing his hands in front of the empty grate. Shivering, I drained my pint glass and left. Next morning – after a tortuous drive around by Laggan Lochs and a hilarious evening in the remote angler's hotel at Tomdoun where it had been

the landlord's birthday and there had been a Kiss-o-Gram girl, a cuckoo's repeated call woke me in my sleeping-bag on the shore at Kinloch Hourn.

I had a headache and the sun was blindingly bright. Everywhere mountains stood pin-sharp against the pale blue sky and the scent of herbs and flowers and seawood was a pungent reminder to be up and on my way before the clouds rolled in and blocked this wonderful day.

Ladhar Bheinn (pronounced Lavenn and a name sounding so like Blaven you may find people bemusedly asking about Clach Glas as you recount your experience on the Hill) is the skyline traverse I completed for this book, which left the biggest impression. I use the word 'bemusedly' because Ladhar Bheinn is not a mountain generally well known like Tryfan, Great Gable or Blaven, but everyone I have met who has visited this wonderful mountain has been impressed with its charisma,

The impressive height of Ladhar Bheinn across Coire Dhorrcail from a point below Stob a'Chearcaill.

especially when the ridge around Coire Dhorrcail is taken. This route over Stob a'Chearcaill, Ladhar Bheinn itself, Stob a'Choire Odhair and back down across the mouth of Coire Dhorrcail to finish from where you began, is not only magnified in shape and aspect by the keenness of the climbing involved, but Ladhar Bheinn's inaccessibility on the fringes of Knoydart is part of its attraction. Also, given a chance, the views are stupendous.

Those mountaineers who have a free-ranging spirit of adventure, like Eric Shipton and Bill Tillman, will always prefer an approach by sea. The Western seaboard gives a wild sense of exploration; Knoydart feels a different place when reached by a canoe, say, across the steely waters of Loch Hourn. Even that huge boat, the Royal yacht *Britannia* takes in this sea loch during visits to the Western Isles. Ladhar Bheinn's finest aspects are after all its northern ones, and no more so than when viewed from the deck of a boat in Loch Hourn.

Yet I was glad that morning that I had not sailed. The walk I was to take along the shore to Barrisdale (and

which was signposted somewhat humorously I was to discover, 'Barrisdale six miles') must be one of the finest in the world for beauty and solitude. This is Gavin Maxwell country, the author living, I had been told, across the water by Sandbeg Bay during much of his most creative writing. The association of ideas became too much for my aching head. *Ring of Bright Water* became Ring of the Nibelungs and the hammering increased, blacksmiths pounding away within my skull as I walked along the shores of the loch.

The pressure of not only taking advantage of this superb morning almost too good, you felt, to last and bound to cloud over, with the summit of Ladhar Bheinn peeping just around the breast of the hillside — but also of tackling the Glen Rosa horseshoe in faraway Arran the following day, weighed heavily on me. Yet wasn't I expecting too much? not only from the weather but from the demands on my ageing body (not to mention the clapped-out Mini)? It would mean that I would have to return to Kinloch Hourn that evening and then drive south.

It took just over two hours to reach

Barrisdale Bay, with Ladhar Bheinn now prominent, rising sheer out of the sea and still unconcealed by the cloud I was sure must suddenly roll down from its lofty heights. The further I progressed along this wonderland of a path — one moment over sand and seaweed as the path skirts the edge of the loch, the next through rhododendrons and heather and gorse and before it climbs upwards only then to descend once again to where an ancient Scots pine laces the path with huge gnarled roots — the more excited I became, almost breaking into a run several times as the sight of the mirror image of the mountains on the far side of the loch shone in the limpid water.

The morning had cleared my head. By the time I arrived at the bothy in Barrisdale, manned by a couple from Sheffield at the croft next door and selling goat's milk and bags of coal, I settled for a carton of the milk as a prudent measure to keep up my reserves. But really I wanted to be going.

Setting off across the saltings with Ladhar Bheinn's crenellated ridge outstanding behind, and with only the whitest of puffs of cloud set in the sky, the climb began abruptly from the flats, zigzagging to the shoulder of Creag Bheithe and offering the most fantastic views into the heart of Coire Dhorrcail with its boulder-strewn floor and granite headwall soaring almost 1,000ft above to the summit of Ladhar Bheinn, still streaked with snow.

It was from a level stretch of the grassy ridge, now tapering ahead, that I now saw the steep buttress of Stob a Chearcaill rearing upwards into the sky like the back of a bucking bronco.

To set foot on this wicked edge was my best moment of all the skylines in this book. It was thrilling, to say the least. With my back to Loch Hourn, as indeed it has been during the approach towards this point, and nothing but near-vertical walls and slabs of rock ahead, stacked high in tiers and with only the slimmest of grass ledges periodically breaking the verticality of the scene, it was an unusually daunting prospect. Not only did the climbing require careful route finding, where I would scale a steep groove or slab to arrive awkwardly on the ledge above – only to find then that that ledge was so narrow it would only just accommodate my body and without any space in which to turn around and sit down and take a breather – every moment on the climb was quite fraught.

It was along the ledges that you had to decide whether to go left or right to try the next lines of possible weakness above, and there was ample opportunity to become spreadeagled against the rock face unable to move upwards or down. There was one such place, a steep groove up overhanging rock requiring my fingers to crimp on small holds and the soles of my trainers to smear on the merest rugosities, which would have been difficult to down climb safely had I subsequently failed above. Nor did the angle relent. With every upwards step you took nearer the top, you knew only too well you were now one step further from the ground.

Although there is an easier route to the summit of Stob a' Chearcaill by traversing round to the southeast for a short way before continuing upwards, those who relish the feeling of space and excitement will be unable to ignore the challenge of its sensational crest. For Stob a'Chearcaill has moments that can be likened to the experience of those Dartmouth naval cadets who had once a week, to climb over the mast of a sailing ship by the rigging. And, who, after climbing the rigging until the deck of the ship below had shrunk to the size of a ruler, were then obliged to go up to the masthead, a bare pole about 6ft high, and sit on top.

Why Ladhar Bheinn left such a strong impression on me, however, was not because of the excellence of the climb up Stob a'Chearcaill. Rather, it was

because the subsequent ascent of Ladhar Bheinn by the connecting ridge, and down, was anything but an anticlimax. Indeed the traverse of the cirque of Coire Dhorrcail became even better as my heartbeat settled down once more, and I walked along the tops as though in a daze, after such a beautiful and satisfying climb.

To my delight, the weather was still holding as I continued first south-west, then north-west, to begin to round the head of the corrie far below to my right. Everywhere you looked, the ranges of hills and seascapes clicked into focus. Skye's Cuillin Ridge across the Sound of Sleat appeared as though it was a cardboard cut-out, while in the other direction, the view back down the length of Loch Hourn, evoked the vastness of the Highlands.

Rugged outcrops abounded on the ridge ahead after dropping into the Bealach Coire Dhorrcail, then climbing out on the steepening incline to the summit of Ladhar Bheinn itself. This succession of buttresses barring the way like citadels break the monotony of the ascent and offer an entertaining choice of scrambling, especially as the ridge is of that kind where you perpetually estimate that the summit is that next high point ahead, only to have it revealed that it is nothing of the kind, and that the summit is still several hundred feet further on, a summit incidentally from where the views excelled anything I had seen in Britain.

A small summit is Ladhar Bheinn's, entrancing to climb on to and equally bittersweet to abandon as you take your leave of the final view of those descending tiers of the ridge that you have climbed, and now face new ones which you are about to descend, down the mighty north-east ridge until you top-out on Stob a Choire Odhair where you drop on down some way further still until, finally, you reach a flattening in the crest and are able at last to

descend without further trouble into Coire Dhorrcail. Here, after crossing to the slopes on the far side way below Stob a'Chearcaill, you can pick up the stalker's path that cuts across the hillside, rounds the breast of the ridge you previously ascended and brings you back to Barrisdale.

As happens after such a glorious day, something occurred that brought me back to earth. I suffered a put-down to which – slow thinker as I am – I would normally have been unable to respond. But I must confess I did think of something that day. Ladhar Bheinn, the Peak of the Hoof (or the Claw), which according to some has a semi-evil presence where people have experienced unsettling moments of a para-psychic nature, finally brought out the old devil in me. It happened just as I was sitting tiredly by the bothy, having tipped the few contents of my sack out on the grass to prepare for that long walk back to Kinloch Hourn (albeit by 'one of the finest in the world').

Two middle-aged walkers just finishing their day approached from the saltings, glancing pointedly at my scarlet long-johns, fell-running shoes and lightweight top – the gear proven by fell runners for mountains large and small.

'Just got out of bed?' enquired the one in moleskin breeches, tartan woollen shirt and big leather boots with sturdy vibram soles. 'Actually,' I said, without losing my temper or relapsing into a sulk, 'I've been on the Hill'. 'Oh, yes?' enquired my oppressor, 'which hill would that be?' 'Just the ridge,' I said, 'The Big Ridge.' 'Ah, but which ridge?' he replied, 'The one we've just done? The traverse of Luinne Bheinn? Followed by Meall Buidhe as well'. But I'm afraid I heard myself cut him short, and without even mentioning the glory of Stob a'Chearcaill's superb edge, 'There's only the one of them, isn't there?' I asked.

Chapter 26
THE SOUTH CLUANIE RIDGE

On the South Cluanie Ridge I encountered the most incandescent mountain I have ever seen, and also a group of gentlemen calling themselves the 'Brigadier', the 'Adjutant', the 'Captain' and the 'Corporal'. From one extreme to the other in the same day, this was surely a case of going from the sublime to the ridiculous, and I accept there is nobody more ridiculous than myself given a chance. If I relate what happened on that day on the South Cluanie Ridge, you will understand.

Perhaps it was the quality of the light that made our celestial peak shine forth or simply the fact that it was during May when the Highlands are deservedly reputed to be seen at their best, but that particular day, along the skyline walk that started from the Cluanie Inn – a lonely outpost above the wild recesses of Glen Shiel which travellers to Skye must breach when main-road motoring from the south (the Road to the Isles, in fact) – I knew that this scene was unique.

The vision was in fact the mountain of Sgurr an Lochain, the penultimate peak along a ridge traversing the crest of the southern wall of Kintail in a westerly direction and incorporating the wonderful heights of Creag a'Mhaim, Anoach Air Crith, Sgurr Coire na Feinne and Sgurr an Doire Leathain. Sgurr an Lochain is the next peak on and there is one more beyond that, Creag nan Damh. But it was the glory of Sgurr an Lochain, faceted and sculpted in ice and snow and with

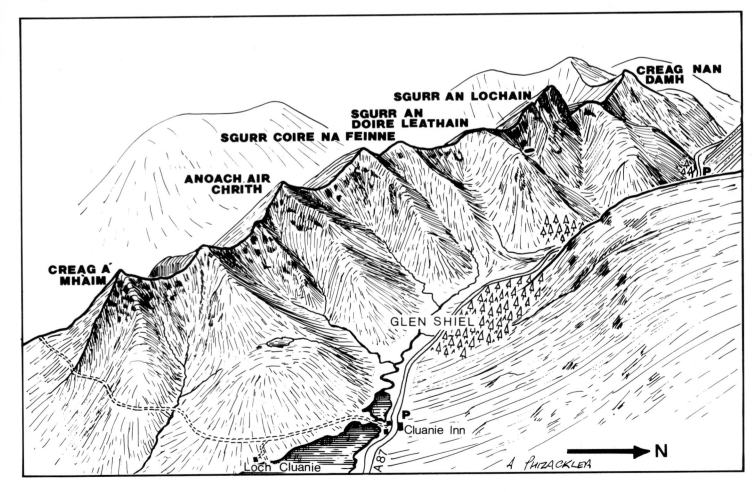

Cornices and sunshine grace the matchless heights of Sgurr an Lochain.

golden light gleaming from its snow-fields and cornices, that held the five of us on the ridge, during that moment, entranced by its dazzling perfection.

Much as I tried to do it justice with my camera, the resulting frames of Sgurr an Lochain can only hint at how breathtakingly it actually looked on a bleak and gale-torn afternoon when the temperature verged on zero and snow devils whirled their shimmering veils in an endless dance along the ridge.

The South Cluanie Ridge is no less perfect than was that one particular peak. Celebrated for the fact that it is a relatively straightforward route by which to link seven Munros in one fell swoop, during which you descend below 3,000ft at only one point, it runs an

enchanted course over the most rugged of Highlands terrain. Across Glen Shiel to the north soars the magnificence of the Five Sisters of Kintail. Ahead, the further you progress, looms the Saddle with its knife-edged Forcan Ridge predominant in the distance. While far away to the south-west, yet so huge it makes its impact, towers the bulk of Ladhar Bheinn. However, these are individual peaks, typical only of a plethora of other leviathans of the Scottish Highlands, rising above a mass of sky-line ridges stretching out as far as the eye can see, with an effect that is staggering.

Some 13 miles in length, the South Cluanie Ridge will take you, say, eight to ten hours to complete, depending on conditions, both of the weather and

your party. As I discovered when I traversed it, expecting only to go half-way along its crest because I was on my own and had no car waiting at the far end.

Imagine my surprise when, having gained the start of the ridge (well, virtually the start) by climbing direct to the saddle between Creag a'Mhaim and Druim Shionnach, I happened to glance behind and saw four middle-aged gentlemen following my footsteps up the steep ice-field I had just ascended.

Counting myself, that made five middle-aged gentlemen now present. However, I at least had had climbing experience, whereas looking now at their combined ascent which was not unlike an illustration from the pages of *Rum Doodle,* it was clear that these gentlemen certainly had not. There was not an ice-axe in sight and purchase on the gleaming ice was instead maintained by hooking their fingers into the imprints left by the toes of my plastic winter boots (but so hard was the ice that these were only the tiniest of imprints, and as insubstantial as if I had repeatedly pressed my denture plate into the frozen snow in lieu of anything better, especially as I had no ice-axe either). Then again, two of the team were showing decided signs of strain. That condition, not unknown among climbers, described as 'Disco Leg' – when the legs begin to tremble and twitch involuntarily, being further galvanized by the high-voltage situation of the impending drop – was all too evident. In addition, two of the group had removed their mittens and even from several feet away I could see their hands were blue with cold and trembling.

A rope, I thought, anything for a

Cascades prelude the walk into Coire an Eich Bhric towards the South Cluanie Ridge beyond.

The Captain on the corniced ridge between Craig a'Mhaim and Druim Shionnach.

rope that I can drop with a loop tied at the end to help them. So alarming was this prospect of wobbling bodies and muffled thumps of repeatedly misdirected boots on the iron hard slope, I found I could not bear to look.

What I had not taken into account was that what these four gentlemen lacked in skill and experience, they certainly made up for in nerve and bare-fingered effrontery. There was a sound of gasping and the occasional nervous trill of a few bars of music whistled as, at last, one after the other they pulled through the final bulging wall of wind-blasted snow that threaded its way between the cornices on to the ridge, eyes bulging and chests heaving.

'Quite a good approach, that,' said the one who, like the Nawab of Pataudi, had only one eye, and the kind of panache you could imagine from someone who still faced the quickest of fast bowlers. 'Thank you. We just did not know which way to go. So we followed you.'

It was true that I had never looked behind. I had set out by taking the old road from Cluanie to Tomdoun from near the Cluanie Inn, then transferred on to the stalker's path across the untamed slopes of Creag a'Mhaim, trying

to avoid the actual peak and instead making a bee-line for the first col in the skyline between the mountain and the remaining crest of the South Cluanie Ridge, reaching out westwards as far as the eye could see. Although this was the easiest approach in my view, the snows of winter remained, adorning the very rim of the ridge for miles with huge cornices, curling like ice-cream spilling over the edge of a cornet and concentrating my attention wonderfully as to how I would at some point break through them and reach the ridge. The idea of glancing behind to see if anyone else was following had never entered my head.

Climber & Hillwalker magazine printed a letter about that time:

Sir,
I am writing to ask if what I am about to relate is unique, or whether there are other ramblers who do the same as we do. We are a gathering of twelve middle-aged men who meet once a year for a weekend in the hills. We started walking in 1960 and have continued to meet annually for the last thirty years . . .

If this quartet I have just mentioned were any indication then, no, they were

THE SOUTH CLUANIE RIDGE · 131

not unique at all. There are probably dozens and dozens of similar groups of men and women enjoying such annual outings, and I had just met a perfect example. The writer of the letter mentioned the members of his group were analytical chemists who started work for the same laboratory in Birmingham. In the case of my newly found friends, however, they had more varied jobs, but met just once a year in the Highlands for ten days of undiluted hilltop climbing, attempting to tick off the Munros with vast enthusiasm.

The Brigadier, the Adjutant, the Captain and the Corporal were the names by which they called themselves. They were from the Midlands and, they said, glad to have met me. They were not climbers, but would I care to walk the South Cluanie ridge with them? As they had a car waiting below the final peak, would I indeed!

Being avid Munroists they insisted we did something I could happily have done without: climb to the very same summit of Creag a'Mhaim at the eastern end of the ridge (which I had been trying to avoid on the theory that as it was the end peak of a ridge which had miles and miles of exquisite skyline to go in the other direction, I would forgo its experience). This ascent and descent achieved, and having returned to the place from where our footsteps could be seen arriving on the ridge through the cornices below, we then began the ridge in earnest.

Led at the front by the driving force of the Captain, he of the black eye-patch and holder of a market stall selling curtain material in Newcastle-under-Lyme, we made steady progress along this magnificent ridge. Peak after peak unfurled itself in the distance ahead as we steadily gained ground above the innumerable corries and two great glens below on either side.

Linear skylines like the South Cluanie Ridge unfold the prospects of their furthest peaks only gradually as you progress along the crest, moving up and down from one summit along the way to the next. Unlike a horseshoe where the opposite arm of the round or cirque offers views of the most distant peaks every time you glance sideways across the intervening valley, a ruler-edge ridge is a more mysterious undertaking as you have no hint of what exactly lies beyond the immediate peak ahead.

It was a mystery to me how the foursome ahead could be so fit. Yet for men who did virtually no hillwalking other than this annual bash, they forged on, the Brigadier (grain merchant) and Adjutant (pharmaceutical chemist) forming a link between the Captain at the front and the Corporal (another grain merchant) who kept up the rear. With me, meanwhile, further behind still, camera in hand, and trying to frame the four of them in the viewfinder through the whirling spindrift. Although, to be honest, when I mentioned this to the Corporal, he laughed in the teeth of the gale. 'Fit? Fit to bloody drop, you mean.' He actually was the one who might be termed the weak link, for he was heavier and somewhat stiffer in his movements, yet his cheerful irreverence and total gutsiness, even with his 'tootsies' aching in the unaccustomed confinement of his rarely used boots, was the kind of stuff I envied.

From the beginning, the corniced splendour of the north side of the ridge, overlooking a series of splendidly rugged corries above Glen Shiel was never ending, apart from occasional breaks where the weight of snow had sent countless tons hurtling into the corries below. Yet the walk along the surface snow immediately to the left of the cornice gave perfect going as we twisted and turned along the meanderings — and occasionally the narrowings – of the crest. However, such was the power of the wind and the amount of snow on the ridge that the scene it presented was midwinter, with the teeth of the wind ripping the frozen surface of the neve into snaking, curling tendrils, while down in the corries below poured spindrift avalanches in great cataracts, falling past slabs and walls until the powerful, persistent wind penetrated and dispersed the mass, whirling it skywards into the path of the next wave.

The shapely summit of Anoach Air Chrith was the first distant objective,

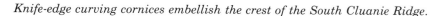

Knife-edge curving cornices embellish the crest of the South Cluanie Ridge.

The corniced splendour of the South Cluanie Ridge in May.

and the limit of our vision. Beyond that, it was a case of 'Something hidden. Go and find it. Go and look behind the Ranges. Lost and waiting for you. Go!' And very Kipling was the scene, too, with the mountain aspect every bit as desolate and barbarous as any of the mountain fastnesses or foothills of the Himalayas that he describes.

Yet unlike skylines such as Sgurr nan Gillean or the Round of Coire Lagan, which are complex crests with a premium on route finding in the most hostile of terrain, here was scenery of the most savage grandeur, but the walking was uncomplicated, a mono-rail of a route through the sky.

The route skirted the cornices for much of the day, though we would swing across the gentler slopes to the left occasionally, especially during the climbs up the undulations of the sky-

line. If Anoach Air Chrith was just such an undulation, the others followed in as serious a vein. All were Munros, and all above an altitude which in inclement weather conditions could be lethal, and most of them involving an ascent from a height of at least 3,000ft and a descent that left you equally exposed at another dip in the ridge, also above 3,000ft.

Beyond Anoach Air Chrith, the tight-rope of the ride curves down before sweeping on up Sgurr Coire na Feinne, followed by a shorter swoop down and then up again on to Sgurr an Doire Leathain. Below the cornice, sometimes now absent but always recontinuing in the distances, the succession of corries passed above Glen Shiel, adjoining amphitheatres remote and isolated. It was from here that the view I first mentioned – that cata-

clysmic view of Sgurr an Lochain – shone ahead.

Had I, as originally planned, only gone midway along the South Cluanie Ridge, I would have missed this glorious moment. Breathing my thanks, I took the photographs knowing I could only do scant justice to the splendour of the scene as we continued on slowly to the top of the next peak. And then, forgoing the last Munro of the ridge, Creag nan Damh, as time was running out, we descended from the peak that preceded it – Sgurr Beag (which as its name suggests is not a Munro) – down a wide, grassy, though steep, northerly spur between the crags, into the valley below. After crossing a gully, we took a footbridge across the river and arrived at the car-park beneath the start to the Five Sisters of Kintail, which is another story entirely.

Chapter 27
THE FIVE SISTERS OF KINTAIL

Franz Schubert, the car radio informed me – as I cranked up the laces of my plastic winter boots in readiness for the Five Sisters of Kintail – had written his most sublime piece of music when depressed, suffering from the advanced stages of syphilis and penniless. I almost said 'I know the feeling', though as far as I knew I did not have syphilis.

The previous evening in the pub near the Eilean Donan castle, a man had sold me a car battery for a fiver. Befuddled and trying to fit it, I had found its terminals were the wrong size. In desperation I forced the jaws of the electrical leads wide open and hammered them on with my Chacal hammer. As I connected the second one, a tingling up the metal shaft of the ice axe and

the resulting blaze of flashes like St Elmo's fire adorned my body and head, enabling me to cut a figure not unlike Frankenstein's monster rising off the slab. In the resulting confusion I split my thumb open with the hammer head of the axe and banged my head on the boot of the mini, bringing tears of pain, frustration and rage to my eyes. When I switched on my motor there was a

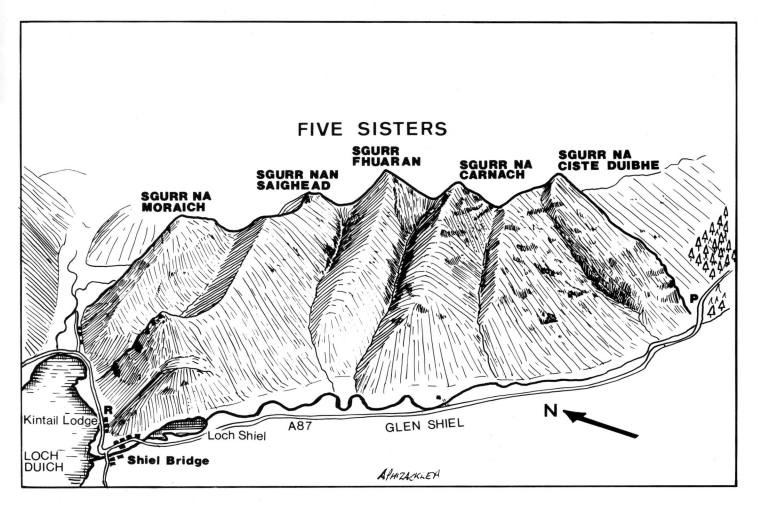

Sgurr Fhuaran, the dominant central peak of the Five Sisters of Kintail.

silhouette across the wild horizons of Wester Ross.

In a similar way that the summits of the Aonach Eagach ridge border the northern side of the road through Glencoe, and Liathach flanks the road through Glen Torridon, so the Five Sisters accompany several miles of the A87 through Glen Shiel, offering those who take the Road to the Isles an immediate presence of large mountains.

Indeed they are massive hills. The north-facing flanks of Sgurr Fhuaran are among the longest continuous slopes of unbroken steepness in Scotland and in general these Glen Shiel slopes sweep up at a uniform incline for as much as 3,500ft in little more than a mile. They demand to be taken seriously, although they are not regarded as unduly difficult.

This is what was on my mind as I switched off the piano quintet, written under such duress and now issuing with similar difficulty from the one intermittently working speaker on the rear window shelf of my Mini. For what I was about to do was also to be under duress. I did not believe in embarking on a skyline of this magnitude at this time of day and in such uncertain weather conditions, but there were photographs to take, given a chance.

The hillside was so running with tiny streams that I had chosen to wear my plastic boots simply to keep dry feet, heavier though they were compared with my fell shoes, which were almost falling to pieces. I had accepted the commission for this book because I imagined taking the photographs would force me to visit places I might otherwise never see. How right I was! But there was so much on my mind I could not always appreciate them at the time.

Even starting up the hill from the lay-by near the Telford Bridge on the A87, and in the wide gap between the plantations, the sign of crossed swords signifying a battle (Glenshiel, 1719) indicated that nothing had changed.

click. A lorry driver told me the worst. I had attached the leads to the wrong terminals and blown the alternator. Alone and marooned in the Highlands, and with my resources at their last ebb, I had to pay £48 for a new one, consoled only by the fact that I had not also entirely wasted the day.

There had been mist, drizzle and humidity in Glen Shiel. It was only as the afternoon wore on that fitful gleams of sunlight broke across the sodden hills, spurring me on to take at least a look along the ridge above, which is so vaunted by mountaineers. This is a tremendous switchback experience, cresting the summits of Sgurr na Ciste Duibhe, Sgurr na Carnach, Sgurr Fhuaran, Sgurr nan Saighead and Sgurr na Moraich as they cut an insane

Though to compare the swish of the claymore and rattle of the musket with my own puny problems of fighting for every gallon of petrol and frame of film without waste will seem relatively puny. Yet there it was. As I clambered on and on up the steep and sponge-like track, the battle motif returned.

It had been, so I had been informed in the pub, a Jacobite Rebellion battle featuring Rob Roy himself and Spanish troops, allies of the Jacobites, who were pursued up the hillside in some disarray. About this time, Eilean Donan Castle, a show-piece of Glen Shiel and a pictorial favourite of chocolate box and calendar manufacturers, was reduced to a ruin by bombardment from Hanoverian ships. Still they battle in the glen, though now it is the shinty matches that bring out the warring instinct. 'Shinty!' you might say, 'Shinty!' Yet it's true.

'No game for taking prisoners,' said the car battery vendor as I studied the poster of a forthcoming event, *Kinlochshiel v. Glengarry* to be played at Kirton. He sipped his whisky and told me that shinty was *the* game in Kintail. 'Many shinty players are scarred for life, aye and there's the odd fatality too.'

I thought about it, finally reaching the ridge that had never seemed to arrive. The slopes had proved unduly convex, suggesting first that the skyline was imminent, only on reaching it for another skyline still to rise beyond and still another beyond that. From the Bealach an Lapain, a level grassy ridge, and with the road a thread in the depths of the glen, I could see only insurmountable problems ahead.

It might have been raining in the glen for several hours, but the ridge rising ahead to the west was starkly crusted with snow and etched with frost. The chill spare beauty of its crest was an awesome thing and something that immediately made the climber's heart skip a beat, with one hideous shortcoming. As might be expected from the gulf of Glen Shiel below where hills shrugged out of the mist and were gone again, and hill burns tore down in peaty torrents to become foaming cauldrons at the trackside, all this was an illusion.

The gloriously bleak and wintery skyline promising such exquisite going along a crisply frozen surface was unconsolidated. Every step you took sank deep into the snow. Sgurr nan Spainteach, the Peak of the Spaniards, which is the next peak on, and is not even counted as one of the Five Sisters, seemed endless. Its undulating ridge was fluted into a crest of fresh snow of extreme sharpness, vanishing into total oblivion as mist descended into the gloom of the late afternoon.

Reeling and ploughing through the soft snow, one thing kept me going: the mist would suddenly clear, the sun would shine. Beyond this Arctic wilderness peeped distant glimpses of Gulf Stream greenery in distant straths, bringing a vision of yellow gorse blooming under a Mediterranean-blue sky.

Beyond Sgurr nan Spainteach, I clambered down steeply into the col below. Sometimes my boots trod banks of snow supported by thin air and the descent deteriorated into a succession of wild slides down the great blossoming mounds of snow deposited at random and through which I crashed into the boulders below, frequently hurting myself in the process as I bruised my shins and banged my knees.

Next, I flailed wildly and forlornly up the final rocky slopes covered in a meringue of snow crystals to the summit of Sgurr na Ciste Duibhe and its large cairn. I was shattered, but could not rest. For at that moment great golden rods of sunlight pierced the skyline further west. Leaning against the cairn, I began to take photographs.

Taking on a project for money has always had its moments of despair, say climbers who have tried it. So I was writing a book . . . but sponsorship for expeditions also commits the climbers to achieving results. Visiting the Isle of Hoy in the Orkneys with Ed Ward Drummond and Oliver Hill for their proposed ascent of St John's Head, and sponsored by a newspaper, the darker side of sponsorship was really brought home to me when I was lowered as ballast on 1,200ft of rope.

This was the only way we could reach the base of the cliff so far below. The first grass ledge in fact was 600ft below the summit overhangs, over which I

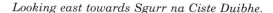

Looking east towards Sgurr na Ciste Duibhe.

Sgurr na Carnach and Sgurr na Fhuaran from the east.

was lowered into thin air like a spider on its thread. Long before I reached this ledge the wind kept spinning me round, twisting the two ropes like the rubber band in a model aeroplane. What I did not know was that the karabiners through which Oliver and Ed were lowering me had, by being used like pulleys, become so hot with the friction that the ropes – in this case Ulstron, as used by yachtsmen (and chosen for the job because it was cheap and the newspaper advance had not been unduly generous) – started to melt and come apart under my weight. I was blissfully ignorant of the fact that far above my two companions were reaching frantically for some dock leaves to squeeze their juice over the

scorching metal and to cool the situation – just.

This memory returned with renewed vigour as I stood in fading daylight on the summit of Sgurr Fhuaran. The way here from Sgurr na Ciste Duibhe had been more straightforward, the snow along the ridge, first to Sgurr Carnach, becoming more consolidated. Then I followed the descent down its steep north slopes until the south face of Sgurr Fhuaran had loomed above, the highest peak of the Five Sisters. By the time I reached the top I was spent. I had run out of film and, personally, was running on empty.

The remaining skyline above the tops of Sgurr nan Saighead and Sgurr na

Moraich, beckoned in the distance. I left them to it – beckoning. The picture of Drummond and Hill, both friendly but wary young men, crushing dock leaves to save my life which hung quite literally by a thread swam into focus as I began to descend the great north-west ridge to Loch Duich in the gathering twilight. The skyline 'not regarded as unduly difficult' had proved too much for me in my state of health. However, I had no intention of going to the extremes of killing myself, something the climber in these most gorgeous of environments – the wild high skylines of our mountains – can so easily do. I know only because I came so close to it myself that day on the Hill overlooking wildest Kintail.

Chapter 28

THE SADDLE OF GLEN SHIEL BY THE FORCAN RIDGE

The Forcan Ridge can — as climbers will tell you its name suggests when placed before the words 'well shattered' — leave you feeling pretty fragile. So too, for that matter, can severing the rope down which you are about to abseil with a penknife. Yet this is in effect what happened when I attempted the Saddle of Glen Shiel by its equally formidable Forcan Ridge. As if that was not bad enough, my day had already been spoilt by the unaccountable behaviour of the Briadier, the Captain and the Adjutant, three of the quartet I met the day before, who now gave the distinct impression that they considered me a madman, and someone to be avoided at all costs.

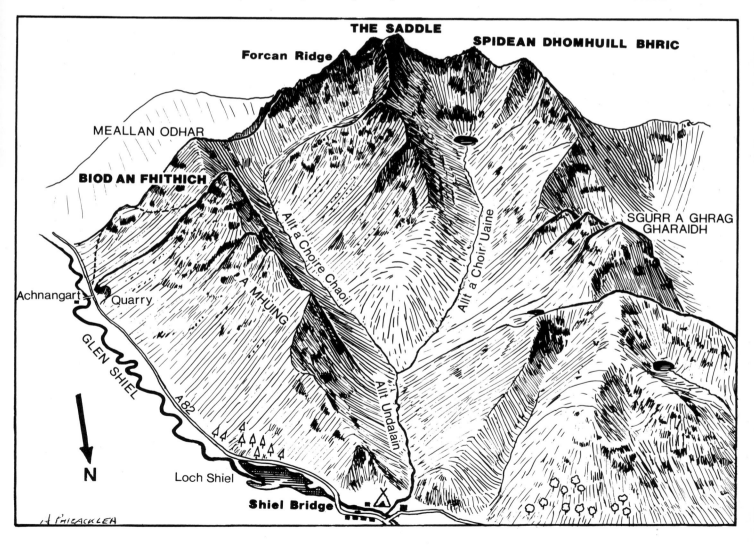

Let us cut to a TV studio in the centre of New York. A chat show is being filmed live, with a famous host, celebrated guests from show business on the sofa, and myself – on a publisher's book tour – about to demonstrate a technique from a book on survival that I had written.

Climbers silhouetted on the crest of the Forcan Ridge with the Saddle beyond.

The subject under discussion is how to escape from a skyscraper window 100m(328ft) above the sidewalk in the event of fire. All you have for assistance is a 50m(164ft) rope. To demonstrate, I tied one end of this to a simulated window a few feet above the stage, stressing the trick was not just to slide down to the end of the rope, but to be able to pull the rope down after you once you have reached the safety of a ledge, because you would need its help again to lower yourself the further 50m to the ground. The question being, since the rope was tied securely at the top to the window, how *did* you pull it down after you?

There would be no vertical drop as such in front of the cameras. It was to be a simulated experience with yours truly standing on a chair, clipping on to the abseil rope hanging from the 'window'. The chair would then be removed, and although I was only a couple of feet from the floor people would get the message when they saw the knife. I had been shown by the Floor Manager how to turn the blade just so and make it gleam in the studio lights, so increasing the sense of drama to the studio audience and eighty million viewers across the USA.

But in this instance the knife would be used for a technique so rare and in fact bizarre, that in nearly forty years of rock climbing I have never seen it put into operation. If you were normally going to abseil down 50m of rock face, you would tie two ropes together and abseil down their twin lines, using them hung over some projection (or threaded through a piton, say) which would take your weight. Then, on reaching the safety of a ledge below, you pull one end of the rope and hope it will run so that you can haul it all through. The only application of the esoteric technique I was about to demonstrate would be in a survival situation with only a single rope for your assistance. Which brings us back to the television studio in Manhattan.

The secret of retrieving the rope in this unusual circumstance, then, once you have abseiled down the first 50m from the window is to have first attached it to the window (or whatever) with a 'sheepshank', i.e. a three-stranded knot used by sailors for shortening ropes. The three strands in fact are the accumulation of taking up the slack, and the middle strand is non-load bearing and useless. While it serves no purpose whatsoever, the remaining two strands take any weight applied.

So . . . if you were to cut the useless middle strand with a knife, once your weight is hanging on the rope and providing you maintain steady tension on the knot as you abseil then that severed sheepshank will still support you as you slide down the rope to the bottom. It is just at the moment you release the rope from your person (attached by a device called a 'descender'), the knot will collapse and your rope will snake down – a few inches shorter but still quite serviceable for any longer abseil subsequently awaiting you below.

Taking the strain then, I assumed the abseiling position, ready to begin sliding down the rope and supported by the descender clipped to my climbing harness. The chair was removed from beneath me and leaning back out into space I braced myself, feet pushing against the wall. The knife flashed as I held it poised. A drum roll broke the silence. I cut the rope.

Unfortunately, in the heat of the moment – not to mention the studio lights – I severed the wrong strand, one of the two load-bearing ones. Within a flash the knot disintegrated and I was catapulted head first across the stage faster than a SAM missile to strike my head on the grand piano on which Stevie Wonder was to play later during the show.

This, unlikely though it may seem, is in effect what happened during my ascent of the Forcan Ridge where a gash in the skyline necessitates an

The ramparts of the Forcan Ridge.

abseil in icy weather. But I had not realized this on setting off that wonderful morning and, as happened on Blaven and Beinn Eighe, I should have done more homework. Because of this a situation developed as a result that became quite fraught.

First let me tell you what had happened previously that beautiful May morning in the Scottish Highlands – a morning so balmy, and with the cuckoo calling, you would not have believed that the previous day we had been battered incessantly by gales along the South Cluanie Ridge.

This glorious morning when I hoped to photograph the Forcan Ridge was only marred at the beginning by the strange behaviour of my three newfound friends. Not only did I get the distinct impression that they considered me a raving lunatic but that they were intent on avoiding me at all costs.

We had made a somewhat flexitime arrangement in the pub the previous evening following our traverse of the South Cluanie Ridge that same day. We would do the Forcan Ridge and, striking while the iron was hot, we would do it after we'd all had a good night's sleep. However, when I reached the car-park in Shiel Bridge the following morning as agreed, there was nobody there. I started up the Saddle alone.

Driving south through Glen Shiel on the A87 and passing the quarry, which flanks both sides of the road, at Achnangart, I reached a parking place from where a stalker's path climbs westwards across an expanse of inhospitable terrain to the col between Biod an Fhithich and Meallan Odhar. It was in the sudden movement of something higher on the mountain, that I recognized my friends of the day before, now matchstick men in bobble hats.

When I realized that the three dots approaching the skyline above were the Brigadier & Co, I shouted my head off from the stalker's path below. But although they hesitated, they began to resume their former speed with all the agility of chamois or seasoned climbers.

Having already accompanied them on the hill, I knew this was not the case, knew without a doubt that they were likely to be aching and sore – like myself – and was in fact surprised to see them so high on the mountain so early. Yet on reflection their burning desire to tick off certain great classic peaks had shone through in our conversation, a recurrent theme being how they had always set their sights on the Forcan Ridge but had previously felt it would be too serious an undertaking. Was that it then? That they were so psyched up to finally climbing the Forcan Ridge that they had developed tunnel vision and quite forgotten about me? Or was it really to avoid me after all?

Quite paranoid at the best of times, my heart sank a little as the ant-like figures crested the skyline and vanished without so much as a wave around a breast of hillside. I knew they would have to slow down when they reached the razor's edge of the Forcan Ridge still hidden some way above, and so I picked up speed to soothe my ruffled feelings. Maybe they *hadn't* seen me.

When I too reached that distant col and looked up, they were just about to disappear around the next bulwark of mountainside beyond and directly below the Forcan Ridge. The faster I ran along the grassy ridge that leads southwards from the col towards the summit of Meallan Odhar, before then veering south-west along a path below and avoiding the very top, the less good it did me. And the more I shouted like the demon of energy I had suddenly become, the quicker they were gone, possibly more convinced than ever that speed was of the essence.

I had moved quickly, that day, thanks to travelling light. I wore fell-running trainers, longjohns, a thermal vest and a yellow T-shirt (though my tracksuit suit bottoms and Ice Warrior jacket were stuffed in reserve in my day sack, should the temperature drop). This is an outfit which will lend you speed on the hills as well as some odd looks from the majority of more traditionally clothed hillwalkers to be found in the Highlands. Indeed, the Brigadier, a man rather acerbic in his manner and looking curiously at my battered pair of Raids shoes and the large flowered patch with which a girlfriend had repaired the seat of my scarlet thermal longjohns was to say, 'The thing is, those things obviously work, I will admit that.'

Despite my relative fleetness of foot and that fact that I was accustomed to mountains, the once-a-year boys from the Midlands were still leading me by a considerable distance. Were these *really* the same team that had progressed, like me, so surely but so slowly along the Cluanie Ridge the day before, albeit battered by gales and snowy squalls?

On the path that cut across below the summit of Meallan Odhar – with splendid views across towards the waterfalls of Choire Chaoil – my friends were nowhere to be seen. Not even in the vicinity of the rugged slopes below the east ridge of The Saddle, the Forcan Ridge itself, now brandishing itself above like a claymore, the blade of this great two-fisted fighting sword slimming appreciably towards the summit of Sgurr Forcan above. I could only conclude that I would never catch them now so determined were they to keep ahead.

Passing beneath the Forcan Ridge, then, I followed the path upwards through the col to find myself approaching the slenderness of the magnificent crest from its left-hand flanks. It is an exposed and airy sight, and as I

gazed upwards in awe I spotted my friends again. By now they were overhead, scrambling up the sharp arête like monkeys. 'Hang on!' I yelled, my insecurities raging, 'Yo! It's me, Tony.' Did they pause? And was that a distant shout? If so, it was unintelligible. Certainly they did not stop long but seemed to increase speed yet again, now precipitating small rock falls which crashed booming down into the depths of Choire Chaoil in their haste to get away. Or were they trundling the rocks at me in the hopes of scoring a direct hit and finishing me off? I stopped myself short. *That* was paranoia. But I still kept a weather-eye open, ensuring I was not in the firing line should the battery increase as a great block sped past a few feet to my right, impinging on the lower crags at such a velocity that sparks flew and there was the acrid smell of gunpowder in the air.

Renewing my efforts to catch up, I finally began the Forcan Ridge itself. Awkward climbing led up a steep groove in the rock and brought me to the crest. Above this there were diversions, left and right, that avoided any difficult bits unless I felt like tackling them direct. Remembering my dismal showing on the Aonach Eagach, I was chary. My trainers were soggy from snow that had freshly fallen overnight and which covered the holds and ledges to some depth.

On the South Cluanie Ridge I had worn Koflach Ultras on my feet, and also my track-suit bottoms and Ice Warrior jacket to withstand the weather. However, this following morning on the Forcan Ridge, everything in the distant valley was green, although the temperature was starting to bite. I began to feel incongruous amongst the snow in my skimpy clothing, yet I was still warm, and this *was* after all fell-running gear; the kind of thing fell-runners in winter would be wearing, so long as they kept on the move.

A fang of granite surrounded by the teeth of upthrusting mountains close by on every side, the Forcan Ridge is

The Captain helps the Adjutant down the crux of the Forcan Ridge – the Gap which appears in the ridge without warning.

municate. So my new-found friends were not ashamed to be seen with me after all, or my rather radical clothing on mountains or perhaps my tiresome manic over-exuberence at times punctuated by periods of dour silence or such a faraway look that occasionally people would pass a hand in front of my eyes and enquire whether I was still there. We greeted each other with camaraderie (the Corporal was confined to the bar as a result of blistered feet).

By now the feeling of exposure was considerable, and the summit of the mountain was drawing near. The sharp peak of The Saddle beckoned just ahead. Everything seemed to be over, bar the shouting. There had been plenty of that, I thought, not knowing that what had gone before was to be nothing compared to the commotion about to follow. I have not climbed for a number of years without obtaining a sixth sense. Shortly after we reached the summit of Sgurr na Forcan, and on the top of the knife-blade at last, that intuition struck. I was well to the rear when I thought I saw something on the rock ahead.

'Edwin,' I called to the Captain (for it was he). 'Is there an abseil sling on that small pinnacle ahead of you?' He replied that he would have a look, quickened his pace, and came to a full stop. So did the Brigadier and Adjutant, now forming a tableau of middle-aged, suburban earnestness, incongruous in the teeth of such savage and rugged settings, their cagoules and rucksacks of the type that might be taken on Sunday rambles on the common and still without an ice-axe, a rope or pair of crampons in sight. It was very *Wind in the Willows* – as poignant and touching as Mole, Ratty and Portly encountering the Piper at the Gates of Dawn. Why they had stopped was immediately obvious. They could go no further.

Immediately below, the ridge fell away into nothingness – a black, shaded gulf plastered with newly fallen snow, glistening with ice and holding all the

quite delectable. Sometimes I climbed it like the rigging of a four-masted barque, hands and feet employed on the netting of pockets and edges provided by the granite. Occasionally, I used the edge as a handrail or cocked a leg over the knife-edge, straddled it and shinned up *à cheval*. The Saddle itself, apparently close enough to touch, its glittering walls of snow and ice stark with jagged rocks, thrust sky-

wards through the mantle of whiteness.

Then I heard a voice through the clear, cold air, 'Hey, it's Tony!' Knowing from experience how sound carries on mountains in the silence of snow and ice, I had previously felt that they must have heard my shouts and yells even though from far below. Yet apparently this was not so at all. I could not speak, though not because of unalloyed joy. I was simply hoarse from trying to com-

hypnotic fascination for my friends of a pit of writhing snakes. On a spike of rock above this yawning abyss was a rope sling from which a previous party had abseiled, presumably the day before, the sling providing – for those readers who are not cognisant with climbing methods – an anchor for an abseil rope. When the rope is doubled through the loop of the sling it can be pulled down later after everybody has completed their abseil down the doubled rope.

The expressions on the faces of my friends spoke of their shock and dismay. Until now, everything had gone swimmingly in their favour. Their one and cherished dream, the ascent of The Saddle by the Forcan Ridge, a certainty. Now they had been robbed. 'We'll never get down there!' said the Brigadier, 'not in a million years'. It was also evident that neither he nor his friends relished the thought of having to descend back down the great arête up which they had so far climbed with such aplomb. Although there are paths by which this *mauvais pas* can be avoided, everything was snowed under.

'Oh, maybe it's not so bad,' I heard myself say, peering over the edge. Then, seizing a large handhold, I lowered myself down until my feet touched a ledge below – a narrow ledge at that, but one that I now saw was repeated on and on downwards into the col below.

Once actually at grips with the climbing it was not so bad. I managed to dust away a powdering of snow, sweeping it clear from the large footholds and ledges beneath. Presently I reached the col some 40ft below, at last being able to look up and see the faces of my friends above, small against the brightness of the sky. 'Come on,' I yelled as someone will on jumping into a freezing pool and even though they are blue with cold, 'It's great down here.' Without further ado, the Captain (he of the eye-patch) clambered down to join me. However, the Brigadier and Adjutant remained above, unconvinced. We

then experienced a hiatus as the Captain and I tried to snare them into descending while the other two at the top would have none of it. I had to admit that they had a point. While the climbing was not difficult, it was sensational. A fall would have the victim bombing straight down in Choire Chaoil, on to rocks and scree, and with the prospect of falling for hundreds of feet further down the wintery hillside. The scene seemed set for a spectacular disaster.

It was – figuratively speaking – as if we had been abseiling using the sheepshank method, and the second one down, the Captain, had cut the sheepshank knot with the knife rather than leaving it for the last man to do. This had allowed the rope to drop into the gap and left the Brigadier and Adjutant stranded above without its aid. There was no actual rope, of course, except the invisible and equally elastic one of 'comradeship'. The bond was there, and an incredibly strong one at that for I have no doubt that these men, if it came to it, would lay down their lives for each other, and now the Captain tried tugging on this emotional link to persuade the others to descend so we could continue to the top of The Saddle while I rested my voice, just urging him on with gestures like the 'You can do it' nods and the old thumbs-up.

'Come on, guys,' I wanted to shout, 'A man with one eye in his fifties and another aged fifty-five in trainers have climbed down. What have you got to lose?' It was a ridiculous question. Visions of pension schemes, portfolios of life insurance investments, homes and families and all the appurtenances of the Golden Years – all the things incidentally that I didn't have – hung over us in a metaphorical cloud. As did, I'm sure, the cost of funeral expenses.

Possessed by an obsession that we would all reach The Saddle's siren call or perish in the attempt, I climbed back up to the top, and suggested that I carry the two remaining rucksacks down, and so it was agreed. I made a

couple of trips to ferry the sacks down into the col. Then the Adjutant lowered himself down inch by inch, followed by the Brigadier and encouraged by the Captain, while I stood well clear in case any falling body should take me with them. It was a situation pregnant with risk, and I knew I had been rash.

Yet I sensed they could do it and that in the circumstances it was the safest action. However, I shuddered at what their wives and grandchildren would have thought if they could see this drama being enacted. A dark thought passed behind me. Had they really seen me coming previously that morning? Was it this irresponsible trait in my character that had urged them to avoid me?

Again I took a back seat with the camera as the three friends, now incredibly relieved and bubbling, were reunited in the col. We shook hands elatedly while the Brigadier and I sat down to recover, and coil the emotional rope between us that had made the descent possible.

We reached the summit of The Saddle without further difficulty and its complex of fine ridges spreading out below made a wonderful resting place. Originally we had intended traversing the cirque over Spidean Dhomhuill Bhric, Sgurr Leac nan Each and Sgurr a'Ghrag Gharaidh to the west and around Choir' Uaine, but the day had taken too much out of us (not to mention the one before it).

We took a shorter route instead, northwards along the lovely and friendly crest of the ridge overlooking Choire Chaoil and with sections of easy scrambling over the roughest of rocks. One last difficulty remained. This ridge becomes a wolf in sheep's clothing beset with crags and scree and extremely steep grass inclines of such a convex nature it is impossible to see the way clearly below. Somehow we successfully descended the western slopes and landed in the welcoming embrace of Choir' Uaine, where a footpath by the river led us laughing and reminiscing back to Shiel Bridge.

Chapter 29

THE TRAVERSE OF BLA BHEINN AND CLACH GLAS

The Ridge cresting Bla Bheinn and Clach Glas is one of Skye's finest mountain chains, both extremely thrilling to execute and suspenseful to the end. Armour-plated like giant turtles, humped and unruly and gashed with ferocious battle scars, yet in other places so biscuit-thin that it is possible to look at distant landscapes or clouds through the pierced form of such a perforation in the ridge (rather like one of Henry Moore's outdoor pieces) — there were indeed occasions along its length when I wondered about getting out from its clutches alive. So gripped did I in fact become when facing its difficulties that it reminded me of a TV thriller written by a friend. In it, prisoners are rioting on the roof of a gaol when a helicopter arrives, rope-ladder dangling, to be grabbed at by everyone

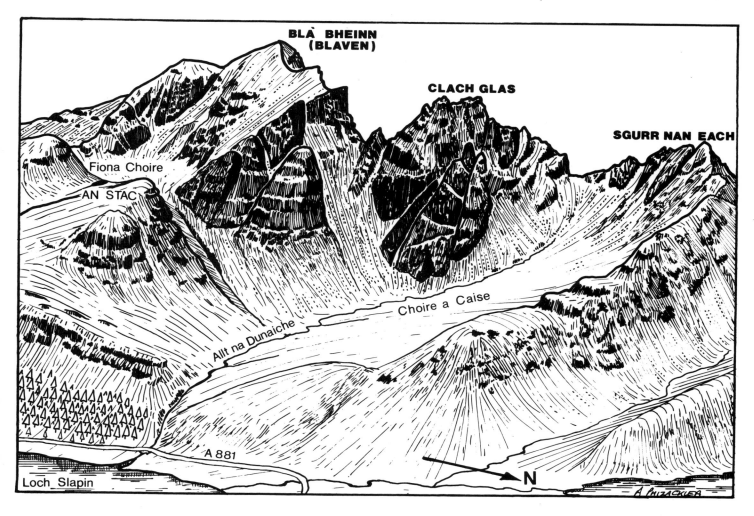

BLÀ BHEINN (BLAVEN)

CLACH GLAS

SGURR NAN EACH

Fiona Choire

AN STAC

Choire a Caise

Allt na Dunaiche

A 881

Loch Slapin

N

A. MUZACKLEA

who sees a chance of miraculous escape.

However, the rope-ladder is whisked out of their reach, and instead the chopper returns again and again to dangle its invitation to one particular prisoner, the only one who is not interested. The upshot of all this is a vicious outcome.

The other men are finally allowed to climb the ladder, the chopper then wheeling away to drop them one after another like bombs on the city below. When it returns, a sniper on board now peppering the roof with bullets as the helicopter in turn braves a fusilade of shots from police marksmen below, 'The Man' reluctantly climbs aboard.

How this could possibly apply to the great and classic sojourn over the peaks of Sgurr nan Each, Clach Glas itself and on past the Putting Green to mighty Bla Bheinn itself – a ridge so mouth-watering in its intensity and persistent with its beauty and challenge – is quite easily explained. Just as in that prison riot story, I ended up on what was in effect an inescapable roof top during its lofty course, was given a chance of release and refused to take it up.

Not once, not twice, not three times, but four times did I turn down its invitation. Only finally when the gods lost patience and threatened to draw the veil of darkness across the proceedings, leaving me stranded high and wet (and rather chilled) on one of the most rugged skylines in the land, did I at last take a chance and accept the offer that had been proferred.

And then? Did I realize my secret fears? Was my reasoning justified? Or was I led further astray, marooned among the jaws of the mountains while facing the embarrassment of knowing rescue teams would be searching for me? (For hadn't I left my car by the roadside and hadn't a lady from the house nearby put me right about the correct path to Bla Bheinn – a sure sign for having a rescue team called out if I was not back by darkness?) Or worse – did I actually perish from the cold and become yet another reluctant victim for a hovering Sea-King helicopter, the disgrace of which would lose me all my credibility for writing a book like this? (And a fate which seemed rather worse at the time than actually dying as I pondered it on the face, while it grew darker by the minute?) Ah, may I prevail on you to wait a little longer – like the outcome of my friend's thriller?

The beginning of my day on Clach Glas and Bla Bheinn – I had been recommended to do them in this order – could not have had a better start. It was a gorgeous morning and the drive had been idyllic. From Broadford on the heel of the 'boot' that forms the Isle of Skye as it rebounds after smashing itself into the mainland with frequent stamping kicks that is peculiarly Scottish whether you are Scottish country dancing or simply 'puttin' the heel in' some poor unfortunate adversary afer a canny head butting has left them lying on the pavement, the narrow road makes its way across the ankle bone to a point just below the shin.

The drive is a delight, pastoral and rustic with its trees and gorse and narrow winding twists and turns over humps and hillocks, terminating in the image of the Clach Glas-Blaven skyline being reflected in the glass-like views of Loch Slapin as the road winds along the waterside – all emerald turf and grazing sheep and cattle and the houses dotted over the landscape.

In my friend's play, the anti-hero is called Felix, and the basic reason he is unwilling to be rescued is because he is of an intransigent nature, masquerading as a fear of stepping from the frying pan into the fire. This too is one of my own weaknesses, a stubborness that is a form of daftness itself, and as I began the walk I sensed that something ahead was waiting to happen that through my own failings would throw me and in one particular way which I will reveal in a moment. For that was when I first glimpsed Clach Glas astride the ridge and the shock brought things about myself into focus that I preferred to forget.

Clach Glas is the Trango Tower – that sheer granite spire of the Karakoram Himalayas – of Skye. I first caught sight of it athwart the ridge after reaching the summit of Sgurr

Bla Bheinn and Clach Glas from the road to Elgol.

Clach Glas and Blaven when approaching from the north.

nan Each at the start of the ridge proper. It had not been easy reaching this point, first taking the wrong path into Choire a'Caise after parking on the west side of Loch Slapin (just south of the bridge over the Allt na Dunaiche), and then following the northern banks of the Allt na Dunaiche along an extremely wet and boggy track. At first there were wonderful waterfalls and pools, then the gorge below gave way to the tumbling burn and the track became progressively boggier still as the heart of Choire a'Caise beckoned ahead. I did not accept its invitation but trended rightwards on to the long and easy south-east ridge of Sgurr nan Each. Although a struggle across the numerous peat hags and bogs at first, it gradually became a pleasant climb on the greenest turf, bright with tiny butterworts, violets, celandines and pink-tinged daisies, and scattered with quartz-white rocks. A short scramble finally brought the summit within reach and the impact of the ridge ahead,

over Clach Glas and on to Bla Bheinn struck home. Narrow and twisting, contorted with pinnacles and jagged edges, its narrowness contrasted with the broad slopes I had just been climbing and brought me up short. Clach Glas rose sheer into the sky above a great drop on either side and entirely blocking the slimness of the ridge now snaking ahead.

Clach Glas I felt in my bones could well imprison me on its brooding heights. It looked forboding. The nearer I approached it – first descending from Sgurr nan Each down on to that north ridge then picking my way along the rim of the narrow skyline, occasionally clambering over gaps and pinnacles, more frequently skirting them to the right – the more it dominated the view. Clach Glas's pointed tower became overpowering as I reached the gully separating it from the ridge I had so far traversed. Then – heart in mouth – I climbed down and then up the op-

posite face, obtaining a purchase on slabs forming the west face and continuing up splendidly rough and steep rocks to the summit of this noteworthy peak, which looks not only inviolate but inescapable.

The thrill of reaching the summit was heightened by finding it was indeed a sharp roof-tree ridge. But I also experienced a twinge of despair as I looked at it, sloping off on either side into the sheerness below. I must have gone wrong somewhere. If, until now, the way to avoid such impasses had been to take them on the right, the right-hand aspect here was particularly forbidding – as straight a drop into the distant glen as from any gaol roof into a prison yard.

However, the left-hand eaves of the roof, were a different matter. Carefully, padding on the rough-cast gabbro, I traversed across like a TV aerial man, silhouetted against the sky and searching for the way down the southern side

The sharp edge on the top of the South Ridge of Clach Glas: The Imposter.

'The pierced form of a perforation in the ridge like one of Henry Moore's outdoor pieces . . .' Looking south along the ridge from the vicinity of Clach Glas.

of this giant rock fang. My hands were taped in plasters because I had torn them on the prickly rock during my past week's climbing efforts on the island and every time I touched a handhold I felt the soreness sting. But my heart was at last settling down. The route had become apparent. First down a cracked slab to the left and then via a sharp arête I now know is called The Imposter. I began to feel relieved. If I was due to meet my come-uppance on this ridge, then at least it would not be on Clach Glas, and as it had looked such a menacing foe and yet had proved extremely amenable – so there was a chance that the rest would be a breeze. What had been the problem?

Unfortunately I let my guard drop. As I descended and then went along the continuation of the ridge below I allowed myself to be further lulled by the excellent scrambling. Although it was still extremely exposed and airy, the way ahead was now obvious with none of the uncertainty about it that having Clach Glas standing in the way had provoked, or so it seemed. After all, wasn't that Bla Bheinn beckoning now almost within reach?

Indeed the relief I had experienced as I found I could clamber down from Clach Glas without undue problem must have been how Felix in the film felt when he saw the chopper wheel away with his four compatriots, and presumed he was finally safe, and could now get on with his hurling down of slates and lighting sundry bonfires on the wreckage of the prison roof. Imagine then his horror when he sees his erstwhile compatriots jettisoned from the chopper into mid air and the whirly bird flying back towards him as the roof around his feet begins to disintegrate into splinters under the impact of his foe's deadly rounds.

For these were also to be my feelings – dismay and shock – as this stupendous skyline then chose to shanghai me too. Though, in my case, the actual confrontation took a little longer to happen. If I thought I had been tested with innumerable invitations along the way, I was wrong. It was on mighty Bla Bheinn itself, the great bulk of the mountain that had been luring me along the crest of this wickedly crenellated ridge like a refuge beyond Clach Glas, that it struck.

From the heights of Clach Glas, its southern face looking on to the northern precipitous face of Bla Bheinn (and a counterpoint actually in two rugged jaws of outstanding grandeur), the ridge narrows again and traverses as before, picking its way tremulously above tremendous drops like a row of teeth. The rock is generally sound, but do beware. Sometimes a handhold on which you seize can rock alarmingly, so test it first. And now, rather than avoiding obstacles to the right as had been the case before Clach Glas, it is best to sidestep them to the left. The Putting Green – an enclave of luminous green, softest-cushioned moss inlaid into a notch in the ridge beneath the frowning eminence of Clach Glas now behind you and glowering over your retreating back – is a haven of lofty solitude.

In the TV play, Felix is a cat burglar, imprisoned not on larceny charge but on the manslaughter of a child-abuser. No one else knows his actual skill of being the man responsible for a series of sensational robberies up the outsides of the most intimidating tower blocks containing luxury flats, save the Big Man with the helicopter to whose notice the flair of our anti-hero has been drawn. He now wants to employ him for his own purposes. Had Felix taken the offer to get into the helicopter quietly, there would have been no story. The fact that his pigheadedness cost the lives of four compatriots to be on his conscience was to be his eventual undoing. As was my stubborness to prove mine.

Mentally blocked by anything remotely logical, bemused by the simplest mathematics (apart for some reason when playing darts), I will only use maps when I have to. And then only after laborious efforts will arrive at the proper configuration of the contours in my mind. The map in this case I had, of course, in my sack, as usual, in case of emergency. In any case, it would not have really helped in what was about to happen. But I had also been stubborn in a refusal to research too closely the mountain skyline along which I intended to traverse and photograph for this book, my reason being that if the skylines were good enough, then they would speak for themselves, and my experience of 38 years of climbing would help me find the way – with a fresh mind.

I realized the folly of this in the case of Bla Bheinn, as its massive, rearing wall of rock faces, chimneys, scree fans and pinnacles beetled ahead beyond the ridge which abutted into it as the tail of a sting ray joins the head. Why hadn't I compromised? Bla Bheinn after all is a giant mountain and, it now filtered into the dullness of my conscious mind, things I had heard vaguely – but deliberately not paid heed too – about its proving complex terrain and indeed being the crux of the ridge were being confirmed. Had I checked a guidebook first then at least I would have known approximately in which direction I should be aiming. For this was not now obvious. While previously I had been tightrope walking, in a manner of speaking, along a slim crest, now I was face-to-face with something massive and which gave no clue as to where a weak point lay.

Furthermore, as the crest along which I had travelled abutted against this great mass, and still with precipitous drops of the most horrendous ruggedness just waiting below on either side, there did not seem to be any clear path to follow. The whole place was a breaking wave of rock and scree confronting me and, as I was to find, it was possible to find it impenetrable.

The immediate problem facing me had arrived after I clambered into a notch in the skyline, the floor of this notch being a continuation of the ridge's crest with nothing but space on either side but now enclosed, as it were, inside a 'box'. Ahead was Bla Bheinn, its actual boundary being this short smooth wall of rock forming the opposite side of the

notch or box or gap and where the sharp ridge – as it had so far been – effectively finished just below this wall, the lip of which in turn was piled high with small pieces of scree like coins in one of those arcade slot machines where you drop in your money in the hope that, as it lands on the heaps of coins overlapping the edge of the chute below, it will dislodge the several jammed together and overhanging the brink and start an avalanche which you will eventually spill into your pocket. In this case the 'coins' were the bits of scree, heaped on the brink of the rock face overhead.

Felix is wanted for the purpose of competing in climbing competitions which, it transpires in my friend's thriller, is set some time in the future. The contests are held on the great mountain walls of the world like the North Face of the Cime Grande di Lavaredo in the Dolomites where stadiums have been constructed and, in a reconstruction of Roman coliseum times, the tens of thousands of seats are packed with the blood-thirsty fans who gloat on the spectacle of the climbers competing ropeless, and falling to their deaths when the rock face proves too much – their bodies dragged away on chains from the scree below by vehicles like space buggies. Felix, the reluctant competitor, faces the keenest competition, however, from himself and his conscience. Besides the killings for which he is responsible, as his opponents fall like flies to their deaths and he continues on to win again and again, it is the deaths of his prison colleagues that weigh heavily on his mind.

So with my own failings of pigheadedly refusing to check a guidebook first – and woe betide you, dear reader, if you feel similarly inclined (although after reading this account you should be aware of the problem involved) – I tackled the wall ahead, at a point approximately level with the top of the Great Prow, a giant needle to the left and one of rock climbing's classic hard climbs.

At first glance it was no more than 20ft high at the most, this Bla Bheinn Bad Step then, despite being above a considerable drop on either side. Although it was apparently smooth, there were holds if you had any knowledge of climbing. The initial pull up on to the first holds was steep, however, and they were flat and wet. It was an awkward move upwards too. And one you felt would be difficult to reverse with any certainty of not falling. I made the move, trainers squirming slightly on the greasy holds and conscious it was starting to spot with rain. I reached up, stepped up and reached again with the help of a crack into which you could just jam your fingers for extra purchase. My hands were almost at the top. But what top? The fringe of scree poised on that brink – and so much so that had anybody on the mountain above been moving across the scree at a higher level they would have deluged me there and then – offered no hope of solid holds at all. Tentatively I reached high

Blaven and Clach Glas viewed from the road to Elgol.

again and buried my hands in the scree, unavailingly coming up with nothing more than a fistful of pebbles. It was the same with the other hand too.

For seconds I deliberated. There were footholds I could step up to again but they were small and skiddy and should I slip my hands would give no support in preserving the status quo until I regained my footing. I could imagine keeling over backwards and the ultimate crash on the mountainside below. The risk was too great. Gently, so as not to trigger a landslide (in fact, I held my breath), I reversed back down to where my first moves from the gap had initially brought me – the footholds I had previously used now scattered with small stones. Then I saw it. A traverse out to the right – airy, true, but leading to a distant foothold and with a clean rock finish above. Within several moments more I was up.

Now I relaxed. With Clach Glas *and* the Bad Step on Blaven past, what more terrors could this skyline hold? Plenty, I was to find. The rain was wetting in earnest, not heavy, but a persistent drizzle which quickly soaked my clothing. Even so, I had on thermal long johns, track suit bottoms, a thermal vest, a T-shirt, a nylon shell top, hat and gloves. Clothing that can become wet but still remains reasonably warm. However, now I wanted to top-out with all speed, the day drawing quickly to a close as well as clouding over and the cloud base sinking lower all the while.

The way seemed surely obvious. Across the scree for some way to the right, then up in drifting cloud to yet more scree. So far, so good. Then up the deep chimney slanting leftwards overhead. I made great headway too. Until, it seemed, I had reached an impasse, bridged across a void on sloping holds. Frustrated, I backed-down and took stock. I had already seen a chimney further to the left and overlooking more scree, but I had initially discounted it. I still did. Now I saw

Peaks along the Cuillin Ridge seen from the Blaven-Clach Glas skyline.

another line to the right of the route that I had tried, and I attempted that, but without experiencing any more luck than on the first attempt. Strange, I thought, it should have been a formality. The top after all was so near. Again the leering slit of the second chimney to the left winked at me. Again I refused its siren call, now traversing away in the opposite direction along increasingly exposed ledges which led amid impenetrable buttresses above to a gorge with steep cliffs and waterfalls.

Again I returned to my patch of scree below the 'obvious' chimney. Once more I discounted the narrow chimney further left and again ploughed up the initial cleft I had tried, this time actually embarking up a holdless ramp on the right wall that seemed to be leading to freedom. Quickly it led me into a hostile region of bristling overhangs and slippery holds. I managed to retreat in one piece, only now at last considering the invitation of the chimney up to the left which I had felt was not the way. Realizing, with advancing twilight, I would have to try everything in front of me, I finally forayed leftwards up the scree and in desperation entered its narrow confines, being in effect a boulder-choked slit that seemed to lead

to nowhere save smooth and overhanging rock above. When finally I had reached a point where I was braced across its jaws and could not climb any higher, I found I was able to see through the slot of the defile and out to the far side. There was a considerable drop below, but a line of footholds and handholds led out across the wall on the right. Hardly able to believe it and almost shaking with relief, I climbed through this 'window' and stepped out on to the shaley slopes of Bla Bheinn, quite near the normal path on the east ridge and an easy walk to the summit.

It was cold, it was blowing, it was almost dark, but rarely has a stark mountain top seemed more welcome than the sight of the valley approaching below with lighted windows and the headlights of traffic just beyond. These, in fact, were waiting their turn. But only after I had descended the normal route of Bla Bheinn, down the eastern side to a shoulder, then by a series of cairns leading – less distinctly lower down – in a series of zigzags to the left of a steeply walled gully. They ultimately landed me in Coire Uaigneich which in turn led me back to the boggy path along the Allt na Dunaiche and back to the roadside.

Chapter 30
THE CIRQUE OF SGURR NAN GILLEAN AND AM BASTEIR

The Matterhorn of Skye, Sgurr nan Gillean rises space rocket-like above the vast launching pad of quagmire surrounding the Sligachan Inn. I will always remember visiting this outpost by a lonely crossroads with a girl friend. We had driven 300 miles holding hands and telling each other what we would do on arrival. What actually happened

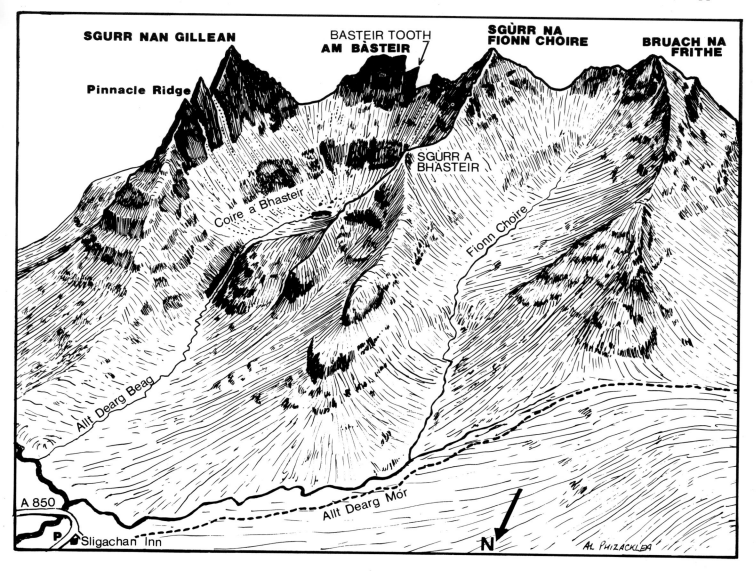

SGURR NAN GILLEAN

Pinnacle Ridge

BASTEIR TOOTH
AM BÀSTEIR

SGÙRR NA
FIONN CHOIRE

BRUACH NA
FRITHE

SGÙRR A
BHASTEIR

Coire a' Bhasteir

Fionn Choire

Allt Dearg Beag

Allt Dearg Mòr

A 850

P Sligachan Inn

N

AL PHIZACKLEA

was I became disastrously half-cut on an empty stomach, tried to bundle her into a wardrobe and received a smack on the head for my pains.

But then Sgurr nan Gillean is known as the Peak of the Young Men. At the time I was fifty-two. Perhaps that explains it. Yet is nothing sacred? Wasn't this also the oasis of Sligachan, beloved by pioneers Collie and Mackenzie, and overlooked by a matchless Scottish mountain?

An elderly Norman Collie – he whom we must also thank for neon lighting and the first practical application of X-rays – was staying at Sligachan when he was approached by two women. What did the Doctor think the weather would do? The great climber glanced towards the streaming window panes but did not answer. When they repeated the question he continued to stare out of the window. 'Can't you use your eyes?' he then said, not unkindly. Perhaps instead of asking, they should just have tapped on the glass of the hotel barometer (after that bedroom encounter my head knows how a barometer feels).

Three elements these, then, that make up the atmosphere of Sligachan.

One, the magical shape of Sgurr nan Gillean – a perfectly proportioned pyramid from wherever you are – and its accompanying peak of Am Basteir on the skyline above. Two, the chances of Skye weather deluging these jagged peaks with very little warning. And three, the madness that can enter the soul when such wild beauty and untamed weather conspire to create a catalyst for the unpredictable.

So enticing is the silhouette of Sgurr nan Gillean, so perfect the view from its summit (of which the Scottish Mountaineering Club guidebook, a work not given to exaggeration, says that on a clear day it offers 'one of the world's greatest mountain views') that my friend and I decided to stroll towards it on arrival as if this was Hampstead Heath. I must have been too smitten to realize what every climber knows. Approach Sgurr nan Gillean from Sligachan and, close as it looks, it will never get any nearer. Neither did the hotel as we returned across the intervening wilderness. The lighted windows remained, it seemed, forever in the distance, as did the candlelit table d'hôte remain a forlorn and unattainable hope.

However, to reach that celestial viewpoint on Sgurr nan Gillean even on the best of days, is no easy thing. Neither is returning from its panoramic summit. Here is a peak beset with difficulties, and one better left alone by anyone who feels unnerved by heights and the feeling of great remoteness.

Indeed to complete the route I suggest, you must expect some serious scrambling as well as quite complex route-finding. Expect too to find the simplest-looking terrain confusing and difficult just when it seems you have surpassed a major difficulty. Allow eight hours at least for safety.

The problems with the Gillean-Basteir skyline are manifest because of the amount of rock that intrudes along the ridges. Seen from the Sligachan Inn, this cirque of Coire a'Bhasteir gives a misleading impression. Sgurr nan Gillean and Am Basteir make up the main arc of the horseshoe while two well-defined ridges – the Pinnacle Ridge of Sgurr nan Gillean and the North Ridge of Sgurr a'Bhasteir – point towards the hotel, cradling between them the tiny jewel of Loch a' Bhasteir, deep within the bosom of the mountains.

It must be said, however, that these same arms embracing Coire a'Bhasteir are seen in a very foreshortened and deceptive way from Sligachan. The Pinnacle Ridge to the left, which is in fact a fiercely serrated skyline, looks anything but except when mist drifts behind the pinnacles. This means you cannot walk and scramble around the crest of this skyline as at first the view suggests from Sligachan. There is just too much rock climbing involved.

The Pinnacle Ridge forms the North Ridge of the mountain, and the difficulties do not end there. The West ridge of Gillean slicing its way down into the col below Am Basteir is another problem, another superb stretch of gabbro blade along which the timid

Sgurr nan Gillean and the Basteirs seen from Sligachan.

scrambler could certainly become overawed. Then again, the sweeping ascent up the East Ridge of Am Basteir – and down again – is no foregone conclusion, appearing a precarious and gripping excursion through outer space all the way to the summit. Am Basteir furthermore is not named the Executioner for nothing; it is brutally sheared off into the steepest cliffs on the west face adjacent to its Tooth, which is another proposition altogether, a great jutting axe-blade of a cliff that is clearly the rock climber's prerogative.

The one Gillean route accessible to walkers is the South-East Ridge – also known as the Tourist Route – which is also a serious proposition, offering some scrambling in tremendous situations. Although it rises around the side of the mountain away from Sligachan and so is not included in that celebrated view from the hotel dining room, I am still including it in this route as it is the safest way down.

The second time I approached Sgurr nan Gillean from Sligachan, I was on my own. It was a Saturday morning and it had been busy on the ferry where I was impatient to reach the mountains before the clear skies greyed over. It was during the May of 1989 and I was committed to taking as many of the Scottish photographs for this book as possible.

In the previous nine days I had traversed (and photographed) The Cobbler, four Glencoe and three Kintail ridges, the Ring of Steall, the Ben Nevis and the Carn Mor Dearg Arête, and despatched the film off for processing. Now I was on Skye. I just did not want this marvellous progression of golden days to stop. 'Speed bonny boat' goes the song, except the ferry that had brought me here could not have been less 'like a bird on the wing'.

'Go on, go on,' I silently urged as it ploughed slowly across the sullen water at the mouth of Loch Alsh while I sat ready to drive off the instant we docked

Sgurr nan Gillean, Am Basteir and Basteir Tooth from Sligachan.

at Kyleachin. Every fresh skyline ticked while the weather lasted was one less to do. And I hoped to traverse Am Basteir and then Gillean that afternoon although the forecast was gloomy. Sgurr nan Gillean marks one end of the main Skye Ridge, the ultimate mountain expedition in the British Isles, a mighty endurance test of half a dozen miles which climbs and drops 10,000ft around eleven scenic corries. Gillean, in fact, might have been sculpted by Nature with this in mind; to serve as a flagship for the Ridge, a peak so dominant it was once thought to be the highest on Skye. Sgurr Alasdair turns out to have that honour and is a worthy contender for shape too, except it only has two great ridges while Sgurr nan Gillean has three. Together with neighbouring Am Basteir then, Sgurr nan Gillean is quite capable of giving a superb expedition in its own right. It is a *tour de force* quite apart from the Skye Ridge which is a mountaineering experience outside the scope of this book.

The walk across the wastelands from Sligachan towards the Coire a'Bhasteir gives you ample time to review how serious this skyline is. Every step and

stumble of the way, more home-truths are driven home: How out on a limb you are; how even this approach – a morass of pools and meandering streams, peat bog, heather like tangled barbed wire and trackless swamp – leaves you vulnerable were mist to come down and you had no compass. Added to which the sight of great crags and rock-girt hillsides drawing ever nearer by the moment gives a feeling of foreboding, especially when you remember the unreliability of the compass in any case due to a preponderance of magnetic rock in the Cuillin.

The actual start is not far west from the Sligachan Hotel, a well-trodden path leading to a footbridge close to what was once a powerhouse for supplying electricity. Once on the far banks of the Allt Dearg Mor, the way becomes increasingly boggy, branching into numerous diversions though all with the same aim in mind: to climb up alongside the Allt Dearg Beag, before crossing over it by another footbridge. With the two Red Streams safely crossed – one the Big; the other, the Little – the path I took approached Coire Riabhach around to the left of the Pinnacle Ridge now looming overhead. However, instead of descending into that next corrie, I followed a deviation upwards once more.

Now you feel the pull of mountains ahead. At first trending in a south-westerly direction, the new path takes you over increasingly rugged ground, including some scrambling, to a point below the first pinnacle of the Pinnacle Ridge which rears up above like a massive cutlass being brandished overhead up to the left. So perfect is the shapely sweep of this great weapon's edge, it is one of the finest sights on British hills, and especially from this angle.

It is a view enhanced by the deepening bowl of Coire a'Bhasteir opening up ahead of you, with yet more ennervating skyline spearing the sky across the emptiness of the corrie with its tiny tarn glinting below. There is such a chaotic display of rock face and scree here that you can well imagine the septuagenarian Dr Collie overhearing younger climbers as they excitedly planned their explorations for the day in the smoke-room of the Sligachan

Sgurr nan Gillean, Am Basteir and the Basteir Tooth from near Sligachan.

Alpine mountain scenery on the cirque of Sgurr nan Gillean and Am Basteir.

and chuckling to himself: 'They'll find a little cairn there.'

This mountain bowl is steeped in character and tradition, enhanced by the crashing splendour at times of rain or melting snow of the waters of the Bhasteir Gorge plunging dizzily below to the Allt Dearg Beag whose headwaters are fed by the tiny lochan from the floor of the corrie – a delectable sanctuary gained by down-scrambling diagonally across the inside retaining wall of the corrie basin.

It is a line that strikes diagonally from below the base of the Pinnacle Ridge down rightwards towards the brink of the Bhasteir Gorge some way beneath. There are scree and boulders to negotiate, but once down by Loch a' Bhasteir, a breather can be taken in this secret place before the next stage is faced, and a steep uphill toil it is. Fortunately, it is short, the slope of screes and broken slabs leading to a deeply cut scree gully that leads unerringly upwards to the delightful –

if all too brief – North-East Ridge of Sgurr a'Bhasteir.

Sgurr a'Bhasteir is the highest point along this satellite ridge. It offers a splendid view of the Pinnacle Ridge of Sgurr nan Gillean across the rugged grandeur of the corrie, and for a complete contrast you need only turn around and gaze behind you into the greenery of Fionn Choire. Fionn is the most verdant of the Cuillin corries with grassy slopes and wild flowers and tradition says that you can jog down it from the summit of neighbouring Bruach na Frithe to Sligachan in an hour.

Poised then between these two extremes, the summit of Sgurr a'Bhasteir commands this ridge which then descends, narrowing towards the Bhasteir Tooth and the col nearby, Bealach nan Lice. So superb is the rock scenery here, it is worth making a detour to the diminutive top of nearby Sgurr na Fionn Choire, the next peak along to the west, for its views back towards Am Basteir.

Photographs taken – and lucky you if there are climbers on the front of the Basteir Tooth, tackling this toughest of all Munros by the formidable Naismith's Route (formidable if they are doing the main Ridge and have yet again had to pull wearily the rope from a rucksack for this sternest of all their tests) – your route now regains the bealach. Walkers with no inclination to rock climb the Basteir Tooth can now follow a path across the scree beneath the steep north face of Am Basteir and up into the next col, Bealach a' Bhasteir, situated below the next obstacle.

The long East Ridge of Am Basteir provides the 'tourist' route to the summit of the Executioner. (This in turn offers marvellous views of the West Ridge of Sgurr nan Gillean, the next to come.) The scrambling involved along the crest is serious and a short descent down steep rock *en route* is awkward. Occasionally there is a temptation to take easier variations on the left, or Lota Coire side, of the ridge especially when descending back down this airy blade (by which time Lota Coire is then to the right). Generally, however, it is best to keep to the crest whenever possible.

Descending Am Basteir, incidentally, the steep drops on both sides are a good initiation into that next problem, the West Ridge of Sgurr nan Gillean. This rises from the ridge a short way beyond the Bealach a'Bhasteir and having returned down Am Basteir's East Ridge you will shortly come to grips with this famous test-piece.

The West Ridge of Sgurr nan Gillean is a serious undertaking, requiring thought and care in choice of route. It is by no means obvious where the best way goes, especially at the start where the rock takes the form of a steep buttress that discourages a direct approach. There is a chimney to the left, another chimney left again, and yet another line of weakness much further left, although this time it is more of a gangway, trending to the right.

That third route is called Nicholson's Chimney. The central chimney is the hardest of the trio; it is the first chimney that you encounter, if you go the usual

Sgurr nan Gillean, Am Basteir and the Basteir Tooth from the vicinity of Sligachan.

Looking from below the Pinnacle Ridge of Sgurr nan Gillean towards Blaven and Clach Glas.

way that provides the key. Very steep and with holds polished by the passage of previous climbers, it involves several awkward moves above the gulf of Coire a'Bhasteir.

The ridge above the chimney narrows, exacerbating the feeling of exposure, something emphasized even more when a large rock tooth, the Gendarme, policed the edge, demanding several obsequious moves to circumnavigate it. The obelisk has since disappeared. Now the way to the summit is unobstructed, save for personal fears that the mountain may still hold some unexpected surprise that could still thwart your arrival on to that diminutive summit with its chance of superlative views.

The descent retains all the tension of the climb, the initial moves down the steep rocks topping the South-East Ridge proving bold above the now un-

familiar terrain. You are now descending another side of the mountain and it feels strange. There is no relenting as the narrowness of the edge plunges on down, the bird's eye view of the landscape below new and disconcerting. Gradually the ridge fills out, thicker in the girth and with the more amenable line of descent on the Lota Coire side.

As its steepness finally relaxes, the descent meets scree to the left, following back round and down through serried, broken crags and into the boulderiness of the corrie below.

The thrust of the return journey, of course, is a sojourn to the north alongside the flanks of Sgurr nan Gillean that will eventually bring you round the mountain back towards the base of the Pinnacle Ridge and where you will meet the footbridge across the Allt Dearg Beag once more.

The Pinnacle Ridge meanwhile looms overhead up to the left, accompanying you *en route* as you continue north with Loch a'Coire Riabhach to the right as you begin the final leg to come full circle, ascending gradually to that point of reference: the footbridge.

The return just from the South-East Ridge to Sligachan is long and arduous in bad weather. It should not be underestimated simply because with the mountain climbing behind you, you naturally may feel the walk back is just a formality.

It can take two hours to return from the footbridge across the Allt Dearg Beag to the hotel. Sligachan indeed never seems to get nearer just as Gillean had kept its distance earlier in the day, but that is the nature of a great mountain day. It never relents from start to finish.

Chapter 31
THE QUIRAING

The Quiraing is an enchanted skyline near the northern tip of the riding boot formed by the Isle of Skye, stamping furiously as it were in good Scottish fashion on the Kyle of Lochalsh with its heel, before disintegrating into bits, these smithereens being Skye's various peninsulas. The long narrow Trotternish promontory is the one topped with Meall nan Suireamach of which the Quiraing is a part. This forms a cluster of towering crags and pinnacles, requiring no more than two or three hours to explore, which provide a magical expedition to a sanctuary unique in the British Isles.

Unlike the jack boot of Italy which is elegant and long, the Skye boot is short and fat, or it was before it flew apart, creating a tattered coastline of between 600 and 1,000 miles in length. Yet it is so compact that nowhere in Skye are you more than 5 miles from a sea marbled in green and blue and so translucent it is like ice. By the same token, it can suddenly flare orange through the ruined castle windows of the Quiraing at sunset. Or blush a rich pink as the sun rises opposite the great battlements of rock. By castle I mean castle, but it is a natural stronghold rather than a man-made fortification. For the Quiraing is a massive pile of jagged

QUIRAING

MEALL NAN SUIREMACH

N

The Table

The Needle

The Prison

A. PHIZACKLEA

volcanic rock, riven deeply into watch-towers and buttresses, sculpted by the forces of nature and overlooking Flodigarry, home of Flora Macdonald.

Pinnacles and rock faces are the physical hallmark of the Quiraing. Unusual in number, magnitude and density, the vertical thrust of this wild rockscape is so thickly spiked with multi-storey crags, each separated from its neighbour by a maze of gullies, chimneys, crags and terraces, that it is possible to become a prisoner among the fastnesses within if you lose the way. The Prison, The Castle, The Needle and The Table are among the features that captivate visitors, literally, but pride of place goes to The Table, a treasured place located deep within this Pillared Stronghold.

The Pillared Stronghold! That is what Quiraing means. In Gaelic the word is Cuith-raing, the word being abridged to Quiraing. It is a name redolent with atmosphere and drama. When Sean Connery puts his sword to the test in *The Highlander*, it was filmed partly on the Table, the surrounding crag walls echoing to the clash of steel and a yawning abyss gaping below. Long before this, 100 years in fact, Victorian tourists travelled to the Quiraing by boat and horse-drawn coach, and mountain guides led them into the heart of this precipitous labyrinth. When the advertising agency employed by Peugeot realized such a venue existed in Trotternish as opposed to Catalonia or Utah, they whisked an estate car by helicopter on to the Table, photographed it

for an ad and ran it for months in upmarket magazines (the silvery car on an emerald pad encircled by a yawning chasm and bristling crags).

The drive from the Skye ferry to the Quiraing is a delight in itself. Starting from Kyleachin which is situated at the heel of Skye's boot (rebounding from one of its frequent kicks into the mainland), it then runs up the calf of the boot via Sligachan and Portree and along the east coast of Trotternish.

Like the Pacific Coast Highway between San Francisco and LA, it is a picturesque route of great beauty and contrasts, threading its way between a wild coastline on the one hand and a precipitous mountain crest on the other. Approaching Portree along the fast road from the Sligachan Hotel, you get

The Table from a second (and smaller) Table above.

an inkling of the magic to come. Tiny white houses with red roofs lie ahead, purple hills bound and leap into the sky beyond and below a great mountain scarp in the far distance rises a needle, a tower so slender and enormous it might be a space rocket on the NASA launch pad. That undulating skyline crest is the escarpment that runs the length of the Trotternish peninsula over Ben Dearg, The Storr, Hartaval, Baca Ruadh, Sgurr a'Mhadaidh Ruaidh, Beinn Edra, Bioda Buidhe and Meall nan Suireamach and below which you will drive to reach the Quiraing. Not that the needle is the Quiraing itself, however, but a prelude to it; the gigantic Old Man of Storr, it was climbed in 1955 by three Sassenachs (Don Whillans, Jim Barber and Geoff Sutton) who left a half-crown coin on the summit before making the descent by abseil.

The Quiraing remains hidden until several miles further on. Then with the northern tip of Trotternish drawing ever closer, the mighty cliffs of the Quiraing finally soar into view beneath the summit skyline of Meall nan Suireamach, the highest peak along the northern section of the scarp. There is a sense of *deja vu* as you glimpse its sharp needles and pinnacles and great flying buttresses of glowering rock, but this is only because the rocks of The Storr have previously hinted at the things to come. Only the settings of the Quiraing are so exquisite, contrasting with the heather and daisy fields below where wild mountain thyme fills the air with an exotic scent and the hum of bumble-bees prevails in summer.

Narrow and twisting as the road from Portree proves, the road that branches off up this mountainside near Staffin is even more so. The passing places for cars become havens, perched increasingly higher up the steepening slopes and affording viewpoints to quicken the heart. On the hairpins looping towards the summit, rocks, scree and even the rotting carcasses of dead sheep can spill on to the road from the crags

The cliffs of the Quiraing plunging down to The Prison from the summit of the road pass (from Brogaig to Uig).

and slopes above, the severity of the bends, gradients and risk of falling objects borne out by the profusion of roadside warning signs.

The road continues over the Trotternish escarpment to Uig (and its ferry to Long Island) on the western side of the peninsula. Here on the windswept summit of the pass, is the place to leave your transport and experience the transition from grasping the steering wheel with both hands to gripping the narrow track that leads towards the Quiraing with both feet, stretching the legs and breathing in the glorious air – heady enough stuff on its own but spellbinding when you glimpse the Outer Isles as blue wisps in the far distance.

This path leading from the roadside to the base of the Quiraing is not difficult, but it traverses mountainous terrain, at one point crossing a narrow ravine, which in flood could prove decidedly awkward. Everything is exposed

to the forces of nature. In high wind or heavy rain it would take on quite a different aspect from the bright green grass and tiny wild flowers reflecting sunlight where rabbits scamper between a honeycomb of burrows, while rocky debris lies below the cliffs like chunks of Tarmac shattered by a pneumatic drill.

Eventually the way leads into a defile. Not only do soaring precipices dwarf you on either side, but they appear ready to keel over and come crashing down from their pedestals of scree and boulders. The Needle, unmistakable among the satellite crags flanking it on either side, beetles overhead to neck-craning heights up to the left. The Prison, a large rock fin, impends above you to the right. Which one is it to be? The Prison, in fact, can be bypassed completely, but it does give you the chance of a trial ascent via its southeastern flanks. Narrow paths ascend the steep and slippery slopes of sweet-

The Needle and its satellite cliffs viewed from across the way below the vantage point of The Prison.

smelling turf to the summit tower, offering a prelude of what is to come when you explore the Quiraing itself, now seen in magnificent close-up across the way. The turreted top of the Prison, though, is by no means a foregone conclusion, proving quite awkward and exposed and best left alone unless you are a capable climber.

Descending the Prison by the same way you climbed it, this foray will have given you an inkling of the complex nature of the Quiraing. The mistake is to imagine the Table will be revealed once you have climbed into any of the many gullies separating the mighty buttresses arranged in line above. The truth is somewhat different. The gullies can only be entered after ascending extremely steep and unstable scree slopes. Even when these ravines are breached they still lead to yet more crags looming top-heavily above, un-

less you choose the one way which is safe.

The Needle is the turn-key to finding the Table, a twist in your route being to keep the giant obelisk on your right after ascending the steep scree slopes beneath it, pock-marked by the impact of countless pairs of boots. Passing around and behind the Needle, you then enter an adjacent cleft leading invitingly upwards between the bulwarks of rock. This narrow gully is the sheep amongst wolves; remember it well for the descent. Not that it seems sheeplike at all. It suddenly appears to end menacingly in a chasm overhanging space. However, this is only a false alarm. The gully, earth-stripped and steep, actually continues to bend back left at this point, leading you out into the daylight of a secluded paradise. Hillocks, mounds, knolls and glades of greenest grass are enclosed by the sur-

rounding walls of the Quiraing. They lead ever higher upwards, until you can go no further.

Suddenly you are on the Table itself, which is a wide expanse of mossy greensward, firm and flat and underpinned by precipices. It is one of the loveliest places I know in the British hills. Yet it is overshadowed by still higher ground. The escarpment of Meall nan Suireamach marches above, unassailable from your lofty eyrie. So near and yet so far. But it does not concern you. The Table *is* the summit for those who visit the Quiraing, and having reached it, the safest way down is by retracing your steps rather than trying available options of steep scree slopes that are unstable and arduous but which beckon seductively as you explore the Wonderland – almost on tiptoe with anticipation – around this High Temple of our hills.

Chapter 32
THE TRAVERSE OF BEINN EIGHE

In Torridon I had traversed three great ridges and on each one I made calamitous mistakes. Perhaps it was exhaustion that finally caught up with me and put me at an all-time low after going all out during the lovely May of 1989 to take the Highlands pictures for this book, when the days were never-endingly bathed in sunshine (with one or two exceptions). This proved to be so much the case that towards the end of the month, golden sunbeams would pierce the fabric of the tent at 5 a.m. while I buried my face in the pullovers I used as a pillow and tried to disregard the voice in my ear saying, 'The sun's there! Ready for you to capture inside the AZ−300! You must go for it! It may never shine again for days.' Torridon came towards the end of that month.

Each morning, having completed a sky-line the day previously, and with the prospect of yet another to come in the hours ahead, I just craved to slide back into oblivion.

In retrospect, Beinn Alligin and Liat-hach might not have been so much mistakes – after all I had taken pictures I felt would suffice and I *had* done their skylines (even if, in the case of

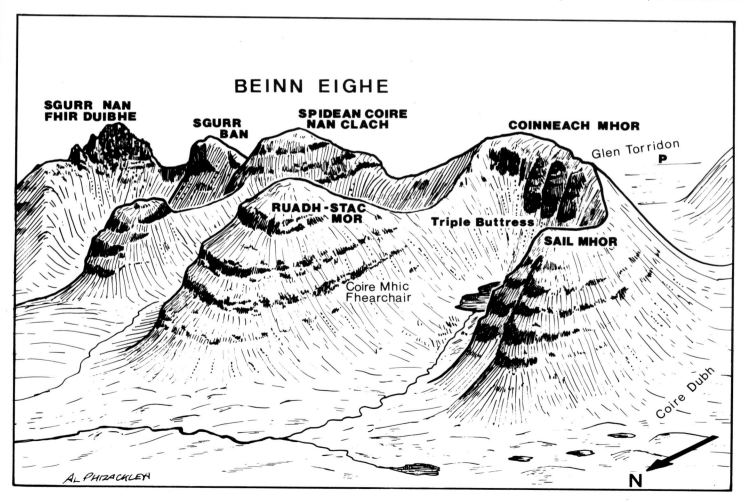

BEINN EIGHE

SGURR NAN FHIR DUIBHE

SGURR BAN

SPIDEAN COIRE NAN CLACH

COINNEACH MHOR

Glen Torridon

P

RUADH-STAC MOR

Triple Buttress

SAIL MHOR

Coire Mhic Fhearchair

Coire Dubh

AL PHIZACKLEY

N

The buttresses and snow-fields of Sgurr Ban seen through the Notch on Sgurr an Fhir Duibhe.

Beinn Alligin, it was only two-thirds). But in the case of Beinn Eighe the error I made might have cost me my life, although I did it on a glorious morning with lots of time in hand, and my reserves of energy resonably high.

The mistake I made this time was criminal. The kind which in the tabloid press would have deserved a 'Lone sailor lands on wrong continent' kind of article being written about me. Again, it was the kind of thinking behind the mistake that in mist or nightfall could have had me trying to descend from the Aonach Eagach Ridge too early or falling into Five Finger Gully on the way down the Tourist Route from the summit of Ben Nevis, both classic errors of the inexperienced.

It was the kind of clanger that I had dropped on Blaven and it could have killed me, perpetrated at another time and in a different place. But then there were times in Torridon when I wondered how I had survived and enjoyed mountains and climbing for so long. Now my solo efforts to get the pictures was showing up my shortcomings. But perhaps it was also fatigue that was the culprit if I was to be fair to myself. After all, no one else was likely to be.

I have gone on at some length here in the hope that it may perhaps draw a lesson for newcomers to the hills. If someone of my experience can make mistakes, so can they. Knowing what crime I had committed might remind them when they too are in danger of making such a decision, though human nature being what it is, I'm sure we usually have to find these things out for ourselves.

My failing on Blaven had been my pigheadness in refusing to even read up about the mountain first, let alone look at a map. I just wanted to see the skyline, to go up and do it. These had also been my tactics with most of the other skylines in the book. If a ridge is that good, was my reasoning, then it will stand out so clearly that the last thing you need is a map to spoil the enjoyment of moving freely on the Hill, unencumbered and enjoying the movement, the crags, flowers and birds, the views, the tremendous feeling of freedom and what does it matter if you know few of the surrounding hills — they're there! Heaven forbid, the carrying of a map in a transparent map case

The precipice – and Notch – of Sgurr an Fhir Duibhe from Sgurr Ban.

on the breast for snap consultation, of the type Clint Eastwood might appear to carry in *A Fistful of Dollars* under his cape.

What the 'The Man with No Name' (for it is he) actually keeps close to his chest is a slab of metal worn under his cloak, much to the annoyance of those who try to shoot him in the heart and find their human target unassailable. Of course, I carried a map in case of emergencies but it remained in the rucksack and only emerged in bad weather. However, you can only get away with this so long, and on big hills you do need to check your whereabouts with reasonable regularity. On Blaven the topography had proved quite complex and I had been too blasé. As to Beinn Eighe, I still grieve about the error of my ways. If only I had looked at the map . . .

As a result, I missed the world-famous view of the Triple Buttress looming across Coire Mhic Fhearchair, a spectacle renowned as a highlight of the Highlands and a gem. As I have said, it was a gorgeous morning. What a fantastic photograph it would have made. I have since seen pictures of the Triple Buttress taken with the humblest kind of camera in Scottish mist and so striking is the setting that they were still wonderful. By what I have seen from these results even a pinhole camera cut from an old cereal packet could not fail to produce good pictures of this magic place.

Again, it was impetuosity that was to blame. I had seen Beinn Eighe the previous day while driving through Glen Torridon from Kinlochewe – its long, undulating ridge dazzling with quartzite screes and keeping pace with the road. This is a marvellous procession of seven tops promising one of the great high-level walks, but with no hint from the scree-covered flanks presented to travellers along the road that on the other side, just around the western end of the ridge, in fact, was the great amphitheatre of Coire Mhic Fhearchair, one of Britain's finest corries and home of the Triple Buttress, arguably the most impressive crag in the northern Highlands, where holiday crowds are drawn to its bowl by its special beauty alone.

Blissfully ignorant of this, it became blindingly obvious as to how I should reach the crest of Beinn Eighe as I stood in the car-park by the road through Glen Torridon. Ahead was the mouth of Coire Dubh Mor. I would follow the path which entered this vast gulf between the hills, and some way into the pass between Liathach to the west and Beinn Eighe to the east (and which unknown to me was the route that eventually curled around the far end of the ridge and into Coire Mhic Fhearchair on the far side of Beinn Eighe), I would cut intrepidly straight up the slopes above to the skyline of my chosen walk. This would bring me on to the crest at a point between Sail Mhor at the western extremity with Choinneach Mhor the next peak along. Could anything be simpler?

That beautiful morning it did not seem so. It was the most plain-sailing ascent of all my days in Scotland. And it began along the track from the car-park, past the ruined croft sited on the way in to Coire Dubh Mor (which attests to the Highland Clearances in the 1800s when tenant crofters were forced off the land by excessive rent increases to make way for sheep), and on still further into the entrance to the corrie.

The quality of the morning lifted the spirits, buoying me up with the vivid greens of the grasses, the spread of purple heather and the tiny birds skimming just above the vegetation. The climb ascended steep grass and scree but with ribbons of grass and turf – which can be pieced together to make a fairy stairway – threading their way up between the silvery slopes of scree falling down which distinguish this mountain (and which can easily extinguish you should you try actually

Beinn Eighe from near the road entering Glen Torridon from Kinlochewe.

climbing them rather than the grass in between).

Had I been rock climbing with a partner that morning, the primary purpose of the rope might have served to tether us to this planet and prevent our bodies floating away into outer space. Yet never for a moment did I consider as I weaved my way upwards between the scree fans that just through the other side of the same mountain was the Triple Buttress itself.

I arrived on top of the ridge approximately above the Triple Buttress, unaware of the immense rock faces underfoot and looking northwards in the same direction as myself, towards a distant Loch Maree and the great wilderness beyond Letterewe on its far shores. The great cartoonist

H.M. Bateman, who specialized in pointing out the crassest of errors, would have found a drawing in it: 'The man who climbed Beinn Eighe from the wrong side.'

Climbers who have known me for a long time may shake their heads at my stupidity (though on second thoughts they may not for exactly the reason that they have known me for a long time). Of course, I had heard about the Triple Buttress on Beinn Eighe and had yearned to climb on it too, only there is so much climbing in Scotland – much of it on hills with similar-sounding names – and I did not associate that Beinn Eighe with the Beinn Eighe as I saw it first from the car window, with its sleek and unbroken horizon stretching along above the moor.

There had been so much to take in during this crowded month in Scotland; I only had the energy that came to me it seemed when actually on the Hill and listening to the motor automatically zooming the camera in my hand as distant views of amazing beauty loomed towards me or receded into the distance at the touch of a button. The ridge between the steep prow of Sail Mhor and Choinneach Mhor being a perfect example, a sharp and curving crest like the scallop of a sea-shell, and so exhilarating.

Although I did not see the Triple Buttress upon which unknowingly I had clambered as I reached the high point above Coire Mhic Fhearchair, I could see into this rugged amphitheatre, a bowl brimful of limpid light, reflected from the remaining snow of winter and the greyness of the rocks. It looked gloriously alpine.

The sunlight retained its golden quality along the ridge. I had it all to myself that Monday morning and it was sublime. Between Choinneach Mhor and Spidean Coire nan Clach – that next magical peak – the going became all stone, occasionally carpeted in a lustrously bright green moss, sometimes interspersed with delightful steps of scrambling, often providing a causeway through the sky, the rockery below the feet all clanking and shifting, and of a deep ochre tint like a Yellow Brick Road.

Below my trainers the rocks squeaked and ground together, pumice-like in their feel and sounding like broken crockery. The boulders along the ridge were also strange. They might have been made from polystyrene, so hollow did they sound as you clambered over them.

The skyline continued, sometimes pink and white like Turkish delight, on to Sgurr Ban, down steeply into a col before swooping upward once more on to the very crest of the impressive cliffs of Sgurr nan Fhir Duibhe. This was a rocky, stony and very steep climb with a little scrambling and panoramic views from its diminutive summit. Further on along its lofty summit crest the ground suddenly opened beneath my feet to reveal a deep gap with vertical sides and a floor comprising large boulders jammed precariously together. Carefully, I clambered down from one large handhold to another, but tugging on them first because the odd one would wobble in its socket like a loosened

A ruined croft marks the start of the walk into the mouth of Coire Dubh Mor and the way round to Coire Mhic Fearchair.

tooth. Then, descent accomplished, I stepped across the chinks of light seen disconcertingly between the poised rocks and climbed out up the other side. However, shortly the ridge began to descend towards the end of Loch Maree and too remote a touchdown for my return to the car.

Reluctantly I turned around and began to reverse the traverse, down into the gap, up the other and steeper side and back on to Sgurr nan Fhir Duibhe. Walking back the whole way along which I had come seemed further and took longer than before. Presently,

though, I stood once more at that point just beyond the top of the Triple Buttress where I had first breasted the ridge and, still quite ignorant of the treasure missed that day, I cut down the scree slopes previously ascended and crossed the moor to the car.

I had missed the Triple Buttress and now I long to return and climb there, although there can never be another morning like the one when I had the mountain to myself and shadows and sunlight chased each other across the depths of Coire Mhic Fhearchair just so.

Chapter 33
THE CLASSIC TRAVERSE OF LIATHACH

My blood-sugar level, blood pressure, resistance to infection, mood and pulse rate presumably at their lowest ebb during their twenty-four-hour cycle, I felt like death as I crouched over my camera on Liathach, shielding it from the rising sun while removing the film I had just ruined and snapping in yet another roll. Then I heard approaching footsteps. 'Hi,' I said absorbed, intent on checking that the leader of the film had been taken up on the spool. 'Hi,' returned a voice and my eyes took in a pair of Walsh Raids fell-running shoes like the ones I favoured during that May in 1989, when I took the photographs for this book.

For a moment that was all I did see,

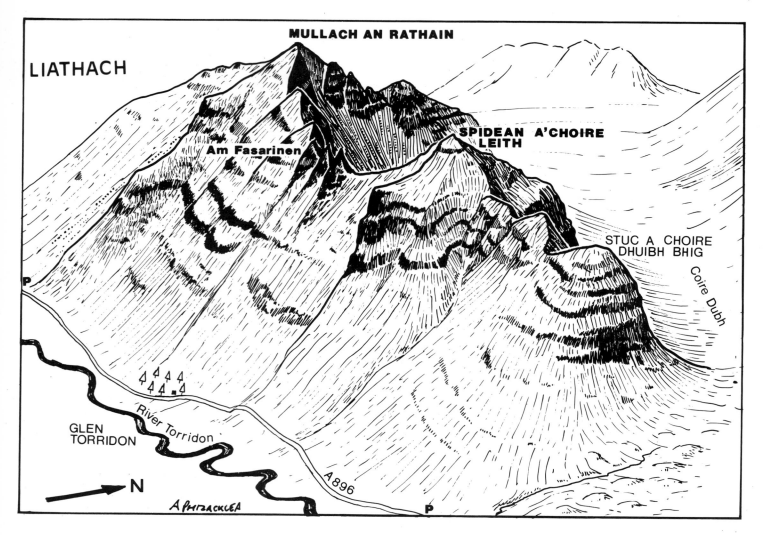

LIATHACH — MULLACH AN RATHAIN — Am Fasarinen — SPIDEAN A'CHOIRE LEITH — STUC A CHOIRE DHUIBH BHIG — Coire Dubh — GLEN TORRIDON — River Torridon — N — A PHIZACKLEA — A896 — P

rather like Ralph in *The Lord of the Flies* who observes a pair of shoes after he collapses on the desert island beach at the mercy of his blood-crazed pursuers. At first he can only take this footwear in as he gasps for breath but then, as he allows his gaze to travel upwards, he realizes they belong to the naval officer who has landed in the nick of time to save him.

As my eyes also followed suit to reveal the person standing before me, they registered he was without a stitch of clothing save the shoes (and a day sack on his back). Totally composed he was too, chatting away despite my confusion at this sudden fully frontal confrontation. I could only try to maintain eye contact and say things like 'Oh, really?' 'Right!' 'Yeah, right!'

He kept glancing towards the clothing I favour on the Hill such as my scarlet underpants (albeit longjohns) and T-shirt, thinking perhaps he was in the presence of another naturist and hoping to persuade me to join in his chilly perambulation. As my nervousness increased so did my rate of verbal diarrhoea, and it was only as he sauntered away that I realized he had been asking what time it was.

This distraction brought me out of myself, for it had happened at a moment when I had reached my nadir in Scotland. The effort of piling out on to the Hill virtually day after day for three weeks was proving excessive. I was becoming punchy. And that morning on Liathach had been a classic example of what can happen when you try to do too much. (Yet considering what was to happen later in the day, it also shows how resilient the human frame can be when forced by circumstance to do the things you must).

Wallowing in self-pity (and not a little terror), I felt I had every cause to do so. Hadn't I been forced out of the pit at 3.45 a.m. in pitch darkness by an insistent image of Cary Grant kneeling over rows and rows of bright red tomatoes with tears in his eyes and wring-

Liathach from near the road through Glen Torridon.

ing his hands? Hadn't I – when all I had wanted to do was sleep, sleep and sleep still more – forced down quantities of muesli and coffee before taking to the Hill?

With Liathach you do this immediately, it being the Leviathan of red sandstone flesh overlaid by a hide of quartzite that stretches for six miles along the northern side of Glen Torridon, a massive horned beast rising so malevolently from the wilderness of moorland below that it would hold its ground in any mountain area in the world on account of its uncompromising shape and compelling presence. The Grey One is Liathach's other name, apposite as you take in the vast flanks of scree and heather towering upwards to the tiers of rock buttresses above, seamed by gullies gashed into black slits and muscular with ancient protuberances at every point.

Once committed to the traverse of Liathach, you can only go forward or back for much of its length. Because it is precipitously buttressed on all sides, and its summit ridge is pinnacled, it is no place for the inexperienced or faint of heart, especially in bad weather. What is an entertaining expedition for the multitudes in summer, becomes a climbing expedition of Alpine difficulty and magnitude in winter.

My express urge to be on the skyline at daybreak had been given a boost the evening before in the hotel bar at Achnasheen, a staging post in the Highlands where after many miles from virtually any direction the weary traveller arrives at this tiny community feeling he might be the only person left on the planet.

Achnasheen is not far from Torridon and farmer Jimmy McLellan who had a striking similarity to Cary Grant, and who was relaxing with a drink, knew all about Liathach. Or Liarakkkk as he called it, rolling his r's and warning me of the dangers. In fact, perhaps

Skyline travellers cresting the Fasarinen Pinnacles leading towards the Mullach an Rathain.

because of my age which was similar to his own and also the fact that I had said, yes, I ventured on the Hill in training shoes he became very solicitious about my safety, saying there had been many bodies brought down from Liarakkkk. 'They're not actually *these* trainers,' I tried to explain, pointing at the footwear in which I visited the pub. 'They're fell-running shoes, handmade in Bolton, crafted on a last, very light, very tough, with a tremendous grip. I mean, we go winter climbing on Ben Nevis and walk up in the trainers, only changing into our plastic Koflach boots when we get to the cliffs.' But it was no use. Trainers are trainers, and for the Hill by far the majority

Looking west to Spidean a'Choire Leith, Liathach's tallest peak.

of the population will have it you must go in boots.

What Mr McLellan said, that focused my attention and limited my refreshment that night to one pint, was about his tomatoes and potatoes. There had been a heat wave in Torridon during that May, the sun blazing down at 5.30 a.m. and – following the ground frost of the evening before – scorching his produce so that he was having to hose down the plants first thing. As I had just arrived from Skye where it rained, what was bad news for him was a tonic for me. To be high on the backbone of the Grey One at such a time would be paradise. The best time for photographs on the Hill, at least I now knew from experience, was first thing in the morning and last thing at night. At 5.30 a.m. next day I would be on Liarakkkk! The weather report that evening assured it.

What plunged me, then, into the depths of the blackest depression happened not as I reached the ridge of Liathach with the sun only just making its appearance over the massive bulk of Beinn Eighe to the east, but that after not only reaching that point and then completing a distance along the skyline that seemed approximately half the length of the ridge, I was required to return empty-handed and totally desolate. I could not believe it. But that early morning there was to be no blazing sun, just a purple haze over everywhere. To make it worse, through my lack of experience I had wasted a film on views that were quite visible but which I realized the more I clicked away would be useless.

Perhaps the visibility would improve during the day. In which case it would have made sense had I climbed to the ridge much later in the morning and got some extra hours sleep. Up here in the half-light of a new day going back and forth like a demented wine waiter seemed insane. Senselesly, I blamed

Mullach an Rathain viewed from Spidean a'Choire Leith.

myself for again making the wrong decision.

However, reaching this point on the ridge in the first place had been the best part. The lay-by from where I had begun is just across the road below the ravine of Allt an Doire Gairbh. The path opposite had soon widened into a regular track, at first taking the left-hand side of the stream, then switching over to the right bank from where it struck upwards with swerves and jinks towards the final headwall of cliffs, breached by a wide gully containing patches of iron-hard and dirty snow – right on to the crest itself.

In daylight that rocket launch ascent up the banks of Allt an Doire Ghairbh into Coire Liath and to just below the top of Stuc a'Choire Dhuibh Bhig looks horrendous. In the darkness which gradually grew lighter, allowing my vision to improve, it was almost a joy.

You saw only vaguely the bulk of the hill ahead and this had a psychological advantage. Just the stars glittering above beckoned you towards them, themselves so far away it did not matter. Also, as the eyes accustomed

themselves to the increasing light, the spectacle of the gorge below the left side of the path was ethereal. Banks of primroses hanging luminous on great black water-streaked walls while the cascades plunged into pools of greenest lime cordial. Rowan trees, their red berries dancing in the draught from the waterfalls, leaned over the maelstrom below. Everywhere small birds twittered and swooped. It was the dawn chorus and the cuckoo was shouting.

I crested the ridge well before 6 a.m. The sun was climbing and I congratulated myself on things going to plan. 'When you reach the ridge,' my friend Ado had said, 'leave your sack in the small col and traverse the short distance of ridge rightwards to the top of Stuc a'Choire Dhuibh Bhig. It overlooks Coire Dubh Mor and Beinn Eighe. It's a great photo.' It was too, but it was then I saw the purple haze.

Even worse was the fact that when it came time to find my sack again, I discovered I had hidden it too effectively. As I had stashed my false teeth inside it during the climb, and was now feeling ravenous after the ascent, I felt this might not be my day after all. All I had to eat in the plastic bag clutched in my hand was a fistful of salted peanuts, which are impossible to chew with just your gums.

I could not help glancing up at the view ahead while conducting my search. By now I had turned my back to Beinn Eighe and the only view forward was westwards along Liathach's crest itself. The three vast pyramidal summits of Bidean Toll a'Mhuic, its subsequent satellite and Spidean a'Choire Leith, still crested with snow, took my attention away from mundane things like false teeth. They looked stupendous. Yet as – rucksack found at last – I raised my camera I knew there was something wrong. The haze that had obscured the sharpness of Beinn Eighe was blurring everything else too.

I had stored my teeth in my sack because my mouth was full of tiny

ulcers – a sure sign of the stress getting to me – and taking them out relieved the discomfort. That pressure was to increase intolerably as I experienced the scrambling up the steep broken ridge of Bidean Toll a'Mhuic. I could already imagine the superb views of Spidean a'Choire Leith from the pointed tip of this peak, but what was the use if it was hazy? It was the correct assumption too. Not only was Spidean's immaculate summit obscured just so slightly by the pall as I finally reached Bidean's top, but so also was – after approaching its eminence up a steep arête still laced with snow – the panorama from Spidean itself, reputedly one of the country's finest view-points and beaming on to Liathach's west summit, Mullach an Rathain, seen to unearthly advantage across the void.

The Mullach, a huge wedge of black rock, furrowed with deep gullies still packed with snow, rises abruptly from a perfect corrie. Fringed by the black

The final climb to the summit of Spidean a'Choire Leith when viewed from the east.

Liathach viewed from near the road through Glen Torridon.

teeth of the Northern Pinnacles to the right, the basin is a sight to see. But not without difficulty that morning.

Yet still I continued taking the pictures as a patient will keep taking the tablets though the prognosis never seems to improve. That was the kind of madness I felt. Nor was it until I had descended a great boulder slope where you picked your way down rock after rock and finally traversed a stretch of grassy ridge towards the pinnacles of Am Fasarinen, that I realized it was a conditioned response and all a complete waste of time. I found myself wishing, oh, for a facility on my camera that would tell me the worth of each snapshot taken (like those pub computer games where a robot voice repeats mechanically 'You are a winner!' when you strike it lucky or, conversely, there is a sound of a flushing loo). But, real-

istically, I knew I had wasted a roll of precious Fujichrome.

The return journey along the route I had already taken was done with a heavy heart. Was this what it was like being on parole with a electronic tag attached to your person so the powers that be could keep track of you? Everywhere I moved was dictated by the optimum position for using my bleeping electronic monster – be it the sun's position, the potential viewpoint or whether a vertical or horizontal picture was possible. Cameras . . .

Back at the nick in the skyline where I had first breached the ridge of Liathach and also fearing for my missing dental plate, I crouched down and replaced the spent film in the camera with a new one. It was at this point I heard the sound of footsteps and encountered the nudist on the Hill. By now time was passing and other parties began arriving. I listened to their conversation as they passed me by, perhaps wondering why this man in longjohns and trainers was sitting with his head in his hands. Suddenly I pricked up my ears. 'Oh, it's good, so good,' said a woman's voice, 'It's getting better by the minute.' I waited until the sound of footsteps clanking on over the rocks had receded and looked through the slits between my fingers, afraid of what I would see, rather like observing a horror movie if you are squeamish, or a wife giving birth.

The day was clear, the hills sharp. Without even thinking about it, I undid the flap of my day sack, withdrew the dreaded Bozo Bag, clipped its waist belt wearily back around me and once more began to retrace my steps first back to Stuc a'Choire Dhuibh Bhig to the east just as I had done first thing. Then, about-turning, I came back, retrieved the once-again cached sack and began the re-ascent of Bidean Toll a'Mhuic. By the time I had reached the Fasarinen Pinnacles for the second time, things were looking up.

'I have a boxful of sunlight here,' I

thought, 'Canned sunlight and pictures to go with it and nothing can take it away once it streams through this pinhole aperture.' My footsteps recovered some bounce.

There were people outlined on the pinnacles, sometimes bent double as they peered down examining where their next respective descents lay, at other times as upright as sentries while posing for photographs. It was a glorious trip to follow, the crest of these crazy gendarmes and towers, and apparently more straightforward than the path which skirts below the pinnacles above Glen Torridon – a sojourn across treacherous grass ledges that can create problems when greasy and/ or covered with snow. At least so I was informed by other walkers. But then the traverse over the pinnacles themselves will prove exacting in such conditions. It was just on that particular morning the rock was snuff dry.

Beyond the pinnacles I slogged on up the brawny shoulder of Mullach an Rathain, the scale of the peaks staggering, which was by now, as I surveyed the wonderful landscape deep into the Coire na Caime to my right, exactly the mode by which I was progressing.

Pausing briefly on the summit of Mullach an Rathain, I stole a glance at the peaks behind me. In a few memorable hours I had gone back and forth along their crest – and back again. Though I also realized neither the mountain nor the morning was yet over. I descended the heather tussocks and tangled grasses to the west of the great stone chute, these steep, rugged slopes following the line of the Allt an Tuill Bhain which drops due south of Mullach an Rathain. It was a tiring descent. But on the road near the National Trust for Scotland Centre a miracle happened. A motor-cyclist stopped and whisked me back to the car-park less than a mile beyond Glen Cottage where the Mini was baking in the sun, its seats too warm for comfort in the midday sun.

Chapter 34

A TRAVERSE OF BEINN ALLIGIN

Doug Scott gave me a nickname that I found not particularly flattering until he told me why. 'The Goose' – for it was this – was a basketball star who had a funny walk. Unaware of this myself, I also have a similar bobbing gait that makes me look odd (and that is only one of the things). Doug had met the Goose when his father took him to see the Harlem Globetrotters at Nottingham Ice Rink. The future mountaineer who was to make an international name for himself on the world's great peaks was then eight years old. Picked out from the crowd to be shown how to take a set shot, he found himself being instructed by the Goose, a beanpole who towered over him as he demon-

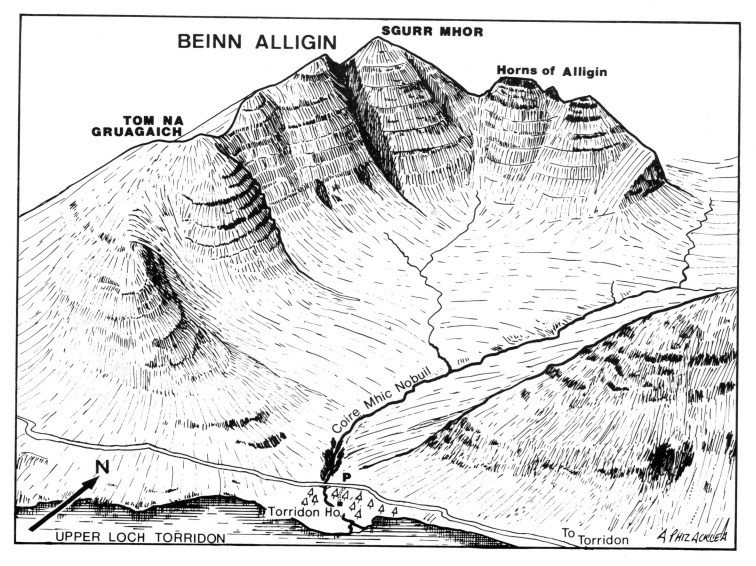

Beinn Alligin and its Black Cleft (Eag Dhuibh) seen from the approach into the Toll a'Mhadaidh.

strated how to aim the ball. 'And,' says Doug, still elated as he remembers the curve of his shot hanging for a split-second before falling towards the basket, 'I got it in.' I am glad I remind Doug of that happy occasion.

By now I should be used to people making fun of my walk. Another was millionaire publisher James Mitchell who spotted it at one o'clock in the morning in New York City. He was on the opposite side of 1st Avenue at the time and gave a shout, audible even over the blaring of car horns which always sound like a brass consort playing a piece by Mozart for wind instruments. I had once climbed with James on Pavey Ark in Langdale, with him in wellington boots and buying me and my girlfriend dinner in the Red Lion at Grasmere. But that's another story. The Manhattan one ended with a drink in a bar and an invitation to come over for breakfast next morning to the Algonquin Hotel.

I thought about this as I finished Ben Alligin and returned down the path to the car. No matter how buoyantly my ridiculous leaping walk may have started that morning, it was not in evidence now. Instead it was the caricature of a drunken and rheumy-eyed shuffle, the hobbling of a broken man, finished and down. I had shot my bolt and experienced the depths of despair during the final passage of that descent.

But it was not Beinn Alligin entirely that had reduced me to this sorry state of affairs. Though it had been instrumental. Rather, the fault lay once more in my own shortcomings.

The traverse of Liathach achieved previously that morning, I had faced the prospect of climbing Beinn Alligin and its matchless ridge over Tom na Gruagaich, Sgurr Mhor and the Horns of Alligin that same afternoon. Not by choice, I assure you. I am certainly no mountain runner, but because – having started the Liathach traverse at 4.30 a.m. and arriving back at the car by 1 p.m. – the sky was still enamelled blue and the sun and the clouds were just right. Having decided to try for the second skyline that day, then, I just had time to lick my wounds, gulp down some muesli and powdered milk.

And, after dozing in the heat of the afternoon for an hour by the car-park below Liathach, I pointed the Mini down Glen Torridon towards the head of the loch.

I was running behind schedule following a disastrous four days in the Cuillins. Yet glorious days I had also had and by doubling up on a skyline a day it was possible to recoup some of the lost time so long as the weather held.

Now was such a chance to redress the balance. I had previously done both the traverses of the Beinn a'Bheithir skyline and the Ring of Steall in a day. The excitement flooded through my tired and aching limbs as I thought of repeating the performance over two of the greatest mountain crests in Torridon. It was a somewhat cavalier attitude to say the least and it might seem heresy to some.

I didn't mean it like that at all. But that's how it may well have sounded. Hoping I had learned from my mistakes on Beinn a'Bheithir and the Ring of Steall then, I was prudence itself as far as my preparation was concerned. The great ridges of Torridon, and their tremendous castellated sandstone mountains, soar upwards with staggering abruptness from the moorland below as though they have been poured into giant blancmange or jelly moulds, allowed to set, then turned upside-down and placed in close proximity on a vast cake tin covered with wild grass, peat and heather, not to mention innumerable lochans and boulders, where you might imagine stags at bay gazing out from the heavy gilded frame of a giant oil painting in a stately home.

Wrinkled and terraced at intervals with horizontal seams and deep vertical gullies, they rise in close proximity to the road that penetrates Glen Torridon from the village of Kinlochewe, away to the east of the Beinn Eighe National Nature Reserve. Beinn Eighe is in fact the first of the Torridonian giants you pass, its long skyline a strand of silver in the sky, followed by – and after a surprise view as you round a bend in the road – the racing yacht keel of Liathach. This, in turn, is followed by – though you have to drive

Beinn Alligin and its Horns (Na Rathanan) from across Loch Torridon.

Looking past the Black Cleft from Sgurr Mhor along the ridge towards Tom na Gruagaich.

right down the glen for this and past the head of Loch Torridon – Beinn Alligin itself.

Driving alongside the loch, the road first has to pass the tail end of the Liathach ridge immediately to the right before Beinn Alligin next rises in its own self-contained complex, also to the right, but well back from the road. It is a lovely piece of highway this, narrow and twisting, the woodland on both sides mossy and green and very Rupert Bear and only affording glimpses of the hills through the foliage.

I locked up the Mini in the car-park near Torridon House, gazed with obligatory wonder at the plunging falls of the river issuing from Coire Mhic Nobuil and finally set my legs in motion again with some reluctance. It was beautiful here. Pines and larch and birch and rhododendrons gave the air a lovely perfume, and the sounds of falling water, a freshness to the air – elsewhere so arid from the heat of the sun.

Across the road, I took the path along the right-hand bank of the river as I headed up Coire Mhic Nobuil. From this point, Beinn Alligin's perfection is unseen, indeed the woods you enter further screen the view. However, once through the trees, and following the path into the barrenness of the valley beyond, the great arena fronting Beinn Alligin and its great skyline – rather like a huge armchair – looms into view to the left, vast, shapely and intensely powerful.

There is a pool up the river, beautiful and deep, landlocked by rock (with the requisite rope swing above the green depths) and with a bridge that takes you over the water towards this forbidden territory – 'forbidden' because it kept occurring to me that I was pushing it a bit. However, I had not yet experienced the dreaded pains in the chest or anything. The exhilaration gained from the surroundings was enough. On I slogged now, up an intermediate track slanting back left towards the left end of the skyline dominated by the great cone of Tom na Gruagaich and the steep groove that ran up to the summit on its end slopes in the form of a hanging valley with a very sloping floor. There was still a cornice of snow across its top.

The ground was spongy, and gave slightly, preventing me from thrusting effectively with those legs that normally gave the bobbing walk associated with the Goose. I felt I was going very slowly, though the sun remained at a reasonable height in the sky. I plodded on, head down save during the intervals when I paused, unable to look away any longer from the majestic mountain now so massive in my sights. Its splendid architecture pulled me on, magnet-like, as gradually I worked my way back across its base to the foot of that final staircase of a corrie to the top, the ground now steepening, becoming firmer underfoot and the grass ever greener.

Now the ground was becoming pock-marked with footmarks, each a pigeon-hole shaped by the pressure of countless pairs of feet that had climbed this way before. Their owners had presumably also reached out with a hand to maintain their balance on the sharpening incline. Clumps of a parsley-like plant dotted the slope, giving occasional assistance if you used them with a pinch grip. Water bubbled downhill from tiny, brimful springs, coursing through the scree and grass. Higher up the corrie, the grass give way entirely to scree and shale, my whole grinding ascent now focussing on the next ochre boulder or gold-streaked rock, say 40yds ahead, which was reached with the head down, only lifting it now and then to take a fix on the next target ahead. This is the easiest way of climbing steep terrain, for your destination is always surprisingly closer when you do look up.

The cliffs of the left-hand side of the corrie fell away below. So too, disconcertingly, did the floor of the corrie, now plunging down ever further as I toiled upwards, my vision unimpeded as I was able to look between my legs so steep was the climb. At last I reached the remnant of an old cornice but now breached by the steps of people who had previously come this way; and then, following the summit slopes of clanking stones and scree, the summit cairn.

Poised abruptly on the edge of space and overlooking the tremendous plunge into the bowl stretching across to the high point of Sgurr Mhor – Beinn Alligin itself – the scale was vast. Without the intervention of some barrier between me and this emptiness, standing as I was on the brink of the hill, my head felt giddy just allowing my eyes to follow the sweeping lines of the great ramparts plummeting down without interruption to the boggy slopes of the Allt Toll a'Mhadaidh, up which I had toiled that hour some time ago. It was one of the great viewpoints of my month.

However, this was only one of several I was to find along the spendidly compact ridge which now surged away around the yawning and cavernous slopes I had just been admiring. Meanwhile, I was starting to shiver. Without thinking, I pulled my Ice Warrior jacket from where I carried it by the slingshot method of doubling it over the rucksack strap beneath an arm. Then I put it on without removing my day sack like a woman can slip on or remove her bra without removing her blouse.

It was, as those conversant with the method know, all to do with the straps – it is rucksack straps we are talking of here, you understand – that you alternately slide off first one arm, then the other, while shrugging on (or off) the garment beneath, first one arm, then the other. But it was a help when you wanted to cover ground steadily and not break the rhythm by stopping, opening a sack, pulling out the jacket and putting it on and so on whenever the air became cooler or, as the case may be, warmer.

The way from the summit of Tom na Gruagaich was now downhill. Down easy stony slopes, then down a sharpening edge with scrambling down rocky steps and always with the great mouth of open space down to your right. The descent completed into the col beyond, the ridge now gradually sloped upwards again by beautiful grassy slopes, traversed if you wished by a well-pounded path.

Padding the soft springy grass with my trainers, I began to feel stronger. My bounding walk, however, was probably not in evidence; the steepness of the ascent had taken it out of me. No doubt the endorphins were now racing round my system, triggered by all the hard work I had been doing that day. My supply of endorphins, however, unlike the day they served me so well on the Ring of Steall, were not to fuel me

quite so effortlessly this time, as I was shortly to discover.

It was after passing and duly marvelling at the views down the tremendous rift of the Black Cleft – Eag Dhuibh – on the long and seemingly endless slopes up Sgurr Mhor that my come-uppance arrived. Perhaps I had been too cavalier in presuming the doing of two giant Torridon ridges would be simply a formality, designed to fit in meekly with my plans.

The breeze was very intermittent. When it vanished my personal temperature soared. Unzipping the black jacket, I shrugged off a rucksack strap, eased my arm out of the sleeve so that the coat hung down my back, replaced the rucksack strap, then shrugged off the other one, preparatory to easing my arm out of the remaining sleeve without breaking a stride. Then I heard the sound of money crashing to the ground. All the considerable amount of loose change in my unzipped inner pocket (accumulated because during my month in the Highlands I changed any Scottish £1 notes that came into my possession into hard cash) cascaded out while it was hanging momentarily upside-down. My worldly wealth, certainly for the next few days, lay scattered by the edge of the vast basin below. Even as I listened I could hear coins dropping like pieces of ice melted by the sun.

Down on my hands and knees, I grovelled for the loose change, When I eventually finished, my pocket seemed a good deal lighter than when I had set out. I felt a fool. I was at least three decades too old to be living out this kind of *Boy's Own* escapist caper.

It was the Peter Pan complex, that was what it was. There is a lot of it about when I think of the climbers I know. All expressing an irresistible urge to become unaccountable. All escapologists at heart. I just had to accept that we were tarred with the same brush, but how great it would be to be responsible and not regarded as an idiot for a change.

Beinn Alligin viewed across Loch Torridon.

Looking through the Black Cleft that splits the south face of Sgurr Mhor, the highest peak of the Beinn Alligin skyline.

It was the hardest toil of the month I now experienced on the treadmill to get me up Sgurr Mhor. Grassy slopes, plunging down into the blackness of Eag Dhuibh, yawned below as I plugged on slowly upwards, pausing every now and then, head always kept down. Presently the angle levelled, I was on top, the very summit of Beinn Alligin itself, and the recipient of such magnificent views that walking on along the ridge culminated in a spot which brought me to a halt.

Directly below, angling out at right angles to my present direction for travel was a narrow crenellated ridge. The culmination of steep slopes angling up from below, it looked so tantalizingly attainable. I realized I was gazing at the Horns of Alligin, but then came the realisation, slowly but surely, that I was not going be able to make their acquaintance from any closer.

'Go on,' a part of my mind urged, 'It's all downhill.' So it was, too, very steeply downhill. I didn't really know what held me back, certain as I was that I would be able to manage not only the descent but also the climb back up on to that narrow saw-toothed edge which looked so utterly appealing, yet which at the same time had an undeniable air of menace about it. I have climbed long enough to know that how a mountain, peak or rock face looks is important. Such an appearance can change from day to day, depending on your state of fitness, mind and form. That evening, as the shadows began to lengthen across the corries, and pin-pricks of light began to appear in those distant valleys, I experienced such an intangible feeling — that if I continued I would be pushing my luck.

Slowly I retraced my steps and began to climb back down the way I'd come, cursing the fact I'd been a wimp. In the distance Tom na Gruagaich looked much further than I remembered. I picked my way back towards it, no longer savouring those views now down to my left, nor those more gentle ones to the right, down the sloping backyard flanks of Beinn Alligin, so to speak. They were still beautiful slopes for all that, the prospect of mountains and lochs beyond quite breathtaking, an endless prospect of mountain, moor and loch.

It is on evenings like this that the climber on the hills can convince him or herself that they are immune from the life in the valleys below. Three thousand feet below, and a mile or two away, are people caught up in their little lives, agonizing over the failure of their car battery, on the verge of divorce, bracing themselves for an appointment with the boss first thing the following morning, quarrelling over the custody of a child or putting the heel in outside bars.

So thinks the hilltop climber, quite overlooking for the moment that they are destined to return to the same trivial daily round themselves on their return to Earth. Ridge-bound on the Hill, in a no-man's land where earth meets the sky, they are possessed by an easy solecism which creeps up on people who have a world of valleys below their feet. The self alone exists – the self, and the Hill.

To the left, Liathach stretched like some great beast, its rump rising above Coire Mhic Nobuil, while Beinn Eighe, disappeared into the distance beyond it, another Leviathan of the glens. Seen through the twilight now descending, their presence comforted and assuaged me. I was after all a Hillman now. I had after all done most of two skylines in a day. I was reasonably sure that the photographs I had taken that evening would stand me in good stead, although I would find it impossible to pretend I had really done all of Beinn Alligin.

So what, said the Hill, so what. I staggered on, more content now, just wanting to be down before dark. The final slopes were killers to the top of Tom na Gruagaich, the snow bank beckoning dimly through the light. I plunged through it, and down the slopes below, inadvertently slide-tackling boulders on the screes.

The path from the corrie followed the one I had originally taken, but then it branched. I took the south fork across some grassy swards to the right, then down on to a wilderness of peat to be led back to the car-park by boggy and eroded tracks. I finally arrived on the opposite bank of the waterfalls from where I had started.

I must have staggered into the Damph Bar like Dangerous Dan McGrew. There was somebody there who knew me. 'What have you been up to?' she asked. 'Liathach,' I said, in what may have sounded a casual voice though really I was finding it an effort to speak. 'And,' I added, 'Beinn Alligin. Liathach was this morning. I did Beinn Alligin this afternoon.' 'You look dreadful,' she said, 'Was it that bad?' I shook my head, feeling the Hillman running in my veins once more. 'Not for this boy,' I managed to utter, 'Not for this boy.'

Chapter 35
THE CIRQUE OF AN TEALLACH

An Teallach is a behemoth of the far north-west and one of the finest half dozen skyline expeditions on the British mainland. One million years ago, as woolly mammoths roamed the Highlands, Arctic ice began to overwhelm the mountains. Only the sandstone pinnacles of An Teallach (and the summit of Clisham in the isle of Harris) were to remain exposed above the ice-cap.

These exquisite tops of Sail Liath, Corrag Bhuidhe, Lord Berkeley's Seat, Sgurr Fiona and Bidein a'Ghlas Thuill, create a saw-tooth scenario that mountaineers dream about during wild-eyed moments. Yet when I almost — almost, please note — completed its famous traverse around the glorious cirque of Loch Toll An Lochain, I saw nothing of this except through a veil of

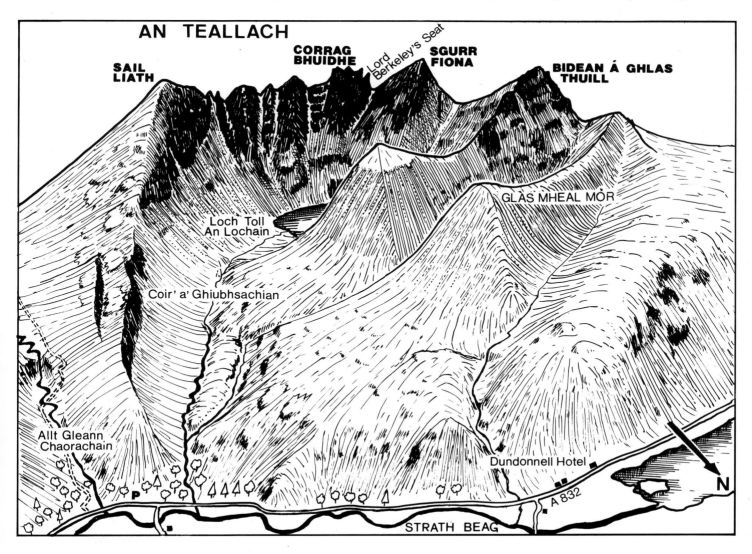

mist which included the tears in my eyes. Only shadowy shapes loomed ahead and only then when you were almost upon them, including one of Al Phizacklea on a sandstone pinnacle engulfed by mighty crags and on the brink of an abyss so that with the palms of his hands upraised, he seemed to be impeaching the very heavens. At the time only my worst fears prevailed. The mountain in fact was to rule my eight hours sojourn along its crest with a reign of unmitigated terror.

It is a role for which An Teallach seems eminently suited, dominating a scene of absolute and utter desolation, a region considered to be the last great wilderness in Britain. Viewed at sunset with its sandstone tops glowing fiery red like the embers of a smithy forge and you have it at its most invincible, rearing as it does over the tiny community of Dundonnell far below.

The Forge it looks like and the Forge it is. An Teallach, The Forge, and such an unearthly sight in certain kinds of light that it can send shivers down the spine. Certainly this applied to Al and myself when we took up its challenge, even though it rained throughout the day.

A story concerning Shenevall, the five-star bothie in Strath na Sealga, under the southern slopes of An Teallach, would appear to bear this out. In the 1950s a group of RAF mountain-rescue team members were preparing a meal here after a day's climbing. There was a knock on the door, and a man stood there, lost and benighted. Was there room for him? Of course. And if he would like, the evening meal would be ready soon. He went upstairs to the floor above, was heard treading on the floorboards and never seen again. There were no upstairs windows and he could not have returned to the door without passing between the people below. Spooky. The RAF team made a pact to keep it to themselves. Several years later one of them overheard a conversation in a pub which tallied uncannily with his own experience. He compared notes with the people concerned. They too had met the man at Shenevall.

It was not, however, anything so sin-

Dawn comes up on the peaks of An Teallach, viewed from near the A832 road to Dundonnell.

ister that ruled my hours on An Teallach with an undiminished fear and trembling – or perhaps it was. It was the spectre of failure that An Teallach made me see, like I had never experienced since becoming a freelance writer in 1961.

As the big cars hurtled past us on the motorway travelling north to Scotland for New Year, throwing up water from the road surface on to our windscreen like a car wash, I was able to muse on this ill-conceived trip – planned on a whim at the suggestion by Al that we do An Teallach and share the petrol – at some leisure.

An Teallach ahead, the focus of our drive, became the focus of what was on my mind with this book. I realized that I had made a serious miscalculation. In banking on completing it within a year, I had been unrealistic. Given rain like this it was going to take forever.

Up to the moment when, shortly after we gained the crest of An Teallach's mighty skyline, Al had rested his hands on top of the pinnacle and mantel-shelfed into a standing position with the deftness of a circus trapeze artist – it had been raining solidly since we had started out on the 300-mile journey after work the evening before.

All the way north to Gretna Green, then through Scotland towards Inverness before arrowing north-west along the Road of Destitution towards our destination of Dundonnell, the rain had pelted down so hard you saw it coming towards you in the headlights as if flung in giant splattering handfuls against the windscreen. There was water all over the road, no more than a strip of tarmac inlaid amongst barren wasteland, and at one point stopping us in pitch blackness when it drowned the motor, the wind rocking the car like a mob of angry soccer thugs. As the eye searched the sea of darkness for the tiniest glimmer of light, there was nothing to draw comfort from save – once we had regained momentum – the occasional gleams of our headlights

on an approaching road sign, suggesting for a moment lighted windows ahead.

And still it rained. Inside the bunk house at Dundonnell the notices in the kitchen appeared to say it all when it came to Highland weather. 'Do not hang wringing wet clothing in the kitchen but in the garage. It should be spin-dried first. Do not cram the spin-dryer too full (it won't dry any faster and uses more current).' Was there any wonder my spirits sank still lower? Even a last look out before sleep had the same individual fistfuls of rain still hurling their way into our faces as we stood at the door under the porch.

Next morning we awoke to the sound of rushing streams, but the storm had blown itself out. After bulking up our digestions with vast amount of muesli and because in winter it is best to get away as early as possible in the morning to allow the most from the daylight hours, we were packed and ready by 7 a.m. The cloud base was around 2,000ft. For a moment I wondered if we should give it a miss. But Al never considered it as he stepped out towards the car.

The rough track which branches south-westwards off the A832 half a mile south of Dundonnell House was a millstream as we began to splash upwards through the inky blackness in our grubby white plastic winter boots. Passing through the woods of Gleann Chaorachain, a deafening torrent of water was plunging down the gorge to our right, while ahead more waterfalls hung suspended above the darkened landscape like streaks of ice. A spark – a spark! – leapt from the ground to the heel of Al's right boot with its rubber vibram sole in mid-stride. Not since the days of rock climbing in nailed boots had I seen this happen (usually on the way back from the pub). Perhaps this bright spark was caused by static electricity. The thought of forked lightning now piercing the moist, humid blackness of the morning and zapping

us on the heights of An Teallach just added to my misgivings.

Higher up the track there had once been a footbridge across the burn that fed the gorge we had passed. Now there only remained a hulk of rotting timber and a couple of posts protruding from the silvery conveyor-belt of flood water speeding past. We took no chances, the power of this water sufficent to bowl over the unwary and transport them down the waterfalls below. Boots off, inner boots off, socks off, longjohns and track-suit bottoms rolled up to the groin and plastic outer boots back on again, we packed everything into the sacks and began to wade, feeling our way gingerly over the uneven stream bed and with my dread of over-balancing and falling in and drowning the camera (uninsured) in my sack growing with every faltering step.

Across on the far side, the brain reeled from the anaesthetically numbing effect of the water on the feet. Al got away first as I retied my boots once more with everything back in place. When I next saw him it was behind a chink of light far up the track as he hunkered down to read the map with his headtorch. First light was just breaking and feeling dreadful already with every passing glance at the desolation of the surrounding view, the feeling was to increase as we broke rightwards from the path to begin ascending a gradual slope of heathery wilderness. For these it seemed were the lower and interminable slopes of our first peak, Sail Liath.

Gradually we approached the top of what was suddenly revealed as an escarpment which – had it been good weather – would have given us a splendid view into the heart of An Teallach's cirque surrounding Loch Toll an Lochain. Instead, mist drifted across the scene and it began to rain. And now, head down to avoid the dispiriting sight of total blankness ahead, we began the toughest part of the day: the ascent of Sail Liath's final slopes, of which there

The Serious 'Bad Step' on Corrag Bhuidhe, An Teallach, in the wet.

were hundreds of feet of them disappearing into the murk overhead.

The only variations to break the monotony were things like slabs of pink sandstone, the white on some boulders looking like quartz through the Stygian gloom but becoming white lichen on closer inspection and a lichen so vividly green on the ground it could have been mistaken for the kind they painted the dials of wristwatches with before it was found to be radioactive. Everywhere there was shite of one kind or another – ptarmigan, grouse, deer or snipe – on the rocks and among the heather. Miss it you did not, not with your head kept well down and every upwards step a measured one.

The slopes steepened ahead, and I found I was pulling myself up with my hands as well as cranking upwards with weary legs. The way ahead was not obvious, being trackless and covered in tangled vegetation. However, at one point a run of scree and rocks gave a temporary respite as clambering up its edges gave relatively solid ground from which to make each laborious step up. You can tell by the angle beneath your boot soles when the incline starts to lessen. This happened, and shortly afterwards we reached the summit.

Now the ground became a mixture that never changed during the rest of the day's traverse: lawn-like turf interspersed with threadbare patches of terrain between tors and pavements of red sandstone, and with sand crunching underfoot like sugar. Often the crest of the ridge was so narrow that any thought of falling was out of the question. We teetered along from one peak to the next, balancing up steeply angled sandstone slabs and walls, always sensationally placed but usually with excellent holds.

Despite the shifting masses of cloud which billowed and eddied past pinnacles and great cliffs stacked ahead in never ending procession, there were glimpses of corries below, of great sandstone walls toppling away down into space from the heights of our aerial causeway through the sky. And whenever you glanced behind you, the cliffs which you had bypassed stood cowled in mist.

As I photographed Al on the pinnacle on to which he had climbed, I thought, 'What's the point?' A persistent drizzle wet the camera within moments, fogging up the viewfinder, and the skylight filter was spotted with droplets as I returned it to its bag. Having spent a lifetime on mountains encumbered only by a rucksack or climbing gear, this additional appendage felt foreign and unwieldy.

With Al it was different. He was a keen photographer. Indeed it was he who now exhorted me to keep taking the pictures, even though the light was at a minimum according to the orange light blinking in the viewfinder.

On Lord Berkeley's Seat, he waxed ecstatic about the incredible nature of our position. However, before we reached this exalted point, first we had to climb the Bad Step, a steep and technical move up a V-groove on the western side of the mountain crest. There are in fact a plethora of paths along narrow terraces on these flanks of the mountain which prove ready options for those who do not want to continue along the very rim of the skyline for the whole way and which lead to the Bad Step. This is what had happened to us; the slipperiness of some of the rock and the exposed situation, especially the imposing terraced arête of Corrag Bhuidhe leading to four exposed towers along the crest beyond, forcing us down to the path below which led to this very point. Not all the paths on their different levels are necessarily viable options, incidentally, but the main path, worn away by the boots of those who had passed this way before is well-marked.

The Bad Step is awkward in big boots. The idea of bowling off this place to go hurtling down the mountainside below, crushing the camera *en route*, was too gripping to contemplate. Al had already clambered up its awkwardness and I followed suit after taking a deep breath, semi-laybacking on a rounded flange of sandstone in the first instance, and then reaching for the handholds he generously pointed out from above.

Above the Bad Step, the path continued along the left-hand flanks of the mountain as before, threading its way in and out of bays among the crimson cliffs and with the skyline always above and to our right. Now, though, we were able to regain the ridge again and, looking back along its rim, could only marvel at its rugged grandeur.

'Just look at that, will you?' said Al. By now he had finished with the retrospective view and was looking once more at the one ahead. 'Yo!' Beyond a pronounced dip into the next col soared the ridge as if in flight, its angle of attack landing it on the pointed turret of Lord Berkeley's Seat. Tears of frustration welled up inside me, of exasperation and self-pity. The scope for photography along this crest was matchless. Yet, wreathed in mist as dense as chimney smoke and with a light register so low that it automatically locked the shutter of my camera, what chance did I have? Especially if it was always going to be like this on my choice of Scottish skylines.

If Al sensed my feeling of fear and hopelessness with everything, he never mentioned it. Nor did he make as much as a comment that if the weather remained like this I would never finish the book within its allotted span. I suppose it was too obvious, but I was grateful all the same. He also said something I find it impossible to think about without laughing. On the summit of Bidein a'Ghlas Thuill, the highest point of An Teallach, we had met another party on the summit who had climbed the peak from Dundonnell.

'Come far?' they asked. 'The Lake District,' he replied. 'Och, that's an awful long way. You'll be up for the New Year then?' 'Hell, no!' said Al. 'We're just up for the day. We'll be back in the Golden Rule tonight.'

Whereas the ridge from Lord Berkeley's Seat down into the col below Sgurr Fiona (which we had climbed to its large cairn before ascending more strenuously up a sharp-edged ridge to that summit of Bidein a'Ghlas Thuill) had been plywood-thin in places, with holes appearing through the crest as if it were fretwork, now the Hill was substantial and solid once more. The narrows of An Teallach were past, we realized. But frustrations were not.

As the rain began to pour down on top of Bidein a'Ghlas Thuill, soaking the Bozo Bag and drenching the barrel of my camera – zoomed to its full 105mm extent in an attempt to snap the atmospheric view – the sound of the autowind motor retracting the glistening wet tube back into the nerve centre of the instrument acted on Al. 'Stop,' he said, showing me how, even in driving rain, it was still possible to wipe away most of the moisture with the cuff of a sleeve. But this wasn't why I was sad – that I could have already wrecked the camera and wasn't it obvious what I should have done? No, it was more than that.

The arm of ridge containing the far side of Toll an Lochain, from Bidean a'Ghlas Thuill to the distant (but to us, invisible in the mist) peak of Glas Mheall Mor, was a famous vantage point for photographs of the immense buttresses and pinnacles of An Teallach just across the way. Yet at that moment you would never have known they were there.

We cut short our full traverse of the cirque around Toll An Lochain somewhere in the vaporous mists below, and descended the northern ridge beyond Bidein a'Ghlas Thuill. Then we picked our way down steep grass and scree into the empty neighbouring corrie of Coire a'Ghlas Thuill.

The corrie was alive with streams of water rushing from crevices in the hillsides, gullies reverberated with the booming sound of waterfalls and we constantly exclaimed what a marvellous climb such and such a spout would be were it frozen in midwinter and we were here to ice climb. The novelty of this began to wear away however as we realized we could not cross the streams frequently barring the way ahead just when and where we required. Many were deep, channelling a force of water that was deadly. We started to concentrate on picking our route through these myriad threads of silver without actually drowning, gradually losing height and finally emerging from the mouth of the corrie onto a prospect of such empty loneliness that I cannot forget it.

The mist still clung to every hillside in sight, and there were miles and

'As I photographed Al on the pinnacle in the pouring rain, I thought "What's the point?"'

miles of them stretching into the furthest distance. The sky was already darkening with the hour. We could only breathe a sigh of relief that there was still some daylight, and use it to descend the rough slopes back down into the Strath Beag, past ubiquitous boiler-plate slabs of pink sandstone and through a wasted land of endless peat. Then, finally, as the trip had begun, it ended with silver birches, pines and rhododendrons and – those months later when the film I had delayed sending was returned – a feeling of the original jubilation. Not all the pictures taken had been the failures I anticipated or so I thought at the time. Later however, my editor told me they were not up to standard.

Chapter 36

THE HIGH-LEVEL CIRCUIT OF THE NORTHERN CORRIES

The ski pole almost took off my ear as it whizzed past and stuck, spike first, in a snowdrift below the great iced cliffs of Coire-an-t-Sneachda. I knew there had to be a catch. We were preparing to traverse a great Scottish skyline. And by a new kind of skiing, the world's fastest growing winter sport. It sounded too good to be true. Stringing together a scenic excursion along the crest of three great Scottish corries – Coire Cas, Coire an t-Sneachda and Coire an Lochain – chiselled deeply into one of Britain's five highest mountains and with all-embracing views in every direction – we would be gliding on skis which, it was said, were only half as costly as those for downhill skiing. Also so adaptable that you could ski mountain tops like mighty Cairn Gorm itself or, come to that, parks, golf courses and even pre-rush hour roads after a night's snowfall. All true, true, true . . .

But the ski pole trembling in the snow bank high above the Glenmore Forest Park said that life was not like that, and Sasha's look of 'To hell with

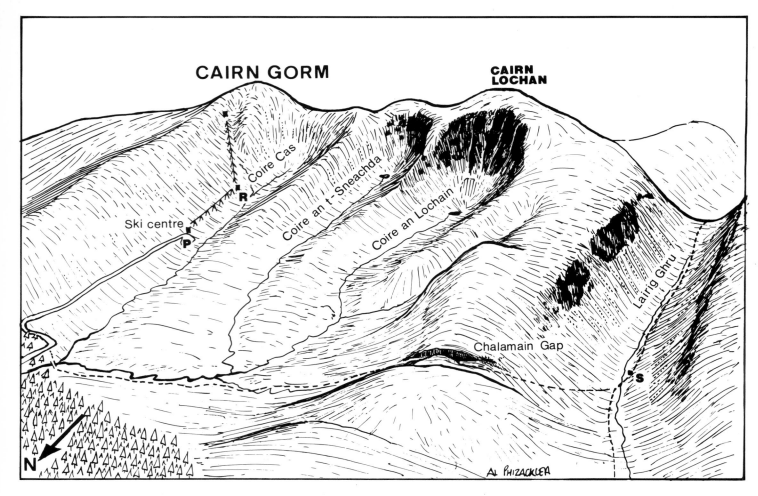

CAIRN GORM   CAIRN LOCHAN

Coire Cas

Coire an t-Sneachda

Coire an Lochain

Ski centre

Lairig Ghru

Chalamain Gap

N

AL PHIZACKLEA

X-C skis, I'm walking home,' confirmed it. When she hurled away her ski poles in disgust, she only just beat me to it.

Things didn't stay this bad beneath the crest of Britain's easiest high-level perambulation (or at least it is usually done by hill walkers and mountaineers). They got even worse. But like a Greek tragedy, they had to before they could improve. They know all about pain and pleasure at the Scottish Sports Council's national outdoor centre at Glenmore Lodge, Aviemore where I had taken this introductory course in X-C – cross-country, or Nordic – skiing.

The Lodge hosts the UK X-C Ski Championships every year in February. Queen's Forest, the shores around Loch Morlich, and the corries and summit plateau of Cairn Gorm have to be among the best X-C ski terrain anywhere. But it's Big Country, and serious, the traverse of the Northern Corries perhaps typifying most of all the excellence of the countryside around here. It is breathtaking, especially, if you get the chance to do it in winter.

The Northern Corries of Cairn Gorm sit like great cinema seats with their backs to the rest of Scotland, England and Wales, facing the Arctic North and the nightly showing of the gigantic ring of fire that periodically leaps 40,000 miles up from the sun's surface to unleash a stream of violent energy causing the beautiful appearance of multi-coloured Northern Lights, or aurora borealis no less.

Just like the particles from this solar storm race across space to Earth 93 million miles away, only to be halted by the vast belt of radiation that shields us from what would otherwise be the lethal effects of such blasts, and which are dragged around a long curving path by the sun's own rotation, in flowing, whirling ever-wider spirals until they reach Earth, the traverse of the skyline of the Northern Corries is potentially extremely harmful and likely to be in-

The blossoming canopies of three UpSki parachutes on the north-east slopes of Cairn Gorm.

jurious to your health. However, by the same token it can – with prudence – be rendered relatively safe, staggeringly lovely and highly exhilarating.

The danger in traversing the Northern Corries lies in the ease of access to what is a high, hostile and disaster-prone environment. It has become the highest yet gentlest skyline in Britain, but only because you can climb almost to the summit of Cairn Gorm by chairlift. It is a wildly contrasting environment from the one below.

Deep in the foothills of the Cairngorms, the remnants of the great Caledonian Forest, whose pines once covered the Highlands, are still there, as are the reindeer that became extinct in Viking times but which have now been re-introduced from Scandinavia. There are sweeping new plantations of sitka spruce and lodgepole pine and high-altitude loch waters with sandy beaches. Capercaillies and black grouse

share the woodland with crossbills, woodpeckers and redstarts. On heather-clad hillsides, golden plover, red grouse and curlew start at the thud of approaching boots. However, it is on the sub-arctic environment of the mountain tops up here, the domain of the eagle, ptarmigan and snowbunting, that winter offers most opportunity for the climber, rambler and skyline skier. For this is the Glenmore Forest Park which includes the slopes of 4,084ft Cairn Gorm, of which our skyline is a fragment.

Extending from as far away as Ben Macdui to Cairn Gorm, this huge expanse is the largest region of high ground in Britain. As such it provides a terrific feeling of space. Because of its emptiness, winds regularly sweep across with great power, often of hurricane force, and in winter such conditions can produce blizzards so severe that crossing this upland massif becomes impossible. Another feature is

A notice that says it all, by the high-level car-park below the chairlift of Coire Cas.

the edge of steep slopes and corries, creating risky avalanche conditions at certain times of year.

Yet despite its hazards, the skyline of the Northern Corries provides some marvellous winter travelling for the experienced and adequately equipped hill-walker, climber and ski-mountaineer. The settings are glorious, the going superb.

The high-level circuit of the Northern Corries takes a delightful line whether you use the chair-lift or not. The skiers' car-park below Coire Cas is the initial starting point. If you decided otherwise, there is no need to use the chair-lift but, instead, you could climb the access road up to the Ptarmigan Restaurant. Or – and as we shall see – there are even other enticing options for getting aloft on the roof of Cairn Gorm.

Inside the Ptarmigan, everyone is cocooned against the vilest weather. If

the chair-lift has provided a rocket-launch into outer space at nearly 4,000ft, the glass-and-steel blister of the restaurant is a space-station. Spindrift flickers beyond the windows like cosmic television interference. Through it, dimly, you can perceive ghostly figures like showroom dummies rising on a conveyor-belt as the ski tows level out, their tight pants pneumatically pleated around the knees like a concertina, or the gas-filled leg of a typist's adjustable chair. Chair-lift passes, clipped to designer jackets like forgotten price tags, flap madly to hint at the power of the wind tearing like the Flying Scotsman across the great mountain plateau, along whose exposed edges would-be traversers of the Northern Corries skyline hope to implement their daring and beautiful route, given a break in the weather.

Yet downhill skiers are probably safer on Cairn Gorm than the most proficient

mountaineer, hill-walker or skyline skier. Although considered 'Aliens' on the mountain by the dyed-in-the-wool climber, the world of the downhill skier being a planet away from that of mountain men like those of the Creag Dhu who man the lifts, that hard-core of Scottish rock and ice climbing (and who, in the back bar of Glencoe's Kinghouse Hotel would send the barman for hot pies while they threw a dart on a piece of string to spear packets of cigarettes from the shelf behind the bar in his absence), their only aim is to swish back down the slopes into Coire Cas on their glossy skis. And if the climate is too hostile? They are prepared to stay put in the Ptarmigan, sip hot soup and stamp their boots in time to Jimmy Shand on the cafeteria radio.

How much more difficult it is for the seasoned hilltop climbers, conversant with map and compass, impatience gnawing, who yearn to distance themselves from the pylons, snow fences and the seething mass of humanity at the soonest opportunity. It is so human to blunder out into borderline conditions, depending on the compass and trusting past successes. If you do this, you forget that your map-reading may well be superb, but the fact that new snow is piling up everywhere means avalanche conditions are likely along the very same skyline crest of the Northern Corries you are hoping to traverse through the great white yonder.

The evening before we skied the Northern Corries skyline, I had met Frith Finlayson, a doyen of Scots skiing, in Aviemore's Red McGregor bar. A few drams later he asked me why I was writing about such a little-known sport as X-C skiing. I told him that a traverse of the Northern Corries had been recommended to me as ideal for this kind of travel. 'Besides,' I said. 'It sounds different.' Frith laughed. 'Oh, it's that all right.'

Hadn't I already discovered this to my cost during the previous three days of rigorous training at the hands of Tim Walker, a Lodge instructor and X-C ski enthusiast?

It was just as well that we practised in the Lodge grounds. 'Tim,' I called, requiring assistance, 'my skis have crossed like seized-up scissor blades.' Tim was kind. He pointed out a little diagram on each ski binding (where foot meets ski) indicating which was 'left' and which 'right'. I had put them on the wrong feet. The bindings – like bicycle pedal toe-clips – let the heels lift high when walking on the slender, skinny skis. There was a snag here too. I tried and went down, K.Od., as a ski shot forward and the other back as slick as car wheels spinning in soft snow.

'I'm sorry,' said Tim, 'It's my fault.' He explained the problem. X-C skis require waxing underneath so that they grip the snow when you climb uphill. To save time he'd pre-waxed everyone's skis the evening before, but had forgotten to give mine a rub. He then did this with a stick of wax along the section known as the 'kicking strip', the 2ft bit in the middle of the underside of each ski. And the difference! Stand on a ski now and it stuck to the snow like chewing gum to rug weave. Kick off from this stationary foot and the other ski – temporarily unweighted (and its waxed kicking strip rising a fraction of an inch) – slid forward.

We began the long-awaited traverse of the Northern Corries from the Ptarmigan Restaurant rather than taking the trouble to ski all the way uphill (something that is relatively simple, if extremely slow, when you get the hang of X-C skiing) because, as Tim said, time was at a premium during the course and using the chair-lift helped give more time for instruction during short mid-winter days. The day before in Coire an t-Sneachda had been the one for sorting out mistakes, and one which had caused Sasha to fling her ski poles away. The problem? Excessive snowballs had built up under her skis because she had not kept up with the ski-waxing that must be done constantly in certain conditions. But that had been only one of the hassles. We had all suffered.

Cairn Gorm winter landscape.

Sparkling mountains shaped glorious contours in a deep blue sky as we left the Ptarmigan's dome and the skiers flocked back down the hillside into Coire Cas in their brightly coloured droves. Snow glittered along the sky-line ahead with a beauty you had to see to believe. This was ultimate X-C skiing, said Tim. You could ski Nordic eight months a year in the Cairngorms if you went high. However, you had to know how to use an ice-axe, crampons and map and compass.

As it was, by the time we had reached the summit of Cairn Gorm by a series of sweeping zig-zags up that final 500ft of ascent, tacking ever-upwards on the skis, the conditions had become thoroughly Grampian. Clouds had descended within moments. Now our world was suddenly different and threatening. We were wrapped in a pea-souper mist, and treading fluffy mashed-potato snow. However, Tim looked pleased. It would help, he said, with our mountain navigation. We soon discovered you couldn't do this successfully on skis. If 'B', 100yd away, is your destination, and you know you walk at 60-double paces to 100yd on average (average step rate), then you should be able to reach it, in theory, by following the compass and counting 60-double paces as you go.

The snag is you can't count paces on skis which glide. Also, if 'B' is a stream junction on the map, it could be snow-plastered in winter, so you will not know when you reach it. The only way to be sure is to carry the skis and walk. In this case, however, 'B' was the cairn at Coire Chais beyond which lay the gradually rising slopes that led southwards along the heavily corniced edge of Coire an t-Sneachda. It was below these that the mist parted, allowing us a glimpse of something startling.

Approaching up the lonely headwall of Coire Cas, a skier was hurtling upwards, towed by a large parachute, its pink and blue canopy blossoming with the updraught that fanned our faces. Only for the nylon mushroom suddenly to gape open in the middle, spill its air and collapse on the brink of the plateau.

A skier uses an UpSki canopy to help blow him along the crest of the Northern Corries.

THE HIGH-LEVEL CIRCUIT OF THE NORTHERN CORRIES · 185

The skier, meanwhile, having been provided with a free tow, regained her breath, understandably relieved that she had been able to stop after all, and not swept on by the wind into eternity.

UpSkiing, she told us, was an American development, now gaining popularity in Europe. Parachutes had been tried to pull skiers before – unsuccessfully. With an UpSki, however, you could deflate the canopy in moments and stop it on a sixpence. Suitably impressed, we put our skis back on as the weather brightened once more and the skyline re-emerged into view. Picking up the rhythm of the double-poling required to thrust us forward was not easy. Yet it gradually came as we began following the precipitous edge of Coire an t-Sneachda, continuing over the top of its eponymous summit and then gingerly gliding down into the col beyond.

The scenery was fantastic. Beneath the crest of the corries, strong updraughts, the same that had inflated the UpSki, had created vertical walls of snow. Great cornices heavy with frozen snow hung out over the precipices of snow and ice, curling like mountain waves over the fantastic drop beneath. But we only glimpsed these. Most of the time, Tim's rejoinders to keep well back from the corniced crest meant the most scenic moments only came after or before it performed sudden twists along its course, allowing us those brief amazing views.

Climbers were slowly making their way along the serrated profile of the Fiacaill Ridge which separates the wide basin of Coire an t-Sneachda from its other neighbour, the steeper and more spectacular Coire an Lochain. This ridge being one of the few rock arêtes in the Cairngorms, it makes a fascinating summer scramble, the rock being ancient pink granite and delightfully exposed.

Finishing near the summit of Cairn Lochan on Fiacaill Coire an t-Sneachda, the Fiacaill Ridge's glassy mantle, that winter's day was a route for experienced climbers only. It can, incidentally, be gained by walking directly from the Coire Cas car-park across the intervening moorland, passing the end of the much easier Fiacaill a'Coire Chais ridge *en route* and avoiding the ski circus of Coire Cas altogether.

Kicking strips correctly waxed, we toiled from the col up the incredibly corniced profile of Cairn Lochan, its summit offering superb views over to Ben Macdui beckoning across desolate snowy wastes which seemed to roll on for mile after mile while to the west beyond the Lairig Ghru, the great arena of Breariach reflected that transparent quality of Cairngorm light beneath the enamelled blue sky. Deep in the corrie below, here and there, pools of ice twinkled at us, exposed by recent winds.

After the exertions of the downhill walk from Cairn Gorm, then the energetic climb back upwards on our skinny skis, it was a relief at last to face the prospect of mostly downhill ahead. Shoulders, upper arms, chest and stomach muscles felt as if they were connected by steel wires, with a constant but not unpleasant ache. We still felt tired but gulps of air kept us going. Glancing behind, our route glittered like a diamond necklace.

Two things stick in the memory: our reluctance to leave the summit of Cairn Lochan before moving on towards the setting sun, past more great ice-encrusted precipices beetling above the distant tarn in the corrie below, then descending north-west down the wide saddle of the Miadan before continuing north down the ridge bounding Coire an Lochain; and a slim woman with long hair silhouetted against the sky circling her thumb and forefinger on the snowslopes on top of Stob Coire an t-Sneachda before sliding down into the col below Cairn Lochan.

An hour later she did the same thing across the sunset-flared ice rink of the walk back to the Coire Cas car-park. We had reached this path, which crosses the wild moorland below the corries, from that same ridge bordering Coire an Lochain, although it had looked easier to descend by the burn falling into the same corrie. This, Tim said, was a common mistake. Why? The slopes above the burn are prone to avalanche, leaving anyone below in a vulnerable and exposed position.

The footpath back should have been a snap on skis, but sheets of ice on the ground and a biting wind made progress difficult. We commiserated with several climbers, stumbling along as one moment they sank into soft snow, the next they found themselves skating on ponds as hard as iron. The gulf between skiers and mountaineers is not as wide as might be supposed. A good day for skiing is often a bad day for climbing, and vice versa. Those competent in both will rarely be disappointed, especially when travelling the magnificently high and snowy wastes of the Cairngorms.

Chapter 37
THE FOUR TOPS

There are only five mountains in Britain which exceed 4,000ft. Four of these lie in the Cairngorms, Britain's greatest, most natural region of ruggedly mountainous land. It is world-famed for climbing and hillwalking, with its web of great whale-backed ridges, the most notorious and challenging hill passes, and spectacular corries, providing some of the best rock and winter climbing. Link then the skylines of these Four Tops (the fifth peak above 4,000ft is faraway Ben Nevis) into one circuit and the result is a stupendous, titanic route for which you should allow 10 hours at least.

Cairn Gorm, Ben Macdui, Cairn Toul and Braeriach are the quartet of peaks concerned, with Cairn Gorm and Ben Macdui lying to the east of the deep trench of the Lairig Ghru pass — that gigantic V-shaped opening in the hills visible from as far away as distant Speyside — while Cairn Toul and Braeriach are to its west. An expedition taking in all four summits requires a long and strenuous outing in remote country, which should only be undertaken after careful planning and by those experienced on the highest hills. The imposing scale of the mountains and the striking contrast between the broad summits and the steep valleys and corries gives a landscape unique in character, subject to very severe weather, and a quick descent is not as

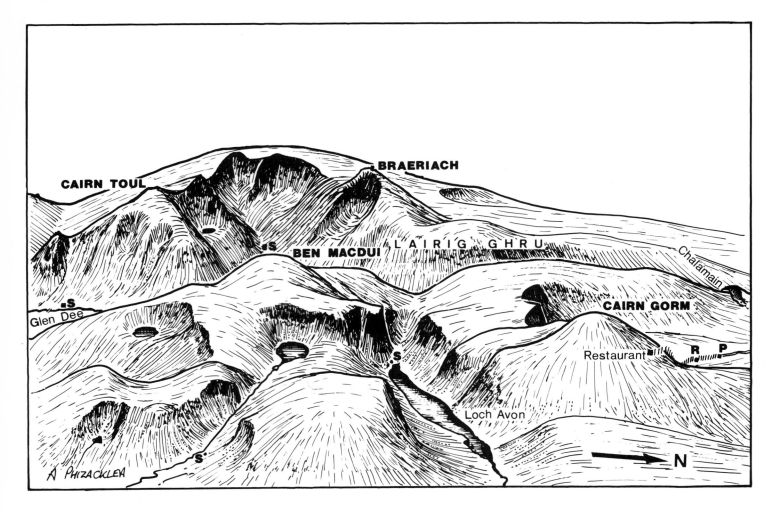

easy as on many sharper British mountains. The terrain is quite featureless in mist and navigation must be spot-on to afford any degree of safety.

To drive home just how remote, wild and desperate the Cairngorms can prove, let's see how a student on a mountaineering course might have written up his experiences of climbing Ben Macdui. Then, having considered just one of the Four Tops, we can go on to the full trip.

'Ye'll need a bottle for tomorrow night,' said the instructor in the pub. 'Then Sammy'll see ye right on the Hill – he's an awful hard wee man.' I dutifully paid up. Ignore inside information at your peril, they say.

Not that the Bells by the bedside next morning was the only reminder of the night before. The fact the rucksack was still to be packed was a headache too. Inside it had to go, besides food and a sleeping-bag; a deadman (a metal plate used for tethering a climber to a snow slope); an ice-axe; a saw; a shovel; a hairbrush; a paperback book; a sack (empty); and a half-bottle of Scotch (full). Each item was necessary, so we had been told by Sam Crymble, our mentor (or, as it seemed that 7.20 a.m., tormentor) and planner of the madcap escapade now imminent.

The adventure in fact was a two-day snow-holing expedition from Glenmore Lodge, outdoor centre of the Scottish Sports Council near Aviemore. As part of the winter mountaineering course, we were to sleep deep inside snowdrifts around 3,608ft on Ben Macdui – at 4,296ft the second highest mountain in Britain. If I met a sticky end in this landscape where a thick blanket of snow covered every discernible feature of the mountain in sight (and you too, if – as photos on the Lodge walls showed – it avalanched) it would be my fault alone. The indemnity presented on my arrival said so. More fool me – or so my buzzing head now

reckoned – I'd signed it.

The gong went for breakfast and seventy students emerged. An hour later we were climbing fast up a desolate glen – by helicopter. Ice chandeliers draped great cliffs, but our faces didn't light up. They were a bit too close – inches away. Our lift was courtesy of an Army helicopter squadron visiting the Lodge to practise mountain rescue techniques. So they air-lifted everyone – four to a chopper to the skyline as part of the operations.

'That way,' said Sam, bringing up the rearguard to link up with a colleague instructor and his charges who had gone on ahead up the mountainside. He pointed up a gloomy snow spout with mist steaming at the top. Everyone stopped to unstrap their ice-axes which, along with monster shovels, were strapped outside their rucksacks. We began to plod uphill, ice-axes dangling like duelling pistols from our mitts, with thumb and fingers round the steel head. We had already had shots at 'falling' on steep snow and ramming the pick into the snow to stop. Ice-axes are also handy for knocking off snowballs which collect below boots like jumbo platform soles, and also for opening bottles at parties. At first the snow was soft. You could hear burns bubbling below, and sometimes you crashed through into malt-brown water. Then it became as firm as hard sand.

Sam took a chunk and squeezed. 'Snow good for making snowballs is fairly avalanche-proof,' he said. I tried. To my dismay the snow crumbled in my mitts. We tramped on up. Sam said there were a few deaths each year in Scotland due to avalanches. Often the victims triggered the avalanches themselves – like walking on a minefield. 'Avalanches can bury snow holes too,' he continued. Seemingly oblivious to my sudden picture of perishing that night under tons of snow in my sleeping-bag while on page 83 of *The Ice-Axe Murders* (the paperback I had packed) he added, 'Even good snow-hole snow can avalanche.'

Hillwalkers silhouetted on the rim of cliffs show their scale above Garbh Choire Mor.

His colleague, the instructor who had gone on ahead, materialized from behind a boulder as if on cue. His first words were sinkers. 'Good snow-hole snow . . . ' It began to snow. I remembered snatches of chat from the previous evening on avalanches. 'Imagine snowflakes falling with tiny arms and legs . . . when they land they interlock, but ageing turns them into blobs . . . start sliding downhill . . . it's called, "destructive metamorphosis".' Too true! My legs felt metamorphosed already. Then we arrived. A steep snow bank shot up into the spindrift like a mini-Eiger. At the top, anorak-cowled figures were shovelling a line of slots into the snow. Our digs for the night. Then the mist closed in again. We kicked footsteps blindly uphill, guided by the

Looking back along the skyline towards Sgor an Lochain Uaine (Angel's Peak), the longest continuous cornice in Britain.

slam of the shovels above.

Whoosh! Wham! We were bombarded by snow blocks as big as kettles. 'AVALANCHE!' screamed the brain for were not – as we had been lectured – falling snowballs a sign of impending avalanche? 'Keep left,' yelled Sam. 'We're in line with the diggers chucking stuff down.' Phew – ah, well. We reached the row of porches to the snowholes. It was like standing on a high scaffold. It looked a long way down for anyone unlucky enough to step back a bit smartish with a shovelful. I ate a Mars Bar. It didn't break so much as 'crack' in two. The cold was terrific. My dentures were frozen in place like no denture fixative could ever achieve.

Sam and I were to share a snow hole and he showed me how to prepare such digs. You each excavate a porch in the snow about 6ft apart, then join them inside the snowdrift by scooping out a hollow – like spooning out the stuffing in a Christmas turkey. One porch is then filled in, leaving just the one entrance open. Then you carve a snow slab quarry in the slope and cut large slabs with the saw which slices them like an electric carving knife cuts pastry. We slid the heavy slabs over the slope like the Egyptians building pyramids to cover the porch down to within a few feet of the ground. Next were added two sleeping benches, ten-candlepower lighting with the candles stuck in niches, the Primus stove standing on a shovel with its handle jammed into the snow, and the deadman, half-buried in the floor as a boot scraper. There was snazzy wallpaper too. Like woodchip pasted horizontally instead of vertically. The lines between, Sam said, were the snowfall levels after each winter storm, completely symmetrical and about 12in apart.

We also insured against domestic hazard. Structural collapse? (Keep shovel and saw by sleeping-bag and link all snow holes with a rope so occupants of any hole whose roof caves in can be found from outside.) Rising damp? (Lumps of snow sticking to clothing will make everything inside wet, so brush your anorak down with a hairbrush before entering.) Gas leak? (Carbon monoxide builds up and asphyxiates snow holers when there is no ventilation so keep the door open all night.) Furniture removals? (Plastic foam pads used as a mattress can skitterbug on the snow floor and shoot out of the open door and away down the mountainside in the night – with you on board, so place sacks beneath to stop them sliding about.)

I was shattered, and Sam cooked. We lay in sleeping-bags as beef curry bubbled on the Primus. Soup and tinned fruit came too. Then coffee (and a wee dram). Instead of TV there was spindrift flickering across the dark doorway, and a host of images in the mind of what was happening outside in the howling wind. Was there really, as Sam had told us, a Grey Man of Ben Macdui, reputedly 60ft high and on the loose on nights like this? Eminent men have sworn he exists . . .

Next day we did Ben Macdui in total white-out. You couldn't tell up from down as there were no identifying rocks or anything. Everyone had to use their compass as we slogged uphill in Indian file, Sam staying at the back and watching us grope onwards into the blankness ahead. Only when necessary did he interrupt with advice like, 'Navigate through the soles of your boots', so you actually feel the tilt of the slope going one way or the other underfoot. 'We need feedback,' Sam then said, and chose two wingers to walk on either side. The rest of us could then tell the uphill slopes from the downhill thanks to our mobile landmarks. Then he cast someone in the role of sweeper to walk behind the single file and check its straightness of direction with the compass. 'Chuck snowballs,' Sam told the front walker. 'If you see them land, we're okay. If not, you're on the edge of an abyss.'

There were frequent conferences on where we were, hunched over maps in the blinding wind, and constant exhortations not to let the force of the wind veer us off-course through sheer pressure despite the compass in our cupped mitts. I don't know how he talked us through. Every time I opened my mouth it was filled with spindrift.

On the topmost slopes, with a featureless vista ahead, we began to look for the summit in the whirling whiteness. We lined up at intervals and groped forward on compass bearings, keeping our immediate neighbours to left and right just in view to make as methodical a sweep search as the gale-force wind would allow. There was a faint whistle. Somebody had found it. A monster cairn. 'As you see,' said Sammy, 'this summit shown on your maps is a scenic viewpoint.' Groans from all. He kicked snow from a brass viewfinder as big as a manhole cover on the trig point. You had to stoop to make out even the markings in the murk. From the summit, we descended slopes dicey with 'grapple' – frozen hail – which, by comparison, makes walking on ball-bearings a piece of cake. To miss ice cliffs just below, Sam counted off paces on a Woolworth's knitting needle clicker, every 'click' meaning two strides nearer safety.

We burst out of the cloud by the ski tow of Coire Cas into another world. The hallucinogenic dots of brightly coloured skiers dazzled us. There were startled glances in the ski car-park as we made our motley way for the pale blue Lodge mini-buses. They didn't faze us now. We might not look so hot, but you feel great after a night in an ice palace, even if you have been destructively metamorphosed in the process.

Without recourse to helicopters, there is still a way to get a flying start to the summit of Cairn Gorm, which is the first objective of the Four Tops. Students from Glenmore Lodge, for instance, kick off the trip this way as part of their course, given good weather. But by the same token, this speedy elevation to the heights can entice people to go for it who are bound for failure. These are the ones who put themselves in danger by being inexperienced, insufficiently fit or over-ambitious. Please bear it in mind. Even instructors from The Lodge have occasionally lost their way on the wide, undulating range of hills that form the Cairngorm plateau, its edges often ending abruptly in the vertical crags of the huge cauldron-like corries scoured by glacial action below. Yet although steep-sided glens, deepened by glaciers, are entrenched into the plateau, only the Lairig Ghru cuts *through* the mountain block, this adding to the difficulties of navigation in mist. Such is the complete desolation of these skylines that Lodge instructors carry not only two maps, just in case, but two compasses as well.

Quite simply, the easy way to begin the Four Tops is to reach the car-park of the Cairngorm Chair-lift Company, a snap of a drive from Aviemore, so saving you a 1,500ft climb through dense forest. A further 2,000ft of climbing is then saved by taking the all-year-round chair-lift to the hemispherical dome of the Ptarmigan Restaurant which, at 3,600ft, is only 500ft from the summit of the mountain. This may seem a soft option, but traversing the Four Tops entails a massive height loss as the route dives from the summit of Ben Macdui into the depths of the Lairig Ghru before roller-coasting back up to the heights of Cairn Toul. The assistance gained by the chair-lift or, failing that, at least the ascent from the car-park by the winding road from the White Lady Shieling to the Ptarmigan, brings things back into proportion.

The Cairngorms are truly Arctic hills and the flora and fauna of these lonely plateaux bears this out: rough-textured boulders are strewn haphazardly everywhere, mosses and dwarf shrubs spread south across the gravel beds of decaying granite and ptarmigans croak their warnings from the scattered rocks of this homeland tundra. Most British hills are splendid from below, but the Cairngorms leave their finest views for those who have reached their skylines and this is apparent on reaching

Cairn Gorm's boulder-clad summit. The gradual slopes from the Ptarmigan Restaurant give no clue what is to come, but having climbed them by the wide path, marked by posts, everything changes. Suddenly panoramas fan out beneath your feet into the great purple distance: whale-backed ridges, separated by ice-scoured furrows and basins – the remnants of an ice age that might never have left.

From the weather station on Cairn Gorm's summit, you descend the stony slopes of the summit dome to the cairn at the head of Coire Cas, beyond which gradually rising slopes lead easily along the edge of Coire an t-Sneachda. Continue over the top to the next col, then bear in a south-westerly direction along a path to Lochan Buidhe, the lowest point on the plateau and the highest named tarn in Britain. To the south, Ben Macdui has been beckoning across the purple wastes, whilst to the west, beyond the Lairig Ghru, the great scalloped amphitheatre of Braeriach forms a superb vista of mountain splendour. Here you will find the 'Eternal Snows', the snow-fields of summer, and the nearest approach in Britain to the permanent snow slopes of higher mountains. As a result Braeriach, together with its neighbour, Cairn Toul, requires great care in winter. Massive unbroken cornices can stretch for several kilometres along their eastern corries and it is a rare summer when there is no snow at all.

The boulder-field of Ben Macdui's summit is reached by taking the cairned track from the lochan as it climbs windswept slopes of gravel and stones, dotted with flowering plants like starry saxifrage and moss campion. Although mountains as far away as Torridon and Knoydart are clearly visible from here on a fine day, it is the immediate summits across the Lairig Ghru that hold the gaze, especially the vastness of An Garbh Coire's great arena with its sharp pointed summit of Sgor an Lochain Uaine, the Angel's Peak, above.

The best way of reaching the skyline on the opposite side of the Lairig Ghru is a relatively direct one. It depends on descending steeply by the Allt Clach nan Taillear (the Tailor's Burn) into

The granite precipices of Coire Bhrochain drop from the summit of Braeriach sheer into the depths of An Garbh Choire.

the bed of the massive trench. This line of descent being located from the summit of Ben Macdui by making for the satellite peak of Sputan Dearg where the plateau between the two tops is the crucial landmark. The required stream descends below. If, incidentally, a large snow patch remains beneath the plateau's rim as late as spring, descend the ridge on the left-hand side of the burn, rejoining the stream further down the hillside. From the point of arrival in the bottom of the Lairig Ghru, cross the youthful Dee and strike strenuously up the mountainside above, following the vague path by the banks of the stream that cuts down Cairn Toul opposite the Tailor's Burn. Climbing steeply you reach a high hanging corrie below the summit of Cairn Toul before striking upwards via the boulder-strewn ridge to the right, which leads to the top.

A glorious skyline now awaits you. Westwards you go to the summit of the Angel's Peak (although the summit can be avoided by a traverse below), continuing along the rim of An Garh Choire, that glorious amphitheatre jewelled with cornices. Skirting round to the north, you reach a small cairn on Carn na Criche, and then, via the spring where the River Dee is born and the tiny rivulets that feed it before the growing stream crashes down the mountainside over cliffs, you press on to the summit of Einich Cairn, continuing in an arc to the summit of Braeriach.

From here it is all downhill at last. Almost. Down the wide expanse of the Sron na Lairig ridge to the Sinclair Hut, down beyond it to the stream. Then, after a steady ascent up the opposite mountainside, you negotiate the granite boulders of the Chalamain Gap – so slippery after rain or when smothered by snow – to take the prominent path that crosses the heathery slopes beneath the mouths of the Northern Corries. This highway in miniature leads you back to the Coire Cas car-park after what surely has been a perfect day.

Looking north from the descent from Braeriach.

Part Three

Wales

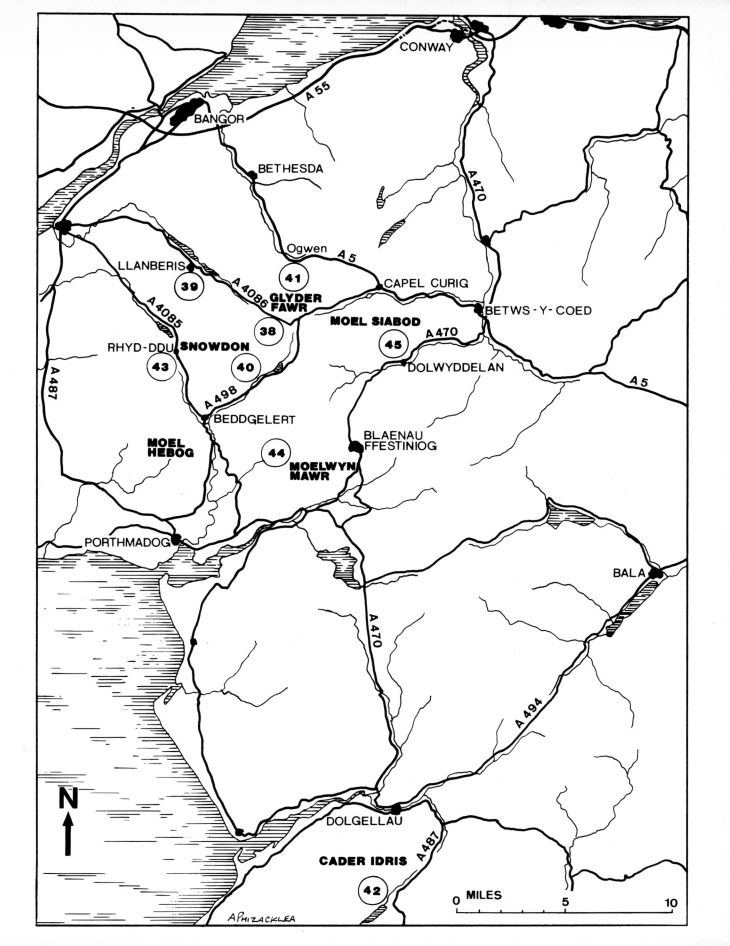

N

0 MILES 5 10

APhizacklea

Chapter 38

THE SNOWDON HORSESHOE

The jade-green waters of Llyn Llydaw were coming up to meet me as I dropped out of the sky below the sharp triangular peak of Snowdon. Only this was at a rather swifter lick than the impression you may receive from the accompanying photo of a paraglider. I had no such canopy. In fact I had nothing. I had just committed a cardinal sin of the mountain climber. I had stepped off the Snowdon Horseshoe and now I was going to pay for it.

How it happened, in fact, was reminiscent of a fun sport played in a certain climbing hut where the roller-board is introduced on wet days or after a return from the pub. To ride the roller-board you balance a short thick plank that rests on a wooden roller the size of a Tesco toilet roll (unused). Then, timed by a wristwatch, you see-saw for as long as you can maintain your equilibrium and contact with the polished wood beneath the stockinged soles of

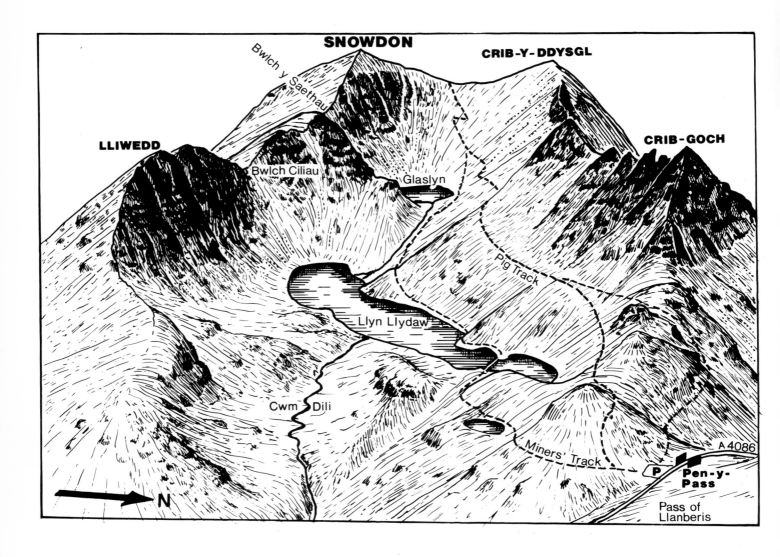

A paraglider pilot flies out from Crib Goch with Snowdon in the background.

your feet. Experts not only keep the roller-board in balance, but flick it around the room like a skateboard. Always, they make it look deceptively simple.

On my first attempt, however, first one end of the board went down as I gingerly applied my weight and the other end went up. Then the end that had gone up fell rapidly down again only to snap back up then down once more – and so on with increasing speed – like a staccato rat-tat-tat of a machine-gun. At the same time these movements grew more violent until – and looking as if a thousand volts of electricity were passing through my body – plank and roller went hurtling in one direction and I was fired through the air like a space shuttle until I crash-landed into someone passing through the room carrying a dish of wet liver.

How my freefall happened on the Snowdon Horseshoe wasn't quite like that, but there was a similarity. A long flat rock I had stepped on with both feet suddenly tilted under my weight and pitched me forward like a child might plunge through an attic skylight head first. I too had fallen, metaphorically speaking, through the skylight filter of my camera for I had been composing a picture when it happened.

As I flew through the air turning somersaults – and the horizon of the greatest mountain south of Glencoe appeared one way up one moment and the other way the next – my one thought was to protect my camera. The longer the fall continued, the more the words of a notice in the climbing hut where I had stayed the night previously had occasion to flash before my eyes. 'CLEANLINESS IS NEXT TO GOD-LINESS' it had said, dropping a hint to departing hut users. How would it apply to me as I hit sharp corners of unyielding rock? But I was not thinking about broken limbs becoming soiled on the earthiness of the ground below and the rapid effects of gangrene. I was more concerned about getting grit in the zoom lens barrel.

As, initially, the shore of Llyn Llydaw below came up to meet me, I had no time to think that it had been in its very same direction I had started out that morning. After first closing the hut door after one last look around to check everything was in order, I'd gone out to the car and taken a quick drive to the top of Pen-y-Pass a few minutes away, the launching pad for Crib Goch and Snowdon.

The Snowdon Horseshoe, in fact, all 7 miles of it and taking say five to eight hours of circumnavigation on average, really begins with the stark East Ridge of Crib Goch. This steep edge, followed by an immense roof-tree of the ridge above, sets the seal on a magnificent skyline, continuing on over further peaks: the problematical spine of Crib-y-ddysgl; the sharp triangular fin of

Snowdon itself; the crest of Lliwedd and down and back to Pen-y-Pass. As everyone says, one of the great days of British mountaineering.

By the time you see Llyn Lyddaw, you are already some way way above it, in the col of Bwlch y Moch, from where the climb up Crib Goch begins and you leave the pathway which has brought you to this point from your point of departure in the Pen-y-Pass car-park. This initial part of your walk is only a mile long – serving both the Horseshoe and the Pyg Track to Snow-don – but it cuts across a mountainside by an impressive path restructured from huge rocks. The views down towards the Three Cliffs of the Llanberis Pass will quicken the heart of climbers, especially the sight of Cenotaph Corner on Dinas Cromlech which is seen to such good advantage, like looking into the pages of a large open book, for so much of the time. It certainly was that fine July morning as I had begun my approach. Ahead of me was the sight of

A cloud-wreathed Snowdon from the Pinnacles of Crib Goch.

Lliwedd from the summit of Snowdon with Glaslyn below and Llyn Llydaw beyond.

the magnificent cone of Crib Goch outlined against a pale blue sky. There were also patches of snow still in evidence.

Not that I had time to think of this as, whirling through the air during my fall, the distinctive peak of Snowdon kept turning upside down – that initial goal which draws you like a magnet along the skyline of Crib Goch. For Crib Goch is the kind of skyline which brings people to their hands and knees in greasy or icy conditions, its steep scree slopes on one side and a pitiless emptiness on the other, exacerbating the exposure.

If you are going to fall on the Snowdon Horseshoe, this airy sojourn is likely to be the place. But no, I had had no trouble on my first acquaintance with Crib Goch that day. I had picked my own way up the steeply rising East Ridge to the summit crest, scrambling up steep bands of rock wherever poss-

ible and sometimes, when forced to retreat, finding another, easier line.

Along the airy crest of Crib-y-ddysgl, too, I had found no problem, though small white arrows had been painted on the rocks. I was told later that this had been done by the Snowdonia National Park Authority, their reason being to prevent walkers from taking diversions over scree and unstable terrain to the left, causing serious erosion and preventable only if the walker keeps to, or as near as possible to, the rocky crest of the ridge, which is the best way I would imagine of traversing the ridge anyway.

And so on to the summit itself, which is called Garnedd Ugain, and with its rounded upper slopes so deceptively dangerous in winter, especially in bad visibility. More than one party of climbers has slipped off the mountain at this spot, in mist and swirling snow. The next stop is the long curving slope

to Snowdon's summit which you finally reach in company with the tracks of the mountain railway – and many, many people. But then the Snowdon Horseshoe is the most popular ridge traverse in Britain, quite apart from the visitors who arrive at the summit by train. And rightly so. Who could begrudge anybody the views displayed that day, a contrast of great mountains and valleys, the coast and the sea.

I had then continued onwards, down the easy South Ridge because having read up on the Snowdon Horseshoe first, for once, I knew better than to try to descend directly into Bwlch-y-Saethau from the summit of the mountain. Instead, I followed the South Ridge down for a short way to an obelisk post, and then descended to the left along a diagonal line across broken slopes, the Watkin Path, in fact – and a dangerous place to be when the ground is hard-frozen. Finally ensconced for more photographs in the Bwlch-y-Saethau, I faced the climb up on to the summit of Lliwedd with less than equanimity. Lured on by the curving, narrowing crest of the ridge, together with the panoramas of its famous north-east face, I found myself at last on one of its two summits in a confused and tired frame of mind. The views across Llyn Lyddaw of Crib Goch were fascinating but even more so I felt would be the vistas of that north-east face beneath my feet with its dark side facing out. I did not know what to do. Then I decided that rather than finishing the ridge in the conventional way – which is, by descending the crest of ridge in an easterly direction before dropping left down to Llyn Llydaw – I would retrace my steps the way I had come and take more pictures, but in the reverse direction along the Horseshoe.

Fatigued now, only the pull of the photographs kept me going the extra distance as I toiled back up to the summit of Snowdon. Not, I might hasten to add, for the aesthetic reason a true photographer might experience, but rather the fear and disgrace of returning with illustrations less than adequate for the book. The more exhausted I became, the more visions of the bailiffs, and the letters from an irate publisher saying the contract for this book is terminated as you have not fulfilled its conditions intruded on my weary brain – all of which somehow made me drag my feet the more, and long to sit down.

The sun and its position in the sky is a ruthless master when you are a photographer. Once more on the summit of Snowdon, this time, with no time to rest, I continued now, skirting beneath Crib-y-ddysgl by the eroded evasive path and back to the Pinnacles and up once more on to the crest of Crib Goch.

To my chagrin the views were not as I had hoped. The viewfinder preferred a fuzzy, hazy scene and frustrated and tired after the long and pointless trip back, I suppose I made my *faux pas* then, though I cannot be sure. I don't remember it as being a trip, more an unconscious motor reaction of a leg for once uncoordinated with the brain, which does happen, but only usually after closing time has been called. And I was falling.

I could feel the somersaults getting faster and faster as my brain registered flashing images of sky, snow and rock. I started hitting rocks sticking out of the slopes whenever I pitched forward from a ledge or terrace. I wasn't scared. I felt quite calm and resigned that whatever would happen would happen. I didn't have any inclination to grab for things, even if I had I was bouncing much too fast to know sky from rock, from one second to the next. I just had an over-riding urge to protect my camera like a mother will clutch a baby to her breast when threatened.

Then I sensed that I was stopping, first on a ledge, then another and finally on a third, each one in succession breaking my fall. I was hanging, back to the mountain, face out, head down, a knee folding over a flake of rock that

A high-wire balancing act on the crest of Crib-y-ddysgl.

was preserving the status quo.

Silence. Should I move, even a little? I didn't want to regain my former momentum again and there were still crags and lots of space below. I flexed my hands, arms, neck and legs. There was some blood about, some tears to the clothing, but nothing broken.

However, I was unable to move. I just hung there paralysed. A blow to the base of the spine had numbed me. Untwisting my legs, I struggled to accomplish a safer position on the ledge. Within a few minutes I was established properly in a sitting position and after half an hour able to stagger upright.

The sun was going down, and it was colder. I was shivering. But it was not until, as I crawled slowly down and down the endless screes to the Pyg Track below that I realized the damage I had done to my face. Until then I thought it had been only my legs and arms and aching body that had suffered,

the sundry impacts reducing me from my previous spriteliness like that displayed in the road signs for Welsh schools where children are shown bounding on their way to school under the caption 'Ysgol' to the stooped, arthritic postures adopted on the signs for old peoples' homes where a couple are bent double over sticks under the words 'Henoed'. But no, I now realized my face had taken a beating too. Running my hands over it I felt its puffiness, sticky with blood and a terrific soreness when I touched parts of it like my mouth or the vicinity of both eyes.

When I returned home people calling at the door recoiled. I looked like something from a bad dream. Two black eyes, a swollen lip, a cauliflower ear, a swollen nose, lumpy forehead and my false teeth chipped. When I told visitors it happened on the Snowdon Horseshoe they smiled, oh, how they smiled. 'Of course it did,' they said, 'Of course it did.'

Chapter 39

THE LLANBERIS HORSESHOE

The Llanberis Horseshoe (otherwise known as The Big Dipper) held a poignant moment for me when I traversed its skyline for the photographs. In my darkest hours, when feeling disadvantaged and challenged – and this was one of them despite the fact I was travelling along one of the great skylines in the land, comparing favourably with the Snowdon Horseshoe, the mountain with which it shares its matchless course – I would gain solace from the fact that 'At least Mo likes me'. It was a reassuring thought, a bit like a lighthouse, a beacon in the dark that made me feel momentarily stronger.

I did not know him particularly well, but he knew me. His unerring insight into human character could be disconcerting. 'Brute strength and ignorance,'

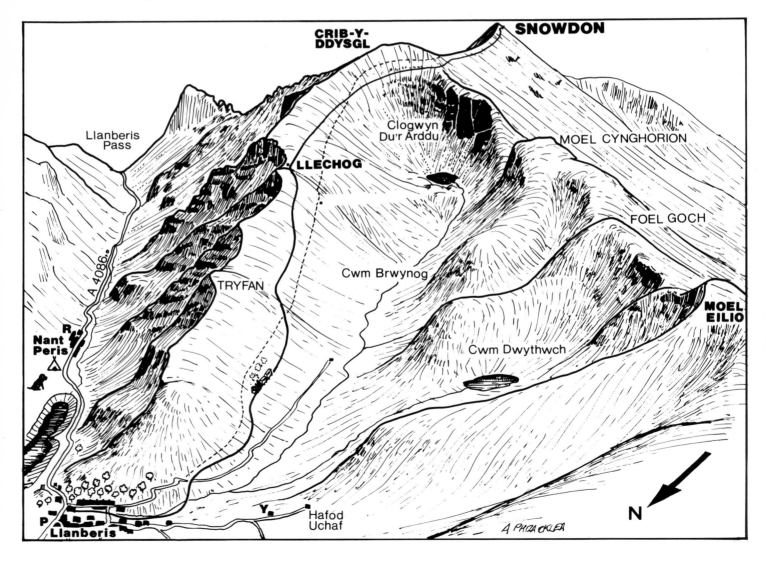

I once foolishly boasted as I heaved away a rock, when the car in which we were making a spirited dash had gone off the road through my misdirection. I'd mistakenly thought that the rock was the obstacle that had been holding us up.

Not a bit of it, however, our predicament was more serious than that. And Mo it was who got us back on the road once more, but only after a prodigious effort as he disappeared under the car in pitch darkness pulling away earth and boulders with his bare hands in an effort unsurpassable by any human being I know, especially as he had only recently left hospital. 'Dunno about the first part,' he said about my feeble claim, 'but I'll go along with the ignorance.' It wasn't so much what Mo said as the timing with which he said it.

The twinkling lights in the houses below gave out a cheeriness I did not share. For Mo was unwell. Somewhere amongst those lighted windows and surrounded by family and friends who loved him to distraction, was the person who impishly would arrive at my door out of the blue, watch me down tools unbidden and whisk me deep into mountain valleys for games of pool with lots of laughs in a variety of bars — laughter, yes, and occasionally tears.

Those would be shed the following morning by me, metaphorically usually, because I just could not handle the poison of alcohol nor the feelings of depression that would follow. Once this had passed, however, the memory of the night before would stay clear and firm. Memories in fact which are still with me and I would not change them in any way.

By the time I had reached this point where the mountainside falls sheer it seems into Nant Peris I had never felt more sober. Perhaps the drinks I'd had the evening before had worn off anyway. I had called on Mo during that previous afternoon, but he was sleeping

The skyline from Llanberis over Moel Eilio and Moel Cynghorion.

and could not be disturbed. It was not until a couple of months later, and the last time I saw him, at a film festival on a ludicrously glorious Sunday (ludicrously because it was a climbing film festival and the audience were itching to be out on the crags) that he said he had actually woken up as I called. But I was walking away by the time he managed to bang on the window and I never heard him. Instead I went to the pub and, being all too human, had taken a few drinks too many on board and so the scenario for the next day was laid: an inefficient start up this, the 15-mile skyline that climbs almost 7,000ft during its terrific horseshoe circuit. First, up Moel Eilio, then along the south-eastern skyline to the summit of Snowdon, returning to Llanberis via Crib-y-ddsygl and the lonely, immaculate crest of the Nant Peris ridge.

While that first part of the skyline is vast and grassy, with its mysterious and remote ambience, the return limb

by the ridge above Nant Peris and the Llanberis Pass is very different. Sharper, overlooking a colossal drop to the one side, on the other it is incongruously accompanied for some of the way by the Snowdon mountain railway with its busy trains transporting visitors up and down the mountain through many months of the year. Indeed, so close to the crest runs the railway at one point that in 1896 a train was blown down into the depths of Cwm Glas Bach and bounced past a startled Pen-y-Gwryd resident – a Mr McFarlane from Glasgow – who fled back inside the hotel for several restorative whiskies.

Between the two extremes, then, the going up over Moel Eilio (and successive peaks along that grassy chain like Foel Gron, Foel Goch and Moel Cynghorion) and the coming down over Gyrn Las, Llechog and Tryfan (yes, another Tryfan) is set a gem. The great crag of Clogwyn du'r Arddu, no less, is a lodestone of British rock climbing from the

The majestic cliffs of Clogwyn du'r Arddu with Llyn du'r Arddu below.

fierce hanging ramparts of the Far East Buttress to the massive, tilted crudity of the West Buttress. It is well named 'The Black Cliff'. Yet see it at dawn or in the sunset and the flush of slanting coppery light turns these precipitous heights into a bronze masterpiece as golden as any Ayres Rock and anything but black. Don Whillans, a climbaholic in his days of pioneering new routes with Joe Brown and other members of the Rock & Ice could not believe I had not been to Cloggy. 'Go there!' he said. 'Just for its looks alone, Cloggy is worth the walk.' If Whillans could say that in his days of creating climbs like Black Cleft and Slanting Slab, the cliff had to be something extra special.

These are the three separate stages then, each with an individual character all of its own. The first from Llanberis to Cloggy and on to the summit of Snowdon saw a complete lack of mo-

mentum in my movements. I seemed to have everlasting reserves of inertia as I plodded uphill past the old chapel and the youth hostel and even after breaching the lush and springy turf of Moel Eilio's Braich Y Foel ridge beyond. This was desperate work, the taking of photographs on the Hill when you had no special desire to. Also, the need to take notes which likewise involved tedious stopping and starting and a concentration of the brain which needed effort. To match my mood, the sun had never looked more remotely like shining. Though I had learned the hard way – by leaving my camera behind only for there to be a few moments of gleaming, golden sunbeams to pierce the clouds on a mountain top against all odds, and you could kick yourself for the oversight – to live in hope.

I found myself thinking of Mo as the views expanded with my gradual increase in height. These were panoramic in every direction though it was a cold,

clear light. To the north-east across Llanberis Pass, the rugged silhouette of a snow-crested Glyders, with the weird wedge of Tryfan jutting over the outline of Glyder Fach, looked stark and wild. Eastwards loomed the summit of Snowdon, also white domed and dominating the grassiness of the ridge that I was destined to travel. The views to the south were quite different; the friendly slopes of Mynydd Mawr and the Nantle mountains with mighty Hebog were touched with cloud, and Trum Y Ddysgyl, standing out like a sentry, rose from woods and fields.

The skyline continues along the lip of the ridge from the summit cairn of Moel Eilio. There are thrilling views down the chaotically riven flanks of Cwm yr Hafod and Cwm Cesig to Llyn Dwythwch as the ridge continues on over the rounded eminences of Foel Gron and Foel Goch. It was on the steep descent from this peak into Bwlch Maesgwm – a good useful route down to the Snowdon Ranger Hostel or back to Llanberis – that I remembered something that for the first time that day made me laugh.

Some toffee I had been eating stuck to my false teeth forcing my jaws together in a lock-tight grip for a moment before, with a horrible sucking sound, the teeth separated from the straining gums. And that triggered it all. The slopes fell away steeply below, offering an astounding view before once more soaring up towards the summit of Moel Cynghorion beyond, but I was remembering a moment that had hardly been to my credit in a pub. I had taken out my dentures and dropped them into Mo's pint of bitter.

In the ensuing silence I saw an expression on his face that warned me of the folly I had committed. It was not the fleeting look that says here is a punch in the face or here comes a head butt. Instead it was almost blissful, to be replaced by innocence as he moved. But I moved faster, desperate now to retrieve the situation. Mo could eat glass – he had indeed already consumed my friend Ed Grindley's spectacles for a wager and Ed had been obliged to buy a new pair (as well as pay up on the bet). If Mo could eat glass, maybe he could eat – well, anything. I grabbed the glass as his hands reached it, the teeth leaping out in the confusion like a fish to land in my lap where I grabbed them and rammed them back into my mouth. Mo just smiled. It cured me of the habit which in the past had led me to skate on such thin ice. But never quite so much thin ice as the prospect of walking around without any teeth whatsoever.

The memory of this gave me a kind of boost, but it was only temporary. The older I get, the more the effect of a previous evening's alcohol takes it out of me in the extreme. It did see me up the broad, grassy slopes of Cynghorion before the effort again seemed to get on top of me. Even the views of Cloggy from high on Cynghorion seemed remote. Then I was descending down more of the steep grassy slopes that had characterized the ridge so far until they are met by the Ranger Path which ascends from Llyn Cwellyn.

The Ranger Path is the popular option to the summit of the mountain, but that day I chose to follow the exposed rim of Cwmbrwynog to the left. Leading to the summit of Clogwyn du'r Arddu, its steep, scrambling gave atmospheric glimpses down a yawning drop below of the silver-rippled waters of Llyn du'r Arddu, cocooned in the hollow below the scree slopes. The long trudge to the summit of Snowdon followed past the notice warning hilltop climbers of the danger of descending unwittingly over the brink of an extremely steep head-wall in bad weather and which has happened all too frequently:

When snow and ice are on the ground it is dangerous to follow the railway tracks beyond this point. Please keep to the Llanberis Path.

Finally I was there, standing on the roof of Wales and almost the last visitor to leave. The Llanberis path may be the safe option and certainly an escape if you are feeling the strain, but to qualify for the remaining 3 miles of the Llanberis Horseshoe, there is a different route to follow. And it is a precious ridge indeed.

Around to the summit of Garnedd Ugain, with its superb view of the Snowdon Horseshoe, I traversed, picking out the highlights from the Pinnacles on Crib Goch all the way round to Lliwedd – the longest cliff in Wales – before heading towards the rim of Cwm Glas Bach and rounding its curve above the great mountain bowl down which the train had gone bounding off the tracks those years before.

On Gryn Las I was lucky. There was still sufficient light in the sky to be able to see one of Snowdonia's finest views, towards the Parson's Nose crag and with the pinnacle ridge of Crib Goch beyond. Then, shortly after this, my footsteps reached the railway tracks for a brief encounter before I veered off rightwards well before the green refreshment shed of Halfway House, once more to clamber upwards. This time to the slabby summit of Llechog, remembering summer days with the trains passing on their 5-mile long journey, the passengers rocking backwards and forwards on their seats like jockeys in the saddle as the juddering momentum of the rack and pinion mechanism jerks everyone to and fro. Until, with the slowing down as the carriages crest the edge of the tremendous plunge to Nant Peris below, passengers leap on to the seats to peer all the better from a standing position over the precipitous edge immediately outside the window, some even trying to get outside to take photographs only to find that the doors cannot be opened from the inside. And you instinctively feel the weight of so many bodies perched high in the train will help to overbalance it, everyone then destined for a

The ridge from the summit of Crib-y-ddysgl to Llanberis, bordering the Snowdon mountain railway.

headlong plunge down the crags below.

The ridge is delightful for its solitude, and above Nant Peris I stood on that other Tryfan, a sharp crest overlooking a pit of space down one of the most steeply mountainous hillsides imaginable. I stood on the short turf those several minutes, then continued on down before the path cuts in to join the mundanity of the Llanberis Path.

I knew I had been in as heavenly a surrounding as ever I will find. The poignancy of the day settled over me as I began the drive back. I could not take my mind off it, the associations of people and places, as I gazed earnestly into the darkness until my eyes were full of black spots and coloured lights and I began to imagine a great mountain ridge was tearing down upon me.

Chapter 40

SNOWDON BY THE NANT GWYNANT HORSESHOE

The Nant Gwynant Horseshoe on Snowdon is like the Dark Side of the Moon to those hillwalkers who think in terms only of popular ridges like the Snowdon Horseshoe, and Tryfan and the Glyders. As the large lorry braked ferociously in the lonely country road, with a hiss of air brakes, and began to career backwards up the road towards my Mini, its reversing lights having suddenly become angry eyes beamed towards me, I began to see that same skyline as the one where I most wanted to be. Two fingers I had waved at that driver as he initially thundered past me, cursing me through the open cab window and fighting the wheel, and those two fingers I now regretted having on my hand. Yet I had not meant the two fingers to be interpreted like that. And now, what previously had

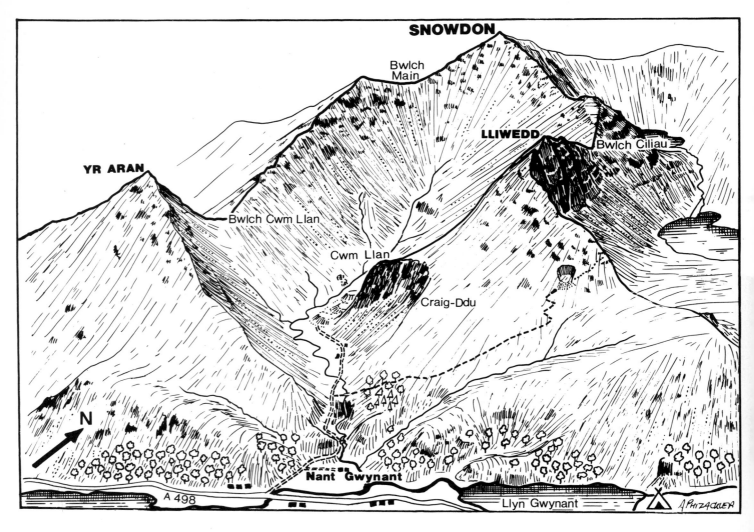

been the focus of my attention – sunlight on the Nant Gwynant Horseshoe – seemed to be light-years away from my reach as I stayed rooted to the spot hypnotized by the onrush of the pantechnicon backpedalling menacingly towards me. Would I live to reach those heights?

Elsewhere in the book I have rated very highly both the Snowdon Horseshoe and the Llanberis Horseshoe (The Big Dipper) – both on the same mountain and both ridges *par excellence*. However, the Nant Gwynant Horseshoe also ranks highly. It is just very different, that's all. The mountain itself is not only immense but so shapely that all three ridges circumscribing its great mass are superb, but the Nant Gwynant Horseshoe is the Cinderella of the three, and you will rarely find it populated. I also found it the most strenuous, and quite magnificent.

Because it has to be looked for to be seen is, I am sure, one of the reasons for its lonely, remote feel. Unlike the Snowdon Horseshoe which is billboarded by Crib Goch's East Ridge, and the Big Dipper signposted by the

Yr Aran from the road to Pen-y-Pass.

Snowdon mountain railway and opening directly on to Llanberis, the Nant Gwynant Horseshoe lies well back from the road and beyond a narrowing of hillsides. It is only by careful perusal, then, that you see the triangular peak of Snowdon from the road through the Nant Gwynant valley, peeping like an Everest way beyond the cwm, bordered by the great hills and looking another world away.

It was this glimpse of Snowdon, in fact, which had brought me first to a screaming halt and which had incurred the justifiable protest by the lorry driver, now looking set to crush my car below this idyllic scenery in the most sylvan and peaceful of Snowdonia's mountain valleys.

My first sight of the Nant Gwynant Horseshoe came as I drove through the valley after descending the serpentine bends of the road from its junction with Llanberis Pass by the Pen-y-Gwryd Hotel. I had almost reached Nant Gwynant when I saw it. Slanting gleams of sunlight struck the far side of a valley turning it into gold while beyond was a triangle of a peak, white with snow and suffused a deepest pink.

Without thinking – you don't when there's a chance of a picture like that – I pulled into the side of the road. Unfortunately, I emerged from the car in such a hurry that the driver's door swung out into the road. There I was standing, camera in hand, and already framing the picture as I pointed the camera towards the goal, when I heard the horn of the approaching lorry, belatedly conscious of the fact that my car was dangerously parked just past a bend in the road with its door sticking out, and that it was too late to do anything about it.

That view of Snowdon is, of course, the one – and I knew this even on the verge of extinction – that makes this walk. This distant, pointed lure is the one that draws you through its foothills into some of the most marvellous mountain scenery.

The path along the crest of Lliwedd seen to marvellous advantage from Snowdon.

It is a skyline known by the *cognescenti* who return to it time and again as opposed simply to climbing Snowdon from this direction by the Watkin Path, an excursion that penetrates the wilder reaches of Cwm y llan but which then climbs up on to the ridge and breaks for the summit rather than circumnavigating the rim of peaks surrounding this vast mountain amphitheatre.

Beginning opposite the car-park at Pont Bethania by the main road at Nant Gwynant, the route follows the narrow twisting road to Hafod-y-llan farm. Then, having gone a good quarter of a mile, you bear left through rhododendrons along the old miners' road and emerge above the stream rushing down from Cwm y llan. Just above the

The slate-slab bridge that marks the start of the climbing for the Nant Gwynant Horseshoe.

series of zigzags, up on to the East Peak of Lliwedd, and with the bulk of the Gallt y Wenallt ridge screening you from the valley with Llyn Gwynant just beyond.

It is a strenuous climb, this ascent, and punishing in the sustained effort required. But I did not know this as I stood that day with the lorry almost on me, and its cab door above the roof of the Mini swinging open with the ogre of a driver preparing to alight as he grasped a length of heavy chain in his fist. And again – as if I still could not prevent the motor reaction of my twitching arm muscles – I again put up two fingers while preparing myself for the worst.

It is when you look up towards the east shoulder of Snowdon from that great skyline crest of Lliwedd, and having traversed over its west peak and down into Bwlch Ciliau (where you meet the Watkin Path rising from the shaley depths of Cwm y llan) that you too may feel similarly fated. The way ahead to the summit looks confrontational and abrasive. Its shattered and exposed front contrasts sharply with the peaceful waters of Glaslyn and Llyn Llydaw far below Lliwedd, which have now appeared in view on its far side.

The obvious way directly to the summit, however, is bypassed by following the Watkin path which strikes diagonally over scree to Y Wydffa, slanting up to the left over shattered terrain, and especially trying in icy or windy weather. It joins the Rhyd Ddu path above Bwlch Main. And so on to the top via a rocky twisting track, jagged underfoot with rocks and passing numerous small outcroppings *en route* towards the Snowdon Mountain Hotel just beneath the summit.

Here, 3,560ft above the precipices and plunging valleys, is the top of Snowdon, alive with flocks of seagulls and the home of big-eared mice that inhabit the summit rocks and cairn. Attracting over 250,000 visitors a year

waterfall, you cross a slate-slab bridge, turning your back as it were on the splendid view of Yr Aran, which is the final peak of the cirque. You then follow a path that branches away towards the slopes which lead, eventually, by a

on average and so exposed to driving rain that research has shown the Snowdon massif suffers the worst weather conditions south of the Scottish border, three times as harsh as Dartmoor and seven times worse than the West Midlands. It has a rainfall equalling West African rain forests and receives a wind speed that can exceed an Inter-City train.

But, as I reflected on these facts that I had learned – and why they had jumped into my mind at such a moment God only knows – the man with the chain in his fist shouted again. Unintelligible, the words flew at me like tin tacks. I could not understand a word. So perhaps he was not swearing. For surely this was Welsh? And had not I been informed that the Welsh only swear in English? Certainly his tone of voice was surely asking did I need help? My sign language must have worked, the two fingers pointed like a pistol barrel at my own head to show I was at fault. The chains presumably had been to tow my Mini with, and a ludicrous sight that would have made had it happened.

I gave the pistol sign to the temple again, shook my head and signalled Sorry–but–I–am–just–an–idiot. He nodded in agreement, shrugged, threw the chains back in the cab and roared off down the road, no doubt thinking he had been right in the first place. Anybody who was stopped in the position where I now found myself, must either have an incapacitated car or a deranged mind. But I now faced the prospect of having to drive out on to what at this point was quite a fast stretch of road totally blind to whatever vehicle just might be approaching on the other side of the bend around which I had caromed to such a sudden stop.

I had had a similar problem after leaving the summit of Snowdon for the remaining half of the Nant Gwynant Horseshoe. I had left it late and darkness was advancing. I desperately wanted to return to the valley in day-

The old quarry workings on the flanks of Lliwedd, attained by the track from the waterfalls on the Nant Gwynant Horseshoe.

light, but felt the risk of rushing would perhaps make me measure my length on the very rocky path as I retraced my steps back down the south ridge. This time, I proceeded beyond the point where you turn off to the left for the Watkin Path and its slanting traverse across that bare and disintegrating mountainside.

First, I had headed in a south-westerly direction, then more southerly as the ridge sank lower towards the valley. I traversed the brink of Clogwyn Ddu, an isolated cliff, and continued along above the great scooped basin of Cwm Tregalan to the left. It was unbelievably atmospheric. Down there the wreckage of tiny quarry buildings spilled amongst the heaps of vast moraines. Was this once a city buried in revenge for King Arthur's death and Mordor's treachery? Bits I had read came to mind. On a skyline as wild as this you could find yourself believing anything.

Down below, the ridge dropped steeply, giving great views of the pyramid of Yr Aran below. I followed the good footpath on down to Bwlch Cwm Llan where the miner's track from the old workings in Cwm y llan crosses to Rhyd Ddu. Then I was face to face with the steep and rugged face of Yr Aran itself,

which offers such a strenuous ascent following the rigorous climbing the day had so far entailed. I reached the summit after a section of steep, broken scrambling. Once there I elected to take photographs in the dying rays of the sun, back towards Snowdon and along its south ridge.

It was then as I perched the camera on a stone, set the self-timer and dashed back to take up my position in the shot, that it came back quite clearly that I was doing a similar thing to that which had rescued me from my predicament on the narrow road through Nant Gwynant the day previously. Then, I had started the car and – leaving the engine idling – had run back to the bend in the road to check no vehicles were once more bearing down on me. Road clear, I had sprinted back to the car, jumped in and driven out into the road, this time clear of any oncoming traffic. However, in the Mini I had only to drive away, whereas after the photo session on Yr Aran, I had still to descend the lovely crest of its south-east ridge, back down into the tranquillity of Nant Gwynant. However, that was a joy anyway, tired as I was. Now at peace with the world, I had only the familiar stress of physical exertion to handle on the way down.

Chapter 41

THE TRAVERSE OF TRYFAN, THE GLYDERS AND DEVIL'S KITCHEN

The bread roll struck me between the eyes in the middle of a reverie. I had been miles away – amongst the rugged and wild glories of Tryfan from which I had just returned that evening. A red film obscured my eyes with the suddenness of it and I reached out to hurl it back. Instead the iron fist of Lobby Butler reached out and seized my wrist with the kind of grip you might take on a Chacal ice-axe after your crampons have slipped off bulging ice, and I desisted. 'If you,' he said kindly, 'throw that back you will start something.' I had heard.

The annual dinner of the North London Mountaineering Club is renowned as one of the livelier does, where in the

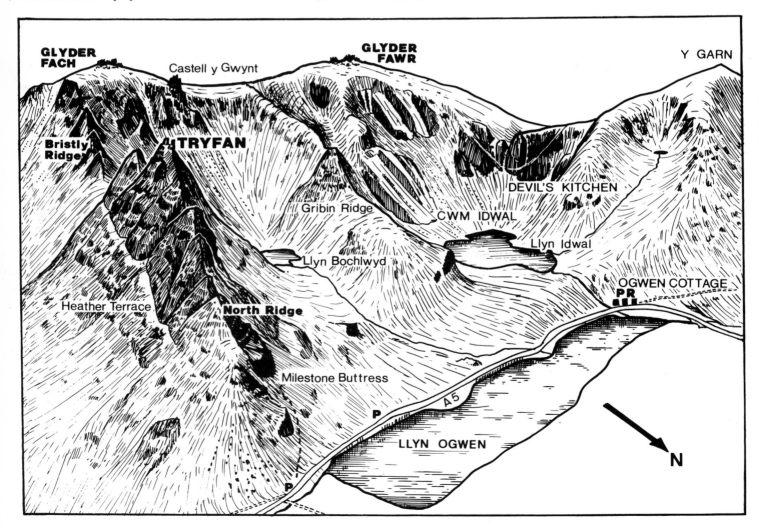

Tryfan from near the A5 to Bangor.

past the flinging of bread rolls and menu cardboard darts has ended with crockery in flight and blood drawn. In other words, a typical good climbing club dinner (the evening included the award of a turd made from plaster of Paris to a woman climber who during the year had been taken short on a rock-face ledge). Lobby was also to be another calming influence when a woman turned to me across the table, and said I looked bored. Actually, I had been enjoying myself thoroughly up to that point when, guiltily, I thought of my daughter Hannah, eleven, and ill in bed at home. The timing was unfortunate. I again saw red – being of a temperament my friend Colin describes as 'Slow thinking and quick tempered' – and said 'What a thing to say to a guest. Typical smart-arsed southerner's remark.' 'Actually,' Lobby said, 'there are quite a lot of northerners here who have moved south to work in London.' Gradually my rush of blood to the head subsided, leaving me feeling foolish and exposed. I could not help thinking of what a friend had said that afternoon on Tryfan, which was in a way symbolized by those famous obelisks of Adam and Eve that stand on the summit so distinctly that they can be mistaken for people.

Tryfan is pronounced Tryvann in Welsh. It is a peak of solid rock which with its associated skyline over Bristly Ridge, Glyder Fach and Glyder Fawr and down into the col above the Devil's Kitchen, gives one of the most superbly compressed and rugged mountain skylines in Britain.

As a result we had had a great afternoon on a skyline jagged with rock, a day to remember, although actually we only climbed and descended Tryfan and my sojourn along the ridge for photographs came later. What he said was apposite and I had not heard it before. 'Mountains are not always good,' he said as we mentioned climbers who had committed suicide and how I had had thoughts of it myself at one point. Their beauty could soften you up for the harsher realities of the world was his drift. With your mind suffused with the romanticism of mountains and still up on the heights, the brutish realities of the world were likely to hit with double the force while you were still under the influence. As, in a way, thanks to my own shortcomings and failings which so often trigger those nasty, sharp shocks, the real world and the way it works bears out. 'Like Adam and Eve,' I almost said as we reached the summit of Tryfan

which rises above the A5 road from Capel Curig to Bethesda and so close to the trunk road it might be a great Cathedral, which in a way it is. With Adam and Eve standing on the topmost eminence, the tradition on reaching the summit is to leap from one to the other.

The gap in between is about the distance across a lift shaft, with similar consequences should the leap fail to materialize quite as successfully as you hoped. What prevents people taking the leap is not the fact that they think it might be impossible but in fact quite the reverse. Rather, the landing point looks rather easy to overshoot so that if you complete your leap only too successfully, you would go sailing over it to crash a hapless victim on to the jagged rocks below.

The process by which a lovely mountain then softens you up into an altogether unrealistic world could be paralleled with this in a kind of way, or that was how I saw it. On the one hand

An ancient sheepfold provides a foreground to Tryfan.

Typical and continuously sustained scrambling up-and-down the North Ridge of Tryfan.

is the urge to jump, with the certainty you surely can do it. Only for the reality to sink in once you are standing on the smallest top which you then think you will have difficulty in getting down from. Again, the parallel – with life on the mountain giving you boundless optimism and faith, only for the reality of the real world to crunch home extra hard when your head is amongst this world of ice-fields and rock pinnacles along a lofty mountain crest.

As I too faced the prospect of jumping, the wind cold and blowing hard, and Richard already having leapt across with accomplished ease I began to wonder and prevaricate. Would I? Wouldn't I? Would I? At this point I had not even left the ground.

Left the ground on the summit of Tryfan, that is. We had left the terra firma of the Ogwen valley an hour previously, parking in the Milestone lay-by below the great spectacular rock buttress of the mountain which, as you approach it from Capel Curig, towers so shapely above the road to the left, so mountainous and yet so easily accessible. It is only when you do it – as we had done – by climbing towards the North Ridge up rough bouldery slopes above the lay-by stile and crossing the

heathery slopes to the left of the famous Milestone Buttress, before aiming for a heather and scree shoulder on the front of the mountain up about a third of its total height, that you meet the North Ridge. Then we pieced together a line of grooves and slabs and chimneys up a rock face that had the delightful quality of going on and on, encouraging you to think that having climbed one facet of the great face you are about to top-out on first the North Summit and then the Central Summit. Only for another sequence of cracks and slabs to spring into view beyond it, offering yet more exquisite scrambling over the space that is developing beneath.

The summit finally reached – the wind so cold that I pulled the cagoule hood up while we paused – Richard leapt the gap. I found it impossible to contemplate. I decided to try when I returned on a better day, and we continued on down the South Ridge, a splendid and easy scramble down the kind of steeply shelving slabs and grooves where the angle is beguiling yet the slipperiness and smoothness of the rock underfoot make you take care.

A little further on along the neck of land connecting Tryfan to Bristly Ridge

ahead, we climbed over the wall linking the two peaks by a stile on the left and, cutting across Heather Terrace, made our way diagonally across the face of the mountain and back down to the floor of the valley. The route finding was generally simple, but in mist or snow the going would be serious as you are traversing big drops.

My return journey to Tryfan followed what had been an unusual ascent the time before, done when nobody was out because of the weather. Now the sun shone. There were plenty of people on the hill, which had been my aim as I would then possibly have figures in the scenes to give a semblance of scale when I took photographs.

Again, I missed leaping from Adam to Eve, the pressure to finish the book too much to risk an accident. I downscrambled to the neck of land from where we had previously climbed the stile and descended back to the valley by Heather Terrace, only *this* time following the stone wall towards Bristly Ridge. First, aiming for the nearest crags before moving 30ft or so right to climb a short gully. At the top of this I scrambled out left over another wall

The Cannon (or Cannon Stone) and the point from where the North Ridge begins to make its presence felt.

A magic moment above the typically rugged scenery of Cwm Idwal and the Devil's Kitchen.

and entered a larger gully which channelled me up on to the ridge itself. The crux of Bristly Ridge is the Great Pinnacle Gap. Having despatched this you continue to the top and on to the boulder-covered summit of Glyder Fach. This is one of the finest viewpoints in Wales, its 'Cantilever Stone' being first noted over 200 years before by Thomas Pennant in his book on Wales.

The path runs westwards across the almost level plateau to Glyder Fawr, and there is ample opportunity in the mist to become lost in a barren and desolate landscape of rock fangs and nothing but stone underfoot between the two peaks. You pass *en route* Castell y Gwynt, the castle of the Winds, a weird collection of rocks resembling a quiverful of arrows or a collection of great spears, their heads pointing to the sky. In good visibility, the pleasure of the traverse is to stay close to the lip of the skyline above Cwm Bochlwyd, inset so atmospherically below, and to follow it round to the top of the Gribin Ridge, which is an excellent alternative to my suggested route to the Devil's Kitchen, with an easy route zigzagging down its west flank until a path leads over scree to a grass shoulder.

However, if you are keen to descend to one side of the chasm of the Devil's Kitchen with its hanging gardens of vegetation on the water-stained cliffs, the descent from the summit of Glyder Fawr descends to the north-west over grass and rocks towards a col above the great defile. From here a sketchy beginning to the path develops into an obvious thoroughfare down scree and slanting slabs, awkward when wet and with several nasty drops below its outer edge.

From the splendid isolation of a mountain crest that presents a wilderness of rock and stone to the traveller, the path descends into the depths of Cwm Idwal, cradled in the bosom of the mountains and striking across a hillside, girt with steep buttresses and slabs which have proved so significant in the history of British climbing.

Do not decry Richard's theory, I heard myself thinking. Do not let yourself be softened by this wild beauty and allow yourself to become vulnerable to the meaner aspects of life to which you are returning. Harden up a little. When I finally returned to the lay-by, happy and glowing from the fray, there were no parking notes on the Mini, nor had it been broken into, and the tyres were still fully inflated. I kicked them to be sure, jumped in and drove joyfully away completely forgetting what I had steeled myself for. The policeman who aimed his 'hair dryer' speedgun at me came 70 miles later.

Chapter 42
THE CWM CAU SKYLINE, CADER IDRIS

The vast northern cliffs of Cader Idris dominate the view from the narrow straits of the Mawddach Estuary, looking every inch of the mile height they are said to be in the local town of Dolgellau, provider of local gold for the royal wedding rings. I was in no mood to check. The pull of its striking skyline impinged on me for a different reason. I just hoped I could find solace on those windswept heights from a bad time I was experiencing, betrayed, I felt, by a friend.

If there seem to have been several periods of depression in the course of writing this book, I reasoned, as I parked the car below the south face of Cader Idris and beyond the wrought-iron gates of the old Idris Estate at Minffordd (where amongst a stately avenue of trees a warning 'Car thieves about!' gave me an unpleasant association of ideas concerning police and the law and my betrayal) – it was with reason.

Until now my years on the hills had usually been for the purposes of rock or winter climbing. This was one of the few times I had broken that habit to venture on mountains as an end in

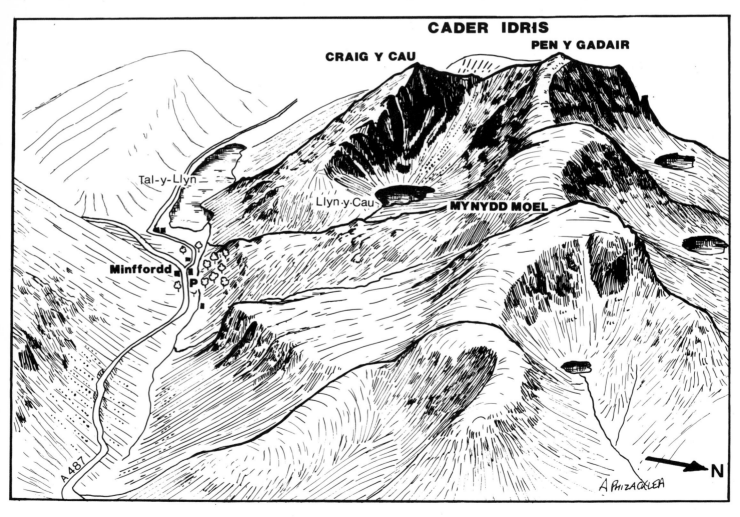

itself. When rock climbing you go with a partner and the bond of mutual trust is forged. But on my own for the purpose of taking photographs for this book, on the theory that I would move faster and be able to concentrate more fully on the task solo, there had been more opportunity to brood. In the company of a climbing friend, he or she would have pulled me out of it. You cannot stay bound up in yourself for long with someone else on the other end of the rope. Perhaps that was why I felt it so keenly. My let-down had been at the hands of a climbing friend, a companion on the rope.

The thoughts had kept intruding all the way to Cader Idris until, on the threshold of the mountain, I made a resolve to put them to one side. The mountain gives its finest view from a distance and I had ample opportunity to study it from the streets of Dolgellau. In fact there was said to be 6 miles of almost continuous cliffs streching from Craig y Llyn in the west, to Gau Graig in the east, although the high point is rather less than they had estimated in the public bar of the Royal Ship. It is actually 2,928ft. But Cader Idris makes a splendid east-west traverse with the deep wooded valley enclosing Tal-y-Llyn on one side and the shining estuary on the other. Ten miles you can go along its crest and they say it is fantastic. But Cader Idris has another rugged and intriguing option for hilltop climbers too.

Cader Idris means the Chair of Idris, possibly King Arthur I had been told in the same pub, and Dolgellauians seem justly proud of it. Seen from a distance to the north, the hollowed Cwm y Gadair looms like a large chair, perhaps symbolizing the number of craggy, ice-ground cwms along the ridge, some still jewelled with lakes. It was the most spellbinding of these I was determined to traverse, the rugged cirque of Cwm Cau, the Hollow Cwm, soaring wonderfully on to the airy crest of crag circling around over the Pencoed Pillar,

via the peaks of Craig Lwyd, Myndd Pencoed, Pen y Gadair (the summit of Cader Idris and highest of the nine tops), Mynydd Moel, and down.

Steeling myself for the steep uphill path through the woods and rhododen-drons, I passed through a scene so halcyon you could imagine nymphs and shepherds cavorting here by the plun-ging water of Nant Cader. However, all I saw, in the mind's eye, and quite forgetting my good intentions, was the flashing blue light of my answerphone before I pressed the 'play' button and heard the robotic but unmistakable sound of an officer from my local cons-tabulary speaking in my absence.

That had been a few days previously. I had spent a disorientating morning in a distant airport, there to meet a friend, the flight being delayed for sev-eral hours. The ensuing crawl, up the M6 in my Mini had taken light years. It was on returning home that the mes-sage greeted me. Its gist was that I had been seen driving in the village with an expired tax disc on my car. Would I call at the police station with my doc-uments. Thank you very much and good day.

Embarrassed and flustered I rushed to the post office to become the arch-etypal figure of fun. H.M. Bateman could have featured me in one of his cartoons: 'The man who answered "Yes" to Question 9 on his vehicle licence application.' Question 9 asks, 'Have you knowingly used this vehicle outside the licenced period?' And I wrote, 'Once – in error.' (Well, they knew, didn't they? A policeman must have seen me driving out of town that morning. It seemed pointless to lie.) 'You can only write 'Yes' or 'No',' said the man behind the counter. And he crossed out my feeble excuse. 'Which do you want it to be, 'Yes' or 'No'?' 'Yes,' I had to say. And he ticked it in the appropriate box. It looked so bad. What I did not know was that things were to get worse before they got better.

All this and more I thought about as

Cwm Cau to the south of the summit of Cader Idris is an atmospheric mountain amphitheatre.

gradually the leafy woodland of the Cader Idris Nature Reserve sank below me and I emerged into daylight to the easy grassy slopes that lead so delight-fully to the dark waters of Llyn Cau.

There is erosion here, of course. This mountain cirque is popular. However, there are variations. I found mine in following the banks of the river rigor-ously over rocks and a little scrambling by waterfalls to the brink of the lake which appears so suddenly and mag-ically in front of the precipices massed behind it like a splendid pyramid, its reflection so often brilliantly reflected in the water.

This crag of Craig y Cau is the jewel in the crown. To its left are the slopes I aspired to of Craig Lwyd which gains you the height, and to its right was the mass of Pen y Gadair and the main ridge itself. Sandwiched in between the two peaks are the buttresses and gullies of lovely grey rock, prominent among which is the Pencoed Pillar on the brink of Great Gully that casts a black shadow marking its presence from the striations of rock in a most distinct way, rather as the chameleon-like presence of the Cioch on Skye's Sron na Ciche crag is revealed by its sundial effect at certain times of day.

The police, I thought, as I continued along the rocky path zigzagging steeply up to the left with the waters dropping away below on my right, had given me a little hope. But I had still become the stereotype for yet another H.M. Bateman-type situation: 'The man who confessed he was driving without a licence disc.' 'I confess,' I had said, placing my driving documents before the policeman on the desk. 'I admit it. I have no excuse – except, well, I have an excuse.' And so I burbled on. The officer inspected my newly purchased tax disc, said he would look into it and that I should come back in three days. When I did, it was still like a nightmare but in a way I had not envisaged.

How it all returned as I tried to focus on the careful footing required while skirting the rim of the crags overlooking the dark waters of Llyn Cau, brooding away those hundreds of feet below the precipitous depths to match my mood. Glimpses of the water, flecked with the white of seagulls flitting across its surface, appeared at regular intervals as I crossed the tops of gully after gully on my own variation of the route which overlooked Cwm Cau.

The rocky summit of Mynydd Pencoed coincided with my simmering mood coming to the boil. Those three days later, the desk of my local police station had been busy with several police officers in attendance. They said they knew nothing about the answerphone message. It must have been a practical joke. 'Though,' said an officer trying to keep a straight face, 'if it was an officer from another force who made the call, please inform him we are aware of the situation.' Now whenever the local police see me they grin. One even beeped the horn of his patrol car as he passed me in the street the other day.

Who could have done this to me? Surely an enemy I had made? If any of my other documents had also expired, he could have seen me in real trouble. Serves me right you say? Of course. But that was not the point. Somebody was getting their revenge, of that I was sure. Yet like so much in life, I decided as I descended from the summit and down into the Bwlch Cau before zigzagging once more up the wide final slopes that meet the wide Pony Track and so lead on to the top of Cader Idris, Pen y Gadair itself, this obvious solution was quite wrong. It had been a friend – a leading light in the mountain rescue team that had once rescued me when I broke a leg on a winter climb – who had caused my grief. And who, I subsequently discovered had admitted the joke that everyone thought so hilarious to a mutual friend, his defence being I was gullible.

'Gullible,' I thought surveying Snowdonia from this tremendous vantage point 'Gullible!' Two days before leaving for the airport I had telephoned him, asking his advice. Having been fined previously in the year for driving an unlicensed car, I wanted to know if he learned anything from his experience – like tips on how I too could temporarily avoid this fate? My tax disc was out of date, yet I had promised to meet this other friend returning from a climbing holiday in Spain. Therefore, I was duty-bound to take my car out on the roads. What should I do? Take the risk? 'Go for it,' he said.

As soon as I was on my way he had disguised his voice and called my answerphone.

If ever a summit view was balm to the soul, it was the view from Cader Idris. That wild panorama of Wales' north and central mountains cut saw-teeth in the sky, while across the Mawddach Estuary, a pale ribbon of Barmouth's sands contrasted with the stark

A view along the northern edge of Cader Idris, looking west to the main summit of Pen y Gadair.

grandeur of Cwm y Gadair plummeting below, that northern cwm of Idris which is seen to such good advantage from Dolgellau.

It quite transformed my soul and angry thoughts fled just as surely as the counselling of Ratty, Mole and Badger in the *Wind in the Willows* pacifies and soothes the agonizing of Toad. There was no longer a revengeful thought left in my being. I was overcome by the knowledge of what a favour I had been done. Had I been stopped by the police, I would have been prosecuted. Now, thanks to him, I was driving once more legally and without a worry. I would thank him personally on my return for the kindness he had shown in going out of his way to make me see the light in such a creative way. Generally, I would turn over a new leaf in the running of my life and in being beatific to all those who oppressed me.

Of course, I did no such thing. Of course, I still feel the occasional vapours when I see him. I have no idea what I may one day do. But it is thanks to Cader Idris that – soothed and calmed by its amazing influence as I descended eastwards from the rocky peak of Pen y Gadair, crossing the top of Fox's Path (the steep descent into Cwm y Gadair) and cresting the northern escarpments by the broad ridge of sheep-cropped turf to the summit of Mynydd Moel before finally descending grassy slopes to rejoin the original route just above the trees – that I will probably not now after all jack his car up in his absence and remove the wheels.

Looking through the Great Gully by the Pencoed Pillar – a celebrated landmark on the cliffs of Cwm Cau – to the northern edge of Cader Idris beyond and with Llyn Cau below.

Chapter 43
A PENNANT HORSESHOE

A poem asks God why he made Cwm Pennant so beautiful and the life of a man so short. I had occasion to think bitterly of those words. It was on this beautiful, beautiful skyline that the power zoom lens of my camera jammed when fully extended and refused to retract inside the camera.

In the heat of the moment I became so certain that the Fates were against me that for several moments I was within an ace of taking leave of my senses. The fact it had let me down was a catastrophe. Everything depended on that camera continuing to work.

The Cwm Pennant Horseshoe, as I completed it, is formed on one side by the Nantlle Ridge, a series of shapely hills, stretching 10km over seven tops between Mynydd Craig Goch and Y Garn, overlooking the sea and separating the quarried vale of Nantlle (pronounced Nantley) from the unspoilt pastoral tranquillity of Cwm Pennant. The route then curves around the head of the valley to tackle the slopes of mighty Moel Hebog after returning over a subsidiary line of peaks including Moel Lefn and back to the point where you began. 'Mighty', of course, is relative. The Nantlle ridge does not exceed 734m in height and compared with Snowdon and its satellites to the east is small

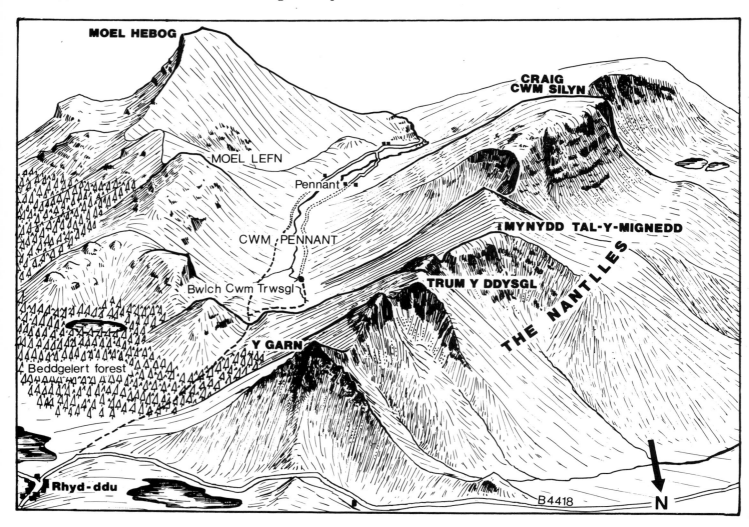

beer but, done in this direction, it gives a long day, say ten hours even.

The Cwm Pennant Horseshoe provides splendid walking on luminous green sheep-cropped sward and with intervals of rocky and narrow crested ridge. Although it can be traversed in either direction, I chose to start from the car-park at Rhyd Ddu on the B4418 and opted for the anti-clockwise circuit. It was clearly popular, this Nantlle Ridge following a maze of tracks leading to the heights of Y Garn and with white arrows to guide you during the early stages.

There have been access problems here, which have been resolved by the National Park negotiating Courtesy Footpaths following a period of local antagonism against the climbing population in general. And there was no shortage of people on the ridge that day revelling in the sunlight, forest scents, marvellous sights and sea breezes.

The climb up to Y Garn's final boulder-field is steep and steady, promising the most beautiful of views. By the time I reached the summit I had already used a roll of Fujichrome. Ration the film in the interests of economy as I tried to, I could not resist taking shot after shot on a skyline as perfect as this. Each time I told myself this would be positively the last picture to be taken until I reached the skyline. Only then for another great scene to loom into view the higher I climbed. Once more I compulsively aimed the camera thinking, 'This has got to be it!'

It was on the best section of the route from Y Garn south and upwards to the cuneiform shape of Mynydd Drws-y-Coed and beyond to Trum y Ddysgl with a tantalizing peep over its shoulder of Mynydd Craig Cwm Silyn in the distance that I had a premonition of the disaster to come. Having taken just that picture, zooming the lens to swim the panorama into ever closer focus, there was a juddering effect as the barrel of the zoom lens travelled

The remote cave of Ogof Owain Glyndwr on Moel Ogof, neighbouring peak to Moel Hebog. It was here the Welsh leader is said to have gone into hiding after swimming the tidal Glaslyn estuary while fleeing for his life.

jerkily back into the body of the AZ-300 in a series of tiny spasms. Panic-stricken, I zoomed out the lens again, pressing first one tip of the rocker switch to effect this, then the other to retract it. This time it worked perfectly. I forgot all about it.

Until, that is, I reached the notched knife-blade of rock of the Aonach Eagach-ish pinnacles of Clogwyn Marchnad leading to the summit of Mynydd Drws-y-Coed – and the technical crux of the Nantlle Ridge – and especially photogenic that morning with a caravan of brightly clothed hill-top climbers pausing and balancing and clambering their way along the narrow, exposed crest above the steep plunging abysses to the north.

It was a marvellous scene as I stationed myself as the last person along the pinnacles and well behind the others, and raised my camera, zooming the lens to bring the figures ahead into lifelike proportions. However, when I pressed the rocker switch to bring back the lens to normal, it refused to withdraw. Like the phallus of a rampant stallion (a small rampant stallion, that is) it stood out obscenely, ludicrously,

now the wrong shape to fit back inside the camera bag and shattering my hopes for the day.

Better go back then, I thought, now plunged into the utmost depths of despair as I clicked the switch repeatedly to no avail. Yet with such glorious sun? With the people available to help give a living scale to my pictures if I felt it necessary? With those views? On automatic pilot I began to progress along the pinnacles as if in a daze, scrambling one-handed because the other hand was required to hold and nurse the camera as I clung first to one hand-hold then another – like the man I had seen climbing up the knotted rope towards me while bivvying in the bothy in Glencoe beneath the main road. The item in his clutches had been a Dewars whisky bottle, but my camera was handled with similar care.

There came a point, however, when I snapped. Beyond the pinnacles, the ridge continues as a narrow arête which soars up to the summit of Trum y Ddysgl, grassy summitted and alluring. It was here I paused a while in the sun futilely pressing various switches and hoping the motor would whirr into action and save my day. There was no such luck, of course, and for a benighted moment I found myself gazing down at my right fist, the fingers of which had closed themselves around the black shiny barrel of zoom lens so that they were wielding it like a mugger might wield a length of lead piping on the point of, I suddenly realized, battering the body of the camera against the ground.

'That would be silly,' said the voice of reason. 'If you did that you would not – supposing the camera were suddenly to work – get that immaculate pic now within your sights of the craggy western face of Mynydd Drws-y-Coed.' Instead, I lowered it gently on my lap and with my head in my hands I confess I said a little prayer. After a few more tries of the obdurate rocker switch the barrel of the zoom lens slid back inside the camera as if nothing untoward had happened.

I switched off the motor and breathed a silent thanks. I had been lucky, I felt, but now was the test. I had found the automatic Powerzoom facility indispensable, particularly when I was tired and it was taking me all my time to guide myself around what seemed

to be the innumerable ridges in this book. Now, the crunch was – would the camera still work? I held my breath, focussed on the next peak along, Mynydd Tal-y-Mignedd, across the adjacent col, and pressed the switch. Slowly the green, grassy outlines of the slopes swam larger into my view as the motor purred. Now for it – I depressed the rocker switch at its other extreme. The barrel slid back without demur.

The views from the monument, built to celebrate Queen Victoria's Diamond Jubilee, on the summit of Mynydd Tal-y-mignedd, are said to include a sighting of three castles from its summit, Caernarvon being one and I think Harlech and Criccieth the other two. Unfortunately, I only discovered this on my return, more taken at this point with the grey and purple decor and waste tips and abandoned quarries of Nantlle and Llyn Nantlle Uchaf, the scars in places fierce and unforgiving.

Now handling the camera with the greatest care and in a fever of suspense whenever I used the zoom facility, I continued on down into the lowest part of the skyline, the next stop being the

rocky twisting north-east ridge of Craig Cwm Silyn beyond that lowly saddle with its pass of Bwlch Dros-bern offering an escape route on fading light or deteriorating conditions.

It was on Mynydd Craig Cwm Silyn that I realized that – looking back along its tortuous and rugged course with affection – the narrow part of the horse-shoe was finally over. Broad slopes of the inevitable green turf and boulders lay ahead *en route* for the final peak along the Nantlles section of the Pennant Horseshoe, the rounded dome of Garnedd-goch. From here, and with its heartstopping view across the Cwm Pennant vale of Moel Hebog itself (a finely shaped peak as befits the Hill of the Falcon), the route continues on over Mynydd Craig Goch. Then down grassy slopes due south before turning east across the Pennant valley via Pont Gyfyng and Llanfihangel y Pennant to the splendidly open incline up to the summit of Moel Hebog by its south-eastern slopes. Leading you to the highest point so far.

The reciprocating ridge north along the far side of the valley is a peach. It descends into the Clover Pass, Bwlch Meillionen, where thickets of ferns and mossy craglets give on to the rising slopes of Moel Ogof and its chaotic rocks and reedy tarns, then on to Moel Llefn and on further still through bog and outcrops to Bwlch Cwm Trwsgl and then Bwlch-y-ddwy-elor – the Pass of the Bier, being the route to a grave-yard.

The final stage of this 15-mile walk, with its height climbed of over 5,000ft, is through pine forest, some of it recently felled, towards Llyn-y-Gader close to Rhyd Ddu. A lovely finale to the trip, it provides a pleasant sojourn along a forest track rich with the scent of pine resin and that pleasurable lassitude that comes at the end of a great mountain day.

Looking back towards Blaen Pennant and the Nantlle Ridge from the descent into the valley before climbing Moel Hebog.

Chapter 44

CNICHT AND THE MOELWYNS

Sir John Hunt, as Lord Hunt was known in those days, first told me about Cnicht and the Moelwyns and the delightful walk over them when I was younger and even dafter than I am now. Elected to climb with him on a climbing club meet where he was guest speaker at the annual dinner, I enjoyed a great day's cragging with him in the rain. He was keen and that was all I cared about, hooked on climbing as I was. But I do remember his saying, 'You would like climbing in the Moelwyns. There is also a wonderful ridge over Cnicht which looks like the Matterhorn'. I remember him mentioning Cnicht because it is the name for knight, its pointed shape resembling a helmet to medieval sailors on Tremadoc Bay.

I also remember something that still had a relevance when I finally visited Cnicht, though it had been some thirty years before when we had roped up below the rock face, and I poured some

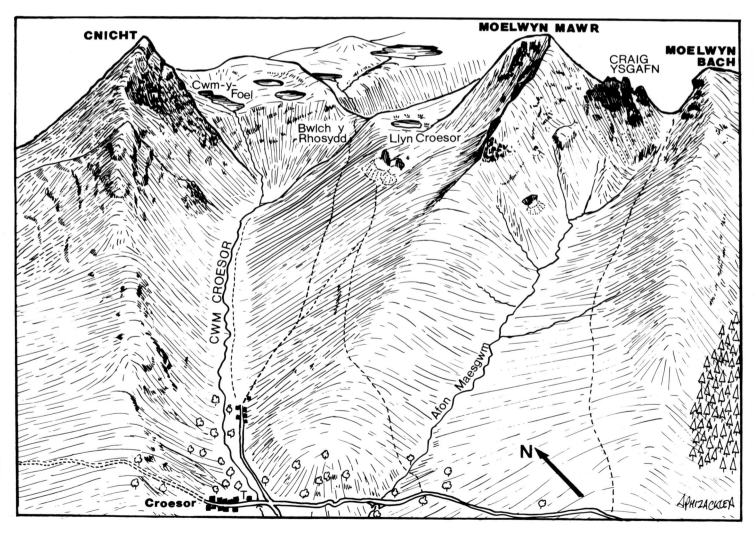

as I did the deed. It would mean a messy rucksack, always a consequence of having two holes in the top of the tin, but what the hell. 'John will do,' he said kindly. Just call me John.'

The relevance of that tale to the morning I kept my long overdue appointment with Cnicht became apparent as I fried bacon and egg in the climbing hut, said to be the building described last century by George Borrow in his *Wild Wales* as a 'wretched hovel'. (Although judging by the sea of Volvo estates outside it might have appeared things were looking up.) My breakfast was ready when a passing hut occupant paused to spit into the frying pan, expecting he said the fat to be so hot his sputum would sizzle off it in a trice. This is supposed to be a test used by great chefs to check the temperature. Unfortunately he was neither a Keith Floyd nor was the pan sufficiently hot and the yellow phlegm stayed there floating on the fat like a tiny oyster. It so put me off my breakfast that I couldn't eat it.

As I 'only' intended traversing Cnicht and its associated peaks in the Moelwyns, I thought it would be easy, a mere formality – breakfast or no breakfast. This was a piece of very foolish thinking.

The Moelwyn group of mountains, of which Cnicht, Moelwyn Mawr and Moelwyn Bach are the three conspicuous summits, lie 10 miles to the southeast of Snowdon and provide an excellent skyline traverse. Though it is inadvisable to try a rugged and complicated tour like this – with its share of scrambling, scree and bogs but most of all, route finding – without a good meal inside you first.

If one thing had stood me in good stead on most of the skylines in this book it has been that I have always eaten a full breakfast first. The importance of this first meal of the day may be inconceivable to those who dash out to work after a quick cup of coffee and clock-in at the factory or switch on their computer terminals, but for me breakfast has to be a priority.

Stream descending between the long western ridges of Moelwyn Mawr and Moelwyn Bach.

tea from a flask. Did he prefer it with milk or without? I cannot remember if, like me, it was with, but I can still feel the small round tin of Carnation condensed milk in my hand as I suddenly became aware of where I was and who I was with; not my usual group of friends, that was for sure, with whom the adding of milk to the tea as and when necessary was effected by the expediency of sucking the milk from the single hole in the tin and spitting it into the cup, or cups, depending on how many required the beverage. Recollecting this in the nick of time, a red flush suffusing my face, I fumbled for my penknife with which to stab another hole in the tin to allow the milk to pour. 'Just a moment, Sir John,' I said

Cnicht (left) and the Moelwyns form the distant skyline to this group shot of Welsh-speaking youngsters at Penryhyndendraeth across the valley.

Besides those three peaks mentioned, another four tops stand behind that western rim of the Moelwyns that fronts the sea, nudging a wilderness of waters and rocks. Y Cyrniau (a fairly insignificant spur), Moel Druman, Allt Fawr and Moel-yr-hydd may be lesser tops but together with the three mentioned they make a great round of Seven Summits in all, providing the most outstanding views, and starting and finishing at the tiny village of Croesor which is accessible from the A4085 road from Penrhyndeudraeth to Beddgelert.

The car-park at Croesor is a popular starting point, too, with Cnicht being the main (and often the one and only) objective of visiting hill-walkers. All of them looked well fed to me as, already feeling more than peckish, I began along the well-marked path which leads to a wide saddle on the south-west ridge and from where a path climbs airily on the narrowing crest to the base of the final steepness – an easy scramble enjoyed by school children and grandparents. The sharply-peaked summit is an illusion, however, being one end of an undulating half-mile ridge, sloping down gently to a saddle. Here boggy slopes glitter in sunlight with the many small lakes, one of the larger ones being Llyn Cwm-y-foel, which is seen to splendid advantage from Cnicht.

A boggy path leads north past the eastern shore of Llyn yr Adar, the Lake of the Birds, and a reflective shield that mirrors the heights of Snowdon in a certain light, but, unfortunately, not that day.

I was feeling insubstantial and disorientated through lack of real food. During my sojourn in the Mamores I had at least already done another skyline on the same day, and the lack of food was due to an oversight. Then a midday topping-up of muesli and the good breakfast I had eaten that morning had kept me going, whereas now, I had not even had that proper start to the day. I was eating on the move to

compensate, but it never quite sufficed. Everything seemed too much effort. I found it a struggle keeping on course which, although in broad daylight, needs care in the Moelwyns and navigation can in fact be trickiness itself to maintain the correct path to your advantage, so you do not lose height unnecessarily nor wander off into a morass of swamp and a rain forest of bracken, grasses and out-croppings of rock.

Beyond the Lake of Birds is the first top above a rocky ridge rising in a north-easterly direction, Y Cyrniau, immediately south of the most eastern tarn of the three Lakes of Dogs. Here is where the mountain watershed between Liverpool Bay and Tremadoc Bay makes its right-angled turn from E-W to N-S, running northward to Pen-y-Gwryd and then over Crib Goch to Rhyd Ddu and the Eifionydd ridges.

The next peak, Moel Druman, lies on the route to the summit of Allt Fawr, the Big High Place at 2,287ft, which is the most easterly point of the route. Moel Druman is an electric light bulb of a summit and, south-east of it, I saw Llyn Conglog looking like a space where a piece of jigsaw puzzle should fit. It was on Allt Fawr, however, reached after a descent and crossing of a moorland slope, that I overlooked the vastness of grim, grim Blaeneau Ffestiniog and its terraces of houses among the waste tips of slate.

Cutting back down to the shore of Llyn Conglog, I found the next 2-mile section particularly taxing. The route-finding keeps you fully occupied, and despite the beauty of the day I felt weak with lassitude. I aimed south-west at the lake's southern tip across open terrain to Bwlch Rhosydd, the pass at the head of the Croesor valley.

Moel-yr-hydd is the next summit, reached by heading east from the ruined buildings in the pass and then slanting leftwards up an easy ridge. Good as the view is here, I found it surpassed on the summit of Moelwyn Mawr which rises west-south-west beyond a lengthy

The tiny summit tarn on Moelwyn Bach.

sweep of typically Moelwyn moonscape. It is one of the best vantage points in Wales giving extremely wide and long-distance views. It is also strategically placed to serve the seventh and final peak of Moelwyn Bach via the rocky ridge descending well over 500ft, due south over the small craggy top of Craig Ysgafan to the col of Bwlch Stwlan between Moelwyn Fawr and Moelwyn Bach, which beetled overhead sufficiently to make me pause.

There were no endorphins for me that day, no second wind, as I staggered slowly up directly towards the weirdly bulging crag to avoid any difficulty by traversing right. Then – and wishing I had eaten the damned breakfast and not been so neurotic about it – I at last descended wearily down Moelwyn Bach's lengthy west ridge back to Croesor.

Chapter 45

THE CIRCUIT OF LLYN Y FOEL, MOEL SIABOD

Woody Allen was criticizing my book and I wanted to thump him. Gazing myopically through his horn-rimmed glasses, the comedian was saying things that would be its death. 'And,' said the man in the middle, 'you say here in your book on survival, Mr Greenbank, you say that when a car goes off the road and plunges down a cliff into a lake with you, your wife and baby on board the first thing you do is switch on the headlights?' 'What's that for?' asked Mr Allen, 'To warn the oncoming traffic?' The audience loved it. There was a wave of applause beyond the studio lights. I was on the Steve Allen chat show in San Francisco in what is known as a 'celebrity guest' role and on a book tour; Woody Allen being the other guest on the sofa. (I am sorry that I never met the man apart from in front of the cameras.) He was giving me a hard time.

I fear having this even more from reviewers and critics with this book. I am afraid they will pick me up on one important fact: I have not included sufficient Welsh skylines. Yet this one particular skyline, and the easiest in my selection of Welsh ridges

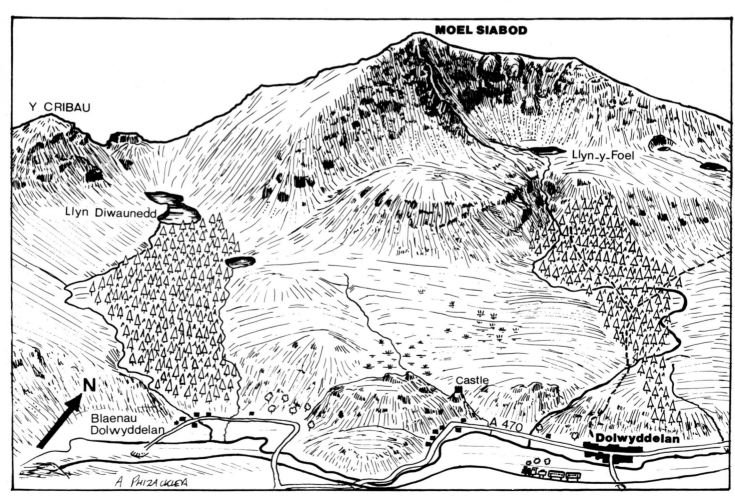

The slopes of Moel Siabod and Dolwyddelan below.

(although remember, please, the vagaries and dangers of mountain weather, especially of snow and ice and how it can transport the humblest hill into a place with thrice the danger), somehow embodies the reason for why I haven't.

The shapely peak of Moel Siabod at nearly 3,000ft dominates a lengthy succession of hills from their northern extremity, while Cnicht it is that guards the south. Between the two, lies a wilderness of trackless wastes, shining with the glint of lakes and tarns and providing in every direction wild, magnificent and mystifying horizons. All the way up Moel Siabod, I was thinking how good it was, and how many other Welsh skylines there were that I had not touched. There were so many summit ridges of variety and beauty like Siabod. Perhaps I should have included more.

Perhaps? Certainly is more the word. The Welsh skylines, large and small, are superb. How could I have left them so short? Mathematics was one answer. I never said these were the best 45 skylines in Britain. How could I do that? These are a selection, and a choice forced on me by breaks in the weather, for time was of the essence. In the final analysis I was forced to include skylines even when it rained throughout my trip and I only managed the photographs by the skin of – in one instance – a poly bag wrapped around the camera.

If Woody Allen could get to me on a book I did not care about, but which I had written for money, what would happen when I was criticized for a book closer to my heart and where the promise of deferred reward was somewhere in the nebulous clouds of the future? 'There are eighteen Welsh skylines you have to include,' my friend Jim had said, jotting them down on the back of an envelope. 'Leave out any at your peril.' As I climbed Moel Siabod I knew exactly what he meant.

This lovely, lonely mountain stands there, remote and sweeping, bounded to the north by the road between Capel Curig and Beddgelert and to the south by the A470 through the narrow Lledr Valley with its tiny fields and woods and tumbling streams. It was from Dolwyddelan in this halcyon vale that I chose to climb it too, following the course of the stream that tumbles from the wind-churned waters of Llyn y Foel secluded in its lofty eyrie, the jewel in the crown as far as this walk is concerned.

The summit of Moel Siabod is gained by a lively, sporting and somewhat shattered ridge that leads directly to the top. Combining this with the walk along the summit crest around the precipitous cove and then back down to Dolwyddelan, it gives a perfect introduction to the hills and perhaps as good a signing off a skyline as you might imagine for this book.

It is in reaching the idyllic haven of Llyn y Foel that an introductory walk has to be taken first. This approach might be likened to walking in to base camp on a Himalayan peak, and Moel Siabod can look most Himalayan from the vicinity of the A5 near Capel Curig as its frozen eastern ridges sparkle in the reddening sun.

The footpath from the narrow road leading steeply up behind the Y-Gardyr Inn in Dolwyddelan and through the forest, flanks the Afon Ystumiau as it tumbles and crashes down the mountainside in a procession of falls from its airy beginnings. I had passed a blaze of colour from rhododendrons and azaleas in the valley, and the forest scent added to the exhilaration of the day. Cuckoos were calling as I left the forest road and slowly climbed higher through the trees after crossing the stream by rickety stepping-stones. Any sign of the

Llyn y Foel viewed from the summit of the crags above.

The 'other' side of Moel Siabod, viewed from Crib Goch and looking back to the east.

precipitous eastern front of the mountain to which I was heading was still a dream on the unseen distant heights.

Finally emerging from the aromatic canopy of the conifers and with open hillside above, knolly with rocks and rugged going underfoot, I at last climbed those final few steps where suddenly ahead the llyn was revealed and with it the splendid rock face scenery of its cwm. I walked around the tarn to the left, climbing the edge of the craggy ridge above for the most thrilling views. The scrambling was excellent and the summit cairn arrived unexpectedly as I negotiated the rocks and boulders, to be rewarded by a fantastic view of Tryfan, its three buttresses rising aloof and sheer above the intervening crest of the Glyders.

'I am staggering along,' wrote a famous man, 'to the end of this job and am glad to have found the strength to accomplish it.' I have definitely plunged into the 'English Peoples' and am now rollicking with the Piltdown Man, Cassivellaunus, the Venerable Bede and other hoary figures. How to make any of this that is (a) readable, (b) original, (c) valuable and (d) true, is known only to the presiding genius of Britain who has not yet imparted his secrets to yours sincerely.

Sadly, I thought about this as I continued around the rim of the cliffs, crossing the very, very broken rocky slabs on the edge of space, and keeping as tentatively to the limit of that boundary as my sense of self-preservation would allow. It was all very Glyderish, and most pleasant walking. Llyn y Foel winked up at me in farewell from below, a solitary dark and brooding eye that gave me a final glance, as I continued on and along the ridge. Gradually the crags gave way to grass and I was able to negotiate my way back down to the path that comes in from Capel Curig and the east, and which led me again to the shores of Llyn y Foel before I descended to Dolwyddelan the way that I had come.

I now knew what Winston Churchill meant when he wrote those words on writing his *History of the English Speaking Peoples*.

Index